lonely planet

WEST COAST AUSTRALIA

Steve Waters,
Rosamund Brennan, Emmylou Dzubiel

Meet our writers

Steve Waters

Steve has been travelling through, hiking, volunteering and working in and writing about northern Western Australia for over 15 years.

Rosamund Brennan

@rosamundbrennan

Based in Fremantle, Western Australia, Rosamund is a freelance journalist focusing on travel, culture and society. If there's a story buried in the bush, hidden in the archives, or carved into an ancient rockface, she will gladly find it.

Emmylou Dzubiel

@emmylou.marie

Emmylou is a Perth-based writer who finds her flow state when hiking serene landscapes, developing recipes, and sharing languages.

PHILIP SCHUBERT/SHUTTERSTOCK

Carnarvon
Shark Bay
Monkey Mia
Denham
Toolonga Nature Reserve
Murchison River
Gascoyne River
National Park
Monkey Mia & the Central West p160
Kalbarri
Kalbarri National Park
Houtman Abrolhos Islands
Mullewa
Geraldton
Dongara-Port Denison
INDIAN OCEAN
Cervantes
Pinnacles Desert
Nambung National Park
Lancelin
Toodyay
Northam
York
Perth p40
Perth
Rottnest Island
Fremantle
Perth Region p82
Narrogin
Hyden
Bunbury
Yallingup
Busselton
Margaret River
Augusta
Manjimup
Pemberton
Margaret River & the South West p108
Denmark
Mt Barker
Albany
Meekatharra
Wiluna
Cue
Sandstone
Mt Magnet
Leinster
Leonora
Laverton
Kalgoorlie-Boulder
Coolgardie
Kambalda
Southern Cross
Norseman
Lake King
Fitzgerald River National Park
Hopetoun
Esperance
South Coast p138
Cape Arid National Park
Dundas Nature Reserve
Plumridge Lakes Nature Reserve
Yeo Lake Nature Reserve
Neale Junction Nature Reserve
Great Victoria Desert
Warburton
Great Victoria Desert Nature Reserve
SOUTH AUSTRALIA
Rawlinna
Nullarbor Plain
Cocklebiddy
Madura
Eucla
Nuytsland Nature Reserve
Great Australian Bight
SOUTHERN OCEAN

Meander the back roads in search of gourmet treasures. Dare to swim with whale sharks. Listen to ancient stories told through Aboriginal art. Immerse yourself in outback gorges and waterholes. Journey beyond where the paved road ends. Let an Indigenous guide show you the country in whole new ways. Discover beaches and coastal stretches just for you. Experience Perth as locals know and love it.

TURN THE PAGE AND START PLANNING YOUR NEXT BEST TRIP →

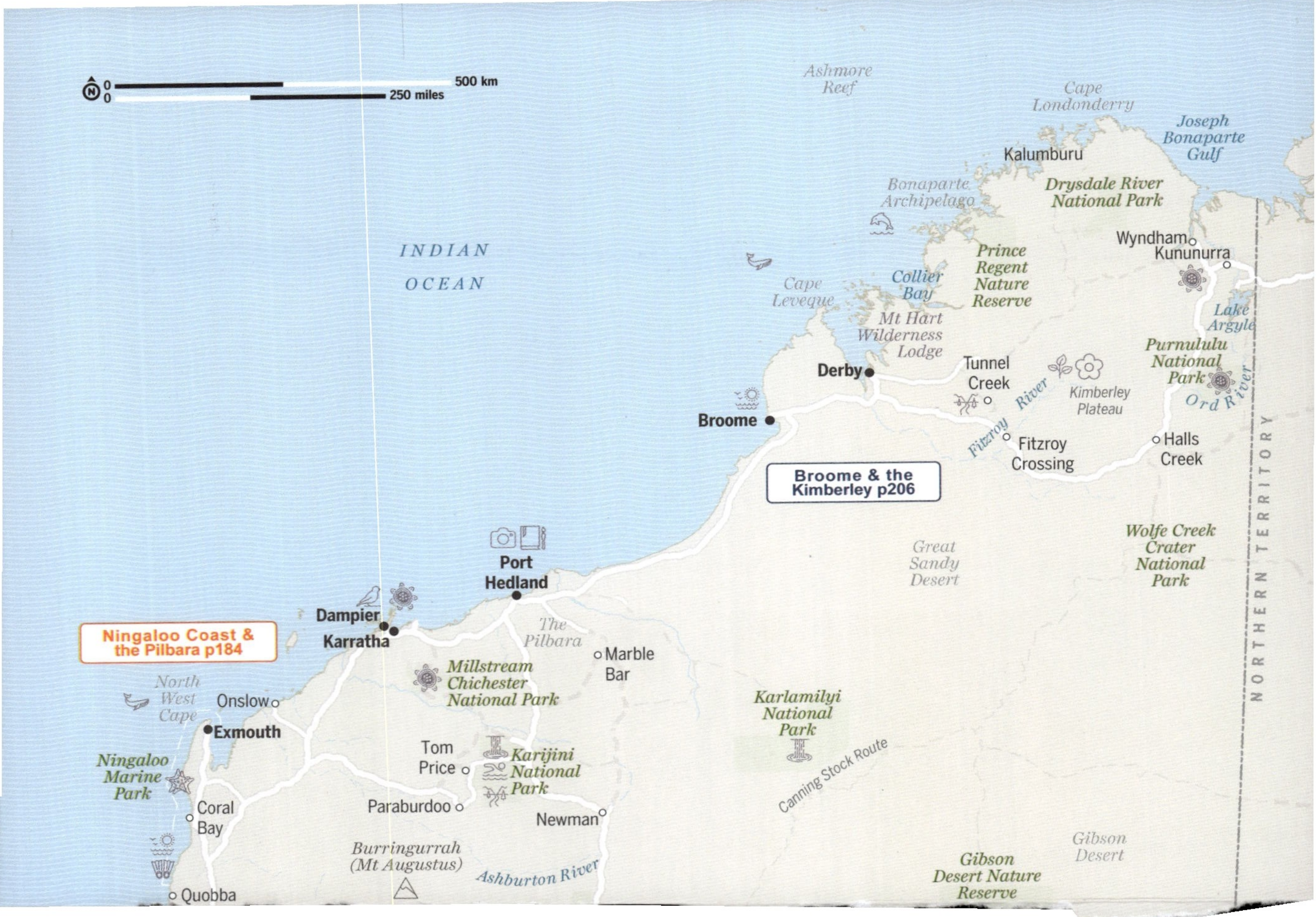

0 500 km
0 250 miles
INDIAN OCEAN
Ashmore Reef
Cape Londonderry
Joseph Bonaparte Gulf
Kalumburu
Bonaparte Archipelago
Drysdale River National Park
Wyndham
Kununurra
Prince Regent Nature Reserve
Collier Bay
Cape Leveque
Mt Hart Wilderness Lodge
Lake Argyle
Purnululu National Park
Derby
Tunnel Creek
Kimberley Plateau
Ord River
Broome
Fitzroy River
Fitzroy Crossing
Halls Creek
Broome & the Kimberley p206
Great Sandy Desert
Wolfe Creek Crater National Park
NORTHERN TERRITORY
Port Hedland
Dampier
Karratha
Ningaloo Coast & the Pilbara p184
The Pilbara
Marble Bar
Millstream Chichester National Park
North West Cape
Onslow
Exmouth
Karlamilyi National Park
Tom Price
Karijini National Park
Canning Stock Route
Ningaloo Marine Park
Coral Bay
Paraburdoo
Newman
Gibson Desert
Burringurrah (Mt Augustus)
Ashburton River
Gibson Desert Nature Reserve
Quobba

Kalbarri National Park (p168)

CONTRIBUTING WRITERS

Fleur Bainger

@fleurbainger

Fleur is a Perth-based freelance journalist, podcaster, writing mentor and radio talker.

Anthony Ham

www.anthonyham.com

Anthony has been travelling and writing about some of the Earth's more far-flung places for more than two decades. He has written or contributed to more than 150 guidebooks for Lonely Planet.

Ariana Svenson

@worldoftravelswithkids *westernaustraliantravel.com*

A proud Western Australian, Ariana is an expert in family travel, who travels the state and globe with her three children.

PREVIOUS SPREAD: KALBARRI NATIONAL PARK (P168).
STEVE WATERS/CONTRIBUTOR

Contents

Best Experiences 6
Calendar 18
Trip Builders 26
7 Things to Know About West Coast Australia 36
Read, Listen, Watch & Follow 38

Perth 40

Jazz Up Your Evening 46
Fremantle Nooks & Crannies 48
The Picnic Spots Locals Love 52
Sculpture-Gaze at First Light 54
A Local's Take on Leederville 56

VISUAL GUIDES

WA's Weird & Wonderful Wildflowers 64
The Biggest, Tallest & Quirkiest 116
Outta this World 152
The Best of the Kimberley ... 218

ESSAYS

Perth's Ambitious Restoration Projects 50
The Boab Transplant 70
Beyond the Quokkas 98
Living on Country 124
Southwest Australia's Biodiversity Hotspot 148
A Long & Complicated History 166
Australia's First Nations People 180
The Pilbara's Great Mining Debate 196
Paradise Almost Lost 224

Street Art Tour 60
Best Free Spots for a Barbecue 62
Under-the-Radar Perth Beaches 66
Savouring Indigenous Flavours 72
A Mystery Tour of Maylands 74
Play the Day Away 76
Listings 78

Perth Region 82

Surprises in the Swan Valley 86
The Pinnacles at Sunset 88
Oddities & Curiosites of Katter Kich 90
Dawn 'til Dusk in the Avon Valley 94
Overnighting on Rottnest ... 96
Easy-Access Roo Spotting 100
Driving Perth's Valleys 102
Eco Eats, Unicorns & Waterfalls 104
Listings 106

Margaret River & the South West 108

A Margaret River Taster 112
Farm-to-Table Trail 114
Go Forest Bathing 118
An Almighty Coast 120
Fun for all Ages in Busselton 126
Explore the Valleys 128
The South West's Artistic Side 130
Margaret River's Underworld 132
Up the Adrenaline Level 134
Listings 136

South Coast 138

The Power of Wilderness 142
A Creative Escape 144
Feel Denmark's Vibe 146
The South Coast for Foodies 150
For Beach Lovers 154
Albany for the History Buff 156
Listings 158

Monkey Mia & the Central West 160

Keepers of the Flame 164
The Cliffs of Kalbarri 168
The Park at the End of the Road 170
A World Heritage Drive 172
Shark Bay's Dolphins & Wallabies 174
The Untamed Coast 176
Listings 178

Ningaloo Coast & the Pilbara 184

More than Whale Sharks 188
The Canyons of Cape Range 192
Epic Adventures Inland 194
Indigenous Art in the Pilbara 198
The Way of the Warlu 200
Pits, Pearls & Pioneers 202
Listings 204

Kangaroos, Lucky Bay (p153)

Broome & the Kimberley 206

Beyond Broome 212
The Inland Reef 214
The Remote Duncan Road 216
The Epic Gibb River Road 220
Deep in the Kimberley 226
Breathless in the Bungle Bungles...........228
The Best of Broome......... 230
Listings 232

Practicalities 236

Arriving 238
Getting Around..................240
Safe Travel 242
Money 243
Accommodation 244
Responsible Travel 246
Essentials 248

Acknowledgement of Country

Lonely Planet would like to acknowledge all Aboriginal nations throughout this country, who have nurtured and maintained the land since time immemorial. This guide was written on, and is written about, the lands of many diverse nations.

We recognise the unique and ongoing connection that Aboriginal peoples have to land and waters and thank them for their efforts to preserve them. We pay our respects to Elders past and present and extend this respect to any Aboriginal or Torres Strait Islander people who may be reading this guide.

We also recognise the ongoing efforts of Aboriginal peoples for reconciliation, justice, and social, cultural and economic self-determination. Sovereignty was never ceded. Australia always was, and always will be, Aboriginal land.

Cultural Sensitivity Warning

Aboriginal and Torres Strait Islander readers are advised that this guide may contain names and images of people who have since passed away.

GOURMET WEST COAST

Australia's southwestern corner is one of the nation's most underrated culinary stars. Margaret River, where the West's reputation for excellence begins, is well known for its wineries, breweries and much more. But far fewer visitors realise until they're here that Perth also has a dynamic eating scene, the Swan Valley is filled with places where you can indulge your taste buds, and Denmark's wine region is like stumbling on secret treasure.

Left Lunch, Cullen Wines (p113)
Right Wine tasting, Margaret River (p112)
Below Bushtucker talk, Swan Valley (p86)

→ MARGARET RIVER WINES

The Margaret River wine region boasts more than 200 (mostly boutique) wineries. The most popular grape varieties are chardonnay and cabernet sauvignon.

GAGLIARDIPHOTOGRAPHY/SHUTTERSTOCK

★ GOURMET ESCAPE

In November, the Margaret River wine region hosts what may be Australia's leading food and wine festival, the Western Australia Gourmet Escape (p113).

RIGHT: MAALINUP ABORIGINAL GALLERY
LEFT: CATHERINE SUTHERLAND/LONELY PLANET

★ SEAFOOD FRENZY

With succulent marron, sweet Exmouth Gulf prawns and the fabled 'barra' (barramundi), WA is a seafood gourmand's paradise. Whalers (p205) in Exmouth serves an unmissable seafood platter.

Best Food & Wine Experiences

- **Create a Tuscan (or Thai) feast at a Wildwood Valley cooking class in Yallingup.** (p113)
- **Choose from 280 wines at the Naked Fox and shop farmers markets in the Swan Valley.** (p86)
- **Taste little-known native flavours in some of Perth's best restaurants.** (p73)
- **Combine wine, food and art galleries along Denmark's farm-gate trails.** (p147)
- **Discover cannabis-based gin and the endemic marron (fresh-water crayfish) in Albany.** (p151)

UNDER THE SEA

Where the Indian Ocean crashes into Australia's West Coast, the sea is a brightly coloured world of astonishing riches. Whales and whale sharks, turtles and dolphins, corals and the weirdly wonderful stromatolites: they're all here in one of the richest concentrations of marine life anywhere on the planet. Whether you're watching from above or diving and snorkelling amid kaleidoscopic underwater hues, this really is one of Australia's best marine experiences.

Left Sea turtle, Ningaloo Reef (p188)
Right Sting rays, Hamelin Bay (p122)
Below Southern Right whale, South Coast (p138)

→ RAYS

There's no better place to widen your marine life checklist than the graceful rays of Hamelin Bay in the South West. Expect smooth stingrays, black stingrays and eagle rays.

ADWO/SHUTTERSTOCK

★ CORAL

It's probably the easiest place in the whole country to snorkel, and Ningaloo won't disappoint, with over 220 species of hard corals on display.

RIGHT: LEA SCADDAN/GETTY IMAGES©; LEFT: EMILY HAMLEY/SHUTTERSTOCK

↑ RESPONSIBLE WHALE WATCHING

If you can't get enough of whales, head to the calm waters of King George Sound, off Albany along the southern coast, from May to October.

Best Marine Wildlife Experiences

- **Swim with magnificent whale sharks from March to August at Ningaloo.** (p188)
- **Spot migrating whales, including the reclusive blue whale, at Augusta and Dunsborough.** (p122)
- **Dive the Indian Ocean's most southerly coral reef at the Houtman Abrolhos Islands.** (p165)
- **Drift snorkel above intricate corals on sublime Ningaloo Reef at Turquoise Bay.** (p190)
- **Search out orcas and southern right whales at Bremer Bay on the South Coast.** (p152)

ABORIGINAL **ART**

One of the best experiences you can have out West is diving into the unimaginably rich world of Aboriginal art. From ancient rock art to modern art centres where you can talk to artists and see their works-in-progress, it's a wonderful introduction to one of the oldest living cultures on the planet.

Left Rock art, Murujuga National Park (p199)
Right Gwion Gwion figures, Ngauwudu (p226)
Below Warmun Arts (p232), Warmiun

→ HOW OLD?

Some Murujuja petroglyphs and Kimberley animal figures have been dated to 50,000 years old, while Kimberley Gwion Gwion (Bradshaw) images go back around 20,000 years and the Wandjina a modest 4000.

NATURE PICTURE LIBRARY/ALAMY

WANDJINA

This creator being is an important cultural entity for the language groups of the central and northern Kimberley and adorns many rock shelters along the Gibb River Rd and Ngauwudu (Mitchell Plateau).

RIGHT: STEVE WATERS/ALAMY, LEFT: STEVE WATERS/CONTRIBUTOR

↑ ART AS CULTURE

Although there's no word in Aboriginal languages for 'art', visual imagery has always served as a connection between past, present and future, and between Aboriginal people and their homelands.

Best Aboriginal Art

- **Discover petroglyphs dating back 50,000 years at Murujuga National Park.** (p199)
- **Spend a day or a week at the Kimberley's unique Aboriginal-owned art centres.** (p232)
- **Explore rock art along the Kimberley's King Edwards River at Munurru.** (p227)
- **Browse works by Wajarri, Noongar, Badimaya and Wilunyu peoples at Yamaji Art.** (p165)
- **Admire works by some of the Pilbara's best artists at Yinjaa-Barni Art in Roebourne.** (p199)

Burringurrah (Mt Augustus), inland from Carnarvon, is two times larger than much better-known Uluṟu.

The Kimberley gorges of Geikie, Tunnel Creek and Windjana form part of an ancient undersea reef dating back 380 million years to the Devonian era.

SUBLIME **SCENERY**

The outback presses right up against this remarkable coastline, and these are some of the most beautiful landforms you'll see anywhere. In places, great gorges and epic monoliths rise from the seemingly endless desert. And in this, as in all things, the northwest is very much the jewel of a gem-studded crown.

Best Outback Experiences

- **Explore the spectacular gorges of the Pilbara's Karijini National Park.** (pictured; p195)
- **Discover why the Kimberley is such a special place in remote Ngauwudu (Mitchell Plateau).** (p226)
- **Disappear into the labyrinths of the Bungle Bungles in Purnululu National Park.** (p229)
- **See the dramatic limestone spires of the Pinnacles at sunset.** (p88)
- **Marvel at one of Australia's most perspective-altering facades at Katter Kich (Wave Rock).** (p90)

IACOMINO FRIMAGES/SHUTTERSTOCK

A DESERTED SHORE

Australia's West Coast wraps from the wild and windy Great Australian Bight in the south to the remote Kimberley in the far north. Its beaches get a fraction of the visitors that flock to the East Coast, so finding a deserted stretch of sand is never a problem. The issue is choosing which one.

→ DUNES OF THE SOUTH WEST

Yeagarup Dunes lie in the Pemberton hinterland. Nearby you can see the awesome basalt columns of Black Point.

Best Deserted Beaches

- **Experience the best of the south at gorgeous Shelley Beach.** (p155)
- **Disappear off the map up north on Eighty Mile Beach.** (p204)
- **Heed the call of the wild at Mandalay Beach in D'Entrecasteaux National Park.** (p155)
- **Seek out striking landscapes overlooking the Southern Ocean in Torndirrup National Park.** (p143)

← EIGHTY-PLUS MILE BEACH

The longest recognised beach on the Australian mainland is actually a lot longer than its name, clocking in at 137 miles (220km).

Above Eighty Mile Beach (p204)
Left Yeagurup Dunes (p123)

CULTURAL ENCOUNTERS

Western Australia is a great place to explore Aboriginal cultures, from coastal 'saltwater people' to the custodians of lakes and rivers to the desert mobs of the interior. Aboriginal-owned and -run businesses are more than willing to showcase their Country, whether by guided tour, a bush tucker class or a window on their art practice.

LEFT: ELEMENTS MARGARET RIVER
BOTTOM: HEATHER RUTH ROSE/SHUTTERSTOCK

★ WAITOC

The **Western Australian Indigenous Tourism Operators Council** *(waitoc.com)* should be your starting point for finding Aboriginal-owned tour operators for the areas you'll be visiting.

Best Indigenous Connections

- **Visit an Aboriginal-owned art centre and discover Indigenous motifs.** (p232)
- **Kayak Shark Bay and learn bush skills with Wula Gura Nyinda Eco Adventures.** (p171)
- **Walk a Songline with the Goolarabooloo along Broome's Lurujarri Dreaming Trail.** (p213)
- **Dive into Margaret River's Aboriginal food culture on a Koomal Dreaming tour.** (p113)

Above Guided tour, Koomal Dreaming (p113), Margaret River
Left Shark Bay (p174)

The banding on the Bungle Bungle domes is caused by cyanobacteria (grey) and iron oxide sandstone (orange).

The Bungles only became known to the public in 1983 after they were filmed for a documentary. Only Aboriginal people and cattle-mustering pilots had known of them previously.

STEVE WATERS/SHUTTERSTOCK

LOST **WORLDS**

You don't have to stray far from the coastal highway to nearly fall off the map. At so many places along this shore, it's possible to leave behind not just the crowds but the modern world, and catch a glimpse of an Australia little changed in the centuries since Europeans first arrived.

Best Remote Adventures

- **See Australia's wildlife as it once was on Dirk Hartog Island.** (p175)
- **Unplug from reality on a three-day hike into Piccaninny Gorge.** (pictured; p229)
- **Lose yourself in a paradise of wildlife and blissful isolation in the Dampier Archipelago.** (p199)
- **Take the 'road' less travelled as you drive the Kimberley's Duncan Road.** (p216)

At last count Perth had a population close to 2.4 million people.

Perth often lays claim to being the world's most isolated city: it lies 2104km (a three-hour flight) from Adelaide, the nearest city.

A SECRET **PERTH**

Perth is the kind of city where a little inside knowledge makes all the difference, be it entering a jazz bar via a phone box, finding the stairs to a secret Fremantle rooftop, or hunting out the best coffee down a Leederville laneway. Some attractions, such as Cottesloe Beach, are so popular that they simply can't be missed, but you can have it all to yourself if you know when to visit.

Left Perth (p40)
Right Cottesloe Beach (p54)
Below Craft-beer tasting

→ EUROPEAN COLONISTS

The first Europeans to come ashore at Perth (on Cottesloe Beach) were Dutch sailors in 1697. Modern Perth was not established until 1829.

BMPHOTOGRAPHER/SHUTTERSTOCK

WADJUK COUNTRY

The land on which Perth now sits has been occupied for 40,000 years. This is the land of Wadjuk, a sub-group of the Noongar people.

RIGHT: LESLIE BRIENZA/SHUTTERSTOCK. LEFT: RUDY BALASKO/SHUTTERSTOCK

↑ PERTH'S EVOLVING DRINKING SCENE

Things change. Northbridge, traditionally pubby, brawly and brassy, now sustains a more idiosyncratic drinking scene. Craft beer reigns supreme in formerly hard-drinking Fremantle.

Best Perth Experiences

- **Get into the swing of Perth's live music at Jazz Cellar.** (p46)
- **Visit Cottesloe Beach's sculpture festival at dawn with just a handful of locals.** (p54)
- **Find your own secluded corner of Bennion Beach, where locals go to escape the crowds.** (p67)
- **Explore the bohemian heart of Leederville by wandering the bars and shops of Oxford St.** (p56)
- **Slip into Darling Darling as the sun nears the horizon for a real slice of Fremantle life.** (p49)

Indigenous Calendars

The four European seasons are not a good fit for many parts of WA; locally, Aboriginal people have been using their own natural calendars for millennia. These range from two to six seasons and are usually broken into sub-seasons. We've elected to use the Noongar six-season calendar for some southern destinations. Search csiro.au, bom.gov.au and goolarabooloo.org.au for 'indigenous calendars' for other groups.

Northern Wet Season

While much of Australia is on holiday, the Kimberley is taking a warm bath. Many businesses close for the duration.

Perth Summer

Perth has one of Australia's loveliest summer climates, with warm temperatures, clear skies and relatively little rain or humidity.

↗ Windsurfing Gero

Summer sees the best conditions for experienced windsurfers at Geraldton's beaches.

→ Orca Pods

January to March is the best time to see large pods of orcas (killer whales) off Bremer Bay in the South West.

p152

DECEMBER

JANUARY

Average January daytime max: 31.4°C (Perth)
Days of rainfall: 2

West Coast Australia in SUMMER

FROM LEFT: JACK KINNY/SHUTTERSTOCK, TORY KALLMAN/SHUTTERSTOCK
MATT JELONEK/GETTY IMAGES, ADWO/SHUTTERSTOCK, STARGRASS/SHUTTERSTOCK

Bunuru Festival

A family-friendly celebration of Indigenous culture from the Undalup Association launches in Pioneer Park, Cowaramup, in mid-February.

▶ australiassouthwest.com/events/undalup-bunuru-festival

All that Glitters

The climate might be wet, but Broome's Mardi Gras, held over two weeks each February, is a riotous celebration of LGBTQIA+ culture.

▶ broomepride.com

→ Perth Music

Late summer sees the excellent Perth Festival and the indie Laneway Festival in Arena Joondalup as live music takes over the city.

▶ perthfestival.com.au, lanewayfestival.com/perth

↑ Fringe World

At Perth's cheekiest arts festival, hundreds of artists perform in parks and pubs across January and February.

Perth (p40)

▶ fringeworld.com.au

FEBRUARY

Average January daytime max: 38°C (Exmouth)
Days of rainfall: 2

Average January daytime max: 33.4°C (Broome)
Days of rainfall: 10

Packing Notes

A hat and sunscreen for warm summer days; an umbrella in the north.

Rain Easing

Things are drying out up north, and by May tourism is back in full swing with most roads open.

Bushwalking South

With easing temperatures and stable weather, autumn is one of the best times to hit the trails in the South West.

↑ Perth Autumn

With summer in the rear-view mirror, it's lovely to be in Perth, enjoying milder temperatures and generally clear skies.

↙ Whale Sharks at Ningaloo

Whale sharks arrive at the Ningaloo Reef in March for one of Australia's greatest wildlife encounters.

Ningaloo (p188)

Margaret River Pro

Watch some of the world's best surfers tackle the gnarly southern swells for 10 days in April at Pevelley.

▸ margaretriver.com/event/margaret-river-pro

MARCH

Average April daytime max: 26°C (Perth)
Days of rainfall: 5

APRIL

West Coast Australia in AUTUMN

FROM LEFT: NYRELLE HAWKINS/SHUTTERSTOCK, CHAMELEONSEYE/SHUTTERSTOCK, SEAN STEININGER/SHUTTERSTOCK, ANNA ALESSIA FRACCALVIERI/SHUTTERSTOCK, LETS GO BEAR TRAVELS/SHUTTERSTOCK

↓ Red Earth Arts Festival

Over 10 days in May, Karratha and surrounding towns come alive for this Indigenous arts festival.

Karratha (p186)

▸ reaf.com.au

← Staircase to the Moon

Come to Broome's Town Beach two nights every month April to October for this alluring natural phenomenon.

Broome (p230)

Ord Valley Muster

Over 10 days in May, Kununurra puts on events such as a huge outdoor concert by the Ord River.

Kununurra (p216)

▸ ordvalleymuster.com.au

MAY

Average April daytime max: 33.4°C (Exmouth)
Days of rainfall: 2

Average April daytime max: 34.4°C (Broome)
Days of rainfall: 2

Outback Cooling

If it's raining on the coast, then rains often linger inland, but temperatures are starting to ease.

Packing Notes

A jacket for evenings in the south, and light, loose-fitting clothes in the north.

The Perth Winter

Perth in winter is generally warmer than Australia's East Coast, but rain is possible and nights are cool.

↑ Wildflowers Emerging

August sees the start of wildflower season, with buds a-blooming across the South West through to October.

Ningaloo Days

It's busy at Ningaloo; while some whale sharks are still hanging around, there are now humpbacks in the mix.

↑ The Best of Broome & Beyond

Milder temperatures, lower humidity and clear skies make this the perfect (and busiest) time in the Kimberley.

Broome (p230)

JUNE

JULY

Average July daytime max: 18.5°C (Perth)
Days of rainfall: 15

West Coast Australia in WINTER

Migrating Whales

Humpback whales are on the move and can be seen from Kalbarri's cliffs all the way to Pender Bay in the Kimberley.

FROM LEFT: AKHDIAN REPPAWALI/SHUTTERSTOCK, CHAMELEONSEYE/SHUTTERSTOCK, ARCHY GREY/SHUTTERSTOCK, INC/SHUTTERSTOCK, LAUREN_GORDONI/SHUTTERSTOCK

↓ Inland Hiking

The winter months are perfect for hiking in Kalbarri, Cape Range and Purnululu, with milder daytime temperatures.

Kalbarri (p168)

↗ Loving the Pearl

Broome's biggest festival, the Shinju Matsuri Festival of the Pearl, kicks off over a two-week period in August–September.

▸ shinjumatsuri.com.au

Average July daytime max: 24.4°C (Exmouth)
Days of rainfall: 3

AUGUST

Average July daytime max: 29.0°C (Broome)
Days of rainfall: 1

Derby Boab Festival

One of the Kimberley's best festivals has concerts, mud footy, tidal-flat dinner parties, art exhibitions and parades.

▸ derbyboabfestival.org.au

Packing Notes

Evenings can be cool and a raincoat may be needed in the south.

West Coast Australia in SPRING

Perth in Spring

The city has a real spring in its step, with warming temperatures and wildflowers blooming in Kings Park.

Roads Less Travelled

Early spring is a fine time to explore the Mid West Coast, and there'll be fewer people than at other times of the year.

↓ Bloom Festival

A month-long flower celebration across the Great Southern has open gardens, wildflower talks, guided walks and myriad other events.

▸ greatsoutherntreasures.com.au/bloom

↖ Space to Breathe

Broome and the Kimberley are winding down in September, most Gibb accommodation closes by October, and locals reclaim Cable Beach by November.

The Kimberley (p208)

SEPTEMBER

OCTOBER

Average October daytime max: 23.5°C (Perth)
Days of rainfall: 6

FROM LEFT: TONY TSL/SHUTTERSTOCK, MATT DEAKIN/SHUTTERSTOCK, BJP7IMAGES/SHUTTERSTOCK, DOMONABIKE/ALAMY, ANJAHENNERN/SHUTTERSTOCK

↓ Sunshine Festival

October is a great time to visit Geraldton for its Sunshine Festival with much beach merriment.

Geraldton (p164)

▸ sunshinefestival.com.au

Nomad Migration

Caravans are all on the move south, away from the pending northern wet season.

↑ Gourmet Escape

Margaret River's culinary celebration is one of Australia's best food-and-wine festivals.

Margaret River (p112)

▸ gourmetescape.com.au

Average October daytime max: 33.0°C (Exmouth)
Days of rainfall: 0

NOVEMBER

Average October daytime max: 33.0°C (Broome)
Days of rainfall: 1

Full Bloom

WA's fabulous wildflowers are in full bloom until early November and appear just inland from the coast all the way north to Shark Bay.

Packing Notes

Loose-fitting clothes in the north; both warm and cool clothing in the south.

PERTH & AROUND
Trip Builder

TAKE YOUR PICK OF MUST-SEES AND HIDDEN GEMS

Perth is both a dynamic destination in its own right and the gateway to a world of natural and culinary attractions. This is the West at its most diverse, with a stirring mix of urban and semi-wilderness to nourish the soul.

Trip Notes

Hub towns Perth, Northam

How long? Allow 10 days

Getting around You won't need a car for Perth or Rottnest Island (the latter is a boat trip away), but grab a rental from the airport to explore the valleys and further afield.

Tips Base yourself in Perth, but factor in overnight stays for Rottnest Island and Cervantes (near the Pinnacles) so you can enjoy both sunset and sunrise.

FROM LEFT: BENNY MARTY/SHUTTERSTOCK, BELLYTUBBY/SHUTTERSTOCK, MARTIN HELGEMEIR/SHUTTERSTOCK

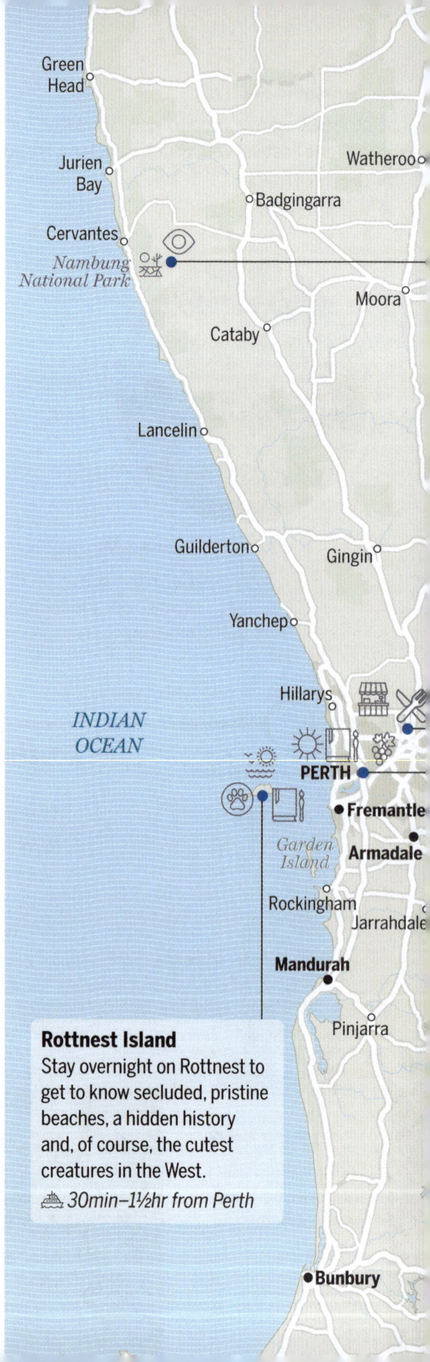

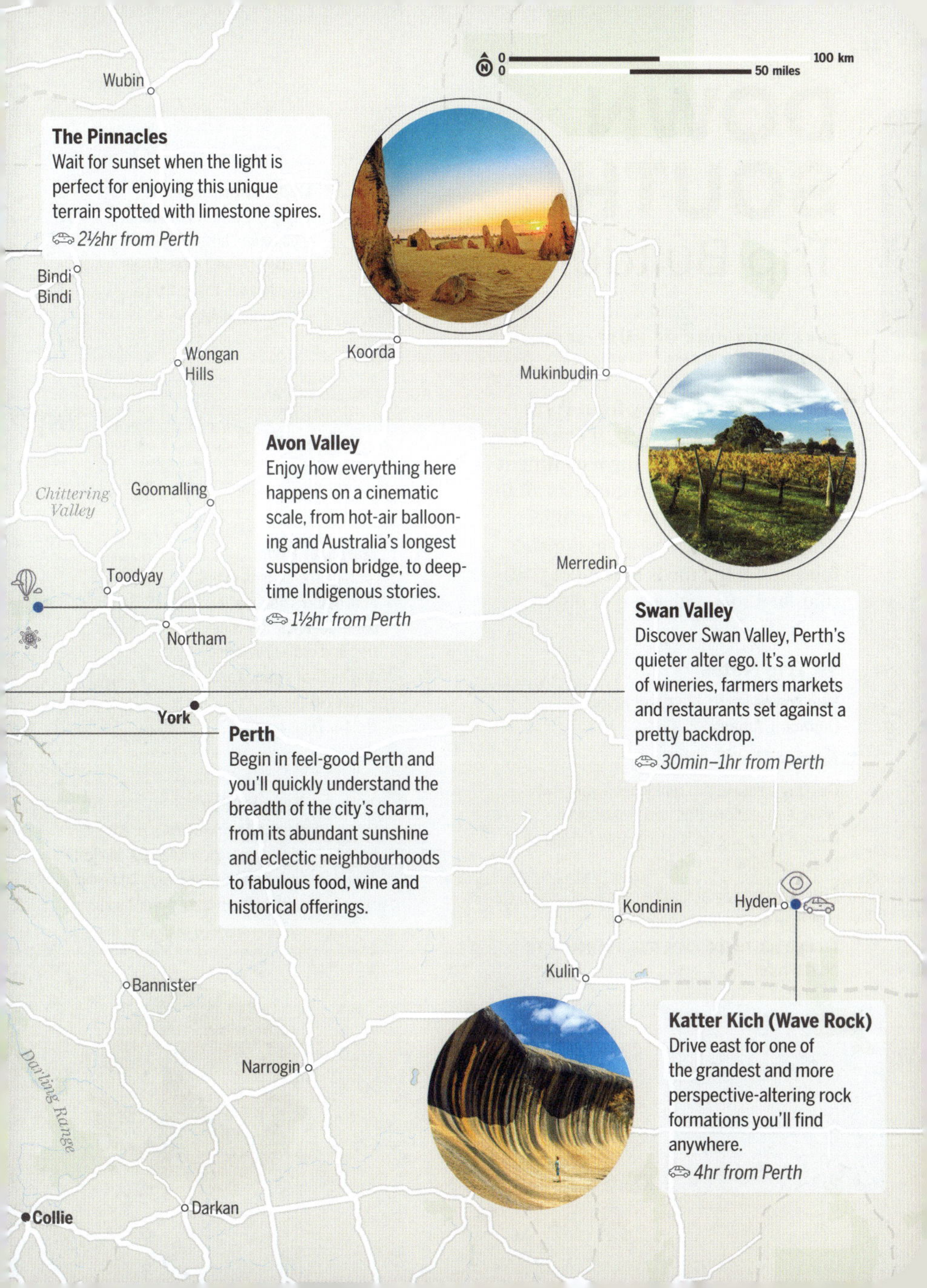

The Pinnacles
Wait for sunset when the light is perfect for enjoying this unique terrain spotted with limestone spires.
2½hr from Perth

Avon Valley
Enjoy how everything here happens on a cinematic scale, from hot-air ballooning and Australia's longest suspension bridge, to deep-time Indigenous stories.
1½hr from Perth

Swan Valley
Discover Swan Valley, Perth's quieter alter ego. It's a world of wineries, farmers markets and restaurants set against a pretty backdrop.
30min–1hr from Perth

Perth
Begin in feel-good Perth and you'll quickly understand the breadth of the city's charm, from its abundant sunshine and eclectic neighbourhoods to fabulous food, wine and historical offerings.

Katter Kich (Wave Rock)
Drive east for one of the grandest and more perspective-altering rock formations you'll find anywhere.
4hr from Perth

DOWN SOUTH
Trip Builder

TAKE YOUR PICK OF MUST-SEES AND HIDDEN GEMS

On this odyssey from Perth through the South West, it can feel as though you're traversing a continent full of diversity. The region has all the hallmarks of the West's magnificence: dramatic landscapes, a passionate food-and-wine focus and quiet roads that lead to a real sense of discovery.

Trip Notes

Hub towns Perth, Margaret River, Denmark, Albany

How long? Allow two weeks

Getting around You really need your own vehicle to explore this vast region; the reward for doing so is being able to take all those enticing back roads.

Tips Plan to stay at least a couple of nights in each place or you'll feel as though you're spending much of your time on the road.

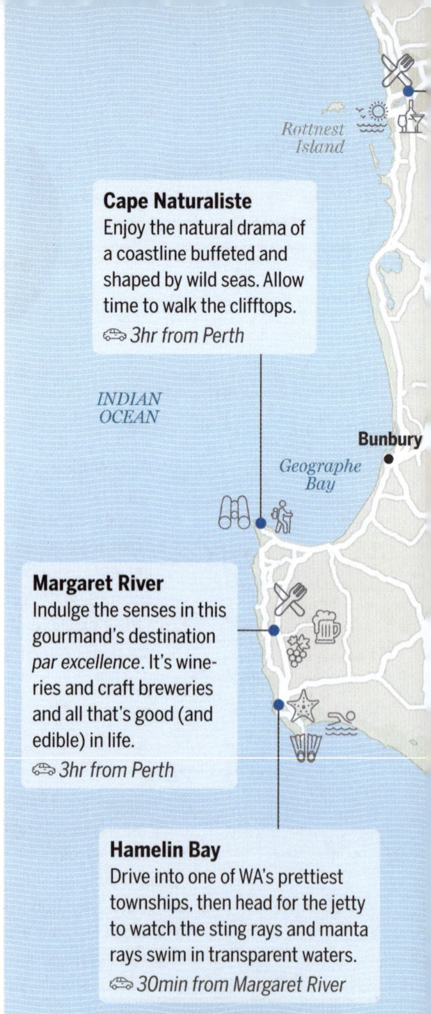

FROM LEFT: YVES DEHOUCK/SHUTTERSTOCK, BMPHOTOGRAPHER/SHUTTERSTOCK, WANDERERS AT HEART/SHUTTERSTOCK

Perth

Dive into Perth's vibrant cultural and culinary life. This is one beautiful city and it's usually bathed in sunshine.

Walpole-Nornalup National Park

Lose yourself in the rivers and ancient forests of giant eucalypts at Walpole-Nornalup National Park.

3½hr from Margaret River

Albany

Feed both body and soul in Albany, an emerging destination for foodies as much as it is a haven for naturalists and historians.

40min from Denmark

Denmark

Discover bohemian Denmark with its markets, cafes, wineries and surrounding country that takes in glorious coastline and forests.

1hr from Walpole

Fitzgerald River National Park

Go on an adventure in Fitzgerald River, soaking up its wilderness feel, incredible floral diversity and inspiring views from East Mt Barren.

2½–3½hr from Albany

PERTH TO MONKEY MIA

Trip Builder

TAKE YOUR PICK OF MUST-SEES AND HIDDEN GEMS

You don't have to travel too many kilometres north of Perth to realise that West Coast Australia is one wildly beautiful shore. The traffic thins, the distances between towns grow, and the views just get better the further north you go.

Trip Notes

Hub towns Perth, Geraldton, Kalbarri, Denham

How long? Allow two weeks

Getting around You could get from A to B by bus, and there are flights (handy for getting back to Perth), but there's really no substitute for having your own vehicle.

Tips Don't be too ambitious about how far you travel each day. Distances are vast, and you'll enjoy it more if you take it slowly.

FROM LEFT: STEVE WATERS/CONTRIBUTOR, ASRUL_ROWI/SHUTTERSTOCK, ANDREAS VON MALLINCKRODT/SHUTTERSTOCK

N 0 200 km
0 100 miles

Francois Peron National Park
Explore beyond the paved road and discover the coast-less-travelled wilderness of Shark Bay's Francois Peron National Park.
15min from Denham

Shark Bay Road
Go kayaking or swimming or just enjoy the stellar coastal views along this World Heritage Drive through a stark, rugged landscape.
4hr from Kalbarri

INDIAN OCEAN

Monkey Mia
Observe wild dolphins, get active on the water and learn local Aboriginal stories at Monkey Mia.
20min from Denham

Kalbarri
Start with clifftop ocean views, move on to some gorge action in Kalbarri National Park, including the spectacular Skywalk, then return to town for a swim.
2hr from Geraldton

Geraldton
Journey through history in and around Geraldton, a bustling coastal hub with plenty of activities to get the adrenaline flowing.
4½hr from Perth

The Pinnacles
Walk amid these weirdly wonderful limestone spires in Nambung National Park; arrive at dawn or dusk for maximum effect.
2hr from Perth

Perth
Soak up the final trappings of city life before you leave it all behind for the long journey north.

EXMOUTH TO BROOME
Trip Builder

TAKE YOUR PICK OF MUST-SEES AND HIDDEN GEMS

This stretch of coastline is a special combination of incredible marine life (Ningaloo Reef), glorious outback parks (Millstream Chichester and Karijini), and gritty coastal towns (Port Hedland) where mining and Aboriginal communities rub shoulders. Put together, it's an opportunity to experience everything good about the West Coast on one long drive.

Trip Notes

Hub towns Exmouth, Port Hedland, Broome

How long? Allow two weeks

Getting around You'll need your own vehicle. A 2WD works, though a 4WD is a better (and insured) ride on unsealed roads.

Tips Skip the Pilbara interior between November and March, when temperatures are unbearable. Camping at Cape Keraudren or Eighty Mile Beach is a pleasant alternative to overnighting in Port Hedland. The Great Northern Hwy is the quickest way south.

FROM LEFT: DVLCOM · WWW.DVLCOM.CO.UK/SHUTTERSTOCK, STEVE WATERS/CONTRIBUTOR, STEVE WATERS/CONTRIBUTOR

Murujuga National Park
Step back 40,000 years at UNESCO-listed Murujuga National Park on the Burrup Peninsula, home to several million ancient Aboriginal petroglyphs.
4hr from Karijini

Port Hedland
Wander among disused machinery, watch impressively massive ships and embrace the rust-red sunset against an apocalyptic industrial skyline in this surprising coastal outpost.
4hr from Karijini

Broome
Delve into local history, treat your taste buds, witness the Staircase to the Moon (p21), and watch the sunset at the one and only Cable Beach.
6½hr from Port Hedland

Millstream Chichester National Park
Stare wide-eyed at the glittering Milky Way from the dark-sky haven of peaceful Millstream and its soothing palm-fringed pools.
4hr from Karijini

Karijini National Park
Discover the magnificent gorges of Karijini hidden in the harsh Pilbara ironstone hills and spinifex plains like rough diamonds.
7hr from Exmouth

Exmouth
Pry yourself away from laid-back Exmouth with its dive shops, craft breweries, beaches and excellent foodie scene on this epic drive into the legendary northwest.

KIMBERLEY TRAVERSE
Trip Builder

TAKE YOUR PICK OF MUST-SEES AND HIDDEN GEMS

The Kimberley is one of Australia's last frontiers, at once Indigenous homelands brimming with culture, Songlines and ancient rock art and a rugged landscape of broken escarpments, boab-studded savannahs, million-acre cattle stations and hidden gorges fringed with rainforest. Shed your city skin, channel your inner explorer and embrace the Australia of legend.

Trip Notes

Hub towns Broome, Derby, Kununurra

How long? Allow at least two weeks

Getting around You'll need a high-clearance 4WD for the Gibb River Rd, or join a Broome-to-Darwin overland tour.

Tips Make a loop from Broome or Kununurra by taking the Gibb River Rd in one direction and returning along the sealed highway. Outside the dry season (May to mid-October), many businesses close and unsealed roads become impassable.

Ngauwudu (Mitchell Plateau)

Discover ancient rock art and the striking Punamii-Uunpuu (Mitchell Falls) on an epic drive to the far-flung Ngauwudu.

6½hr from Mt Elizabeth

Emma Gorge

Float on your back and soak up the feeling of being far away from it all in one of the Kimberley's prettiest waterholes.

1hr from Kununurra

Kununurra

Paddle along the mighty Ord, stretch your legs in Mirima National Park or just relax under the mango trees while your vehicle's repaired.

6hr from Mt Elizabeth

Mt Elizabeth Station

Stay on a fair-dinkum outback cattle station and watch how things are done in the heart of the Kimberley.

6hr from Derby

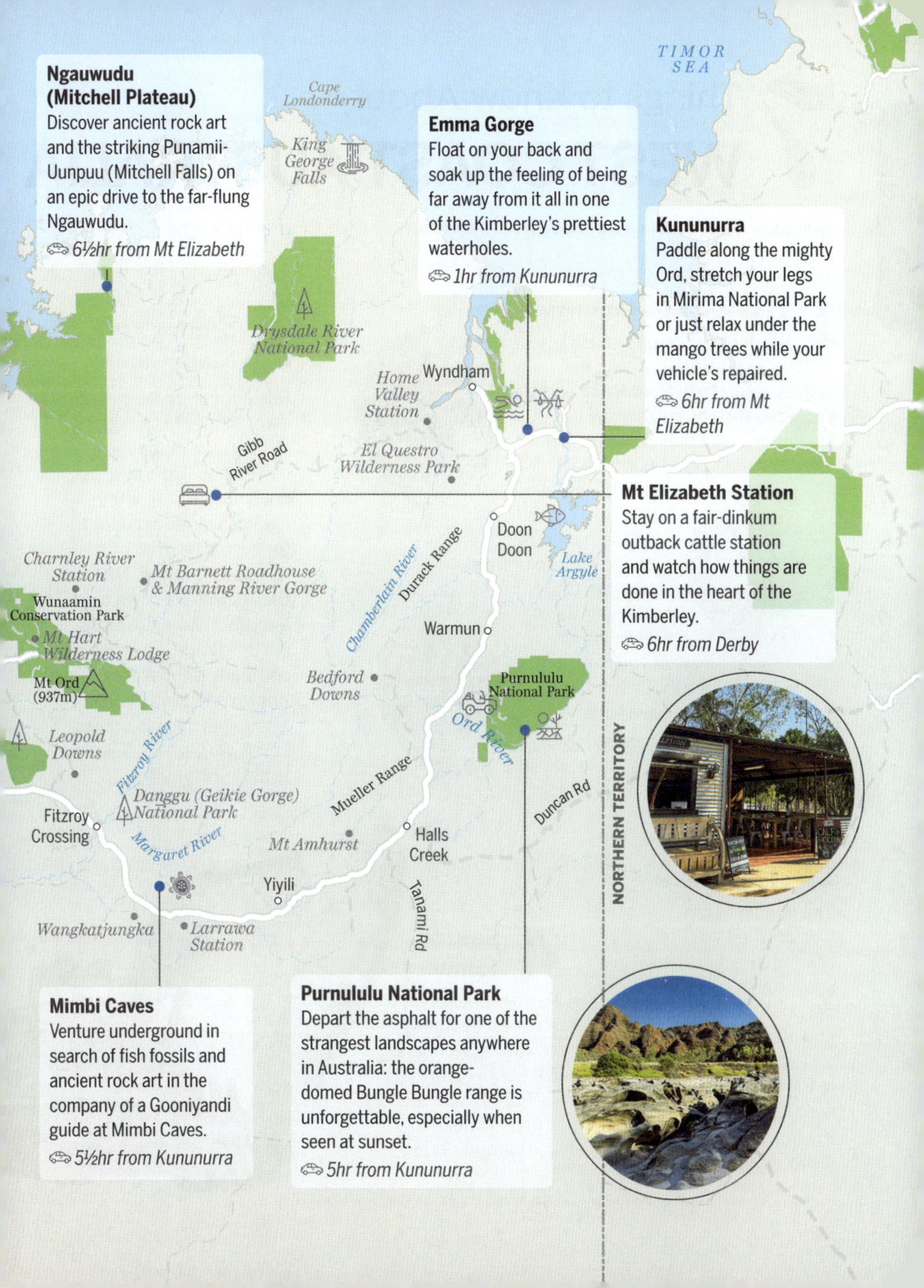

Mimbi Caves

Venture underground in search of fish fossils and ancient rock art in the company of a Gooniyandi guide at Mimbi Caves.

5½hr from Kununurra

Purnululu National Park

Depart the asphalt for one of the strangest landscapes anywhere in Australia: the orange-domed Bungle Bungle range is unforgettable, especially when seen at sunset.

5hr from Kununurra

7 Things to Know About WEST COAST AUSTRALIA

INSIDER TIPS TO HIT THE GROUND RUNNING

1 This is a BIG Country

Western Australia's south is relatively compact, but take the coastal road north from Perth and you'll see the country's scale is staggering. By the time you reach Kununurra you'll have driven over 3000km. That's longer than from Madrid to Oslo or from New York City to Denver. Be realistic about what you can achieve in the time you have available.

▶ See more about getting around (p240)

2 Mining's the Main Game

Resource-rich WA makes a lot of money from digging stuff up and shipping it overseas. The state government's mining royalties alone account for over 20% of all of its public revenue. Then there's the infrastructure – roads, power, hospitals, ports – that the big mining companies subsidise. Approximately half of all Australian mining jobs are in WA. Go visit the Pilbara (p184) and you'll soon

3 Booming Expensive

The mining boom transformed WA (particularly Perth and areas north) into one pricey destination. Plan carefully or you may find the fuel, food and accommodation prices in the outback deflating your wallet.

▶ See more about managing your money (p243)

4 Sunny Times

Perth is officially the sunniest capital in Australia, averaging 8.8 hours of daylight per day. No wonder it doesn't need to use summer time.

1 ECELOP/SHUTTERSTOCK, **2** MAFU77/SHUTTERSTOCK, **5** ZPANTUNA/SHUTTERSTOCK, **7** KOHKENGZA/SHUTTERSTOCK

5 When the Doctor Calls

Between November and March, a cooling southwesterly wind can blow across WA's coastal towns due to a temperature differential between land and ocean. In Perth it's famously known as the 'Fremantle Doctor' because that's the direction the wind comes from (and it makes you feel better). Temperatures can drop several degrees. Geraldton, Carnarvon and Albany all have their own 'doctors'.

6 Talking Strine

Aussies love talking slang (Strine), and WA is no exception.

sandgroper – denizen of WA

mate – universal term to address someone you know or don't know or whose name you can't remember: *'Hey, mate, where's the loo?'*

loo – toilet

bevvies – drinks

arvo – afternoon: *'Hey, mate, wanna have a couple of bevvies this arvo?'*

FIFO – mining parlance for workers that fly-in to work then fly-out back home each roster

hi–vis – fluorescent orange, yellow or pink reflective work clothing; the 'Pilbara tuxedo'

shout – buy a round of drinks: *'It's your shout, mate'*

bush chook – emu; also slang for the local Emu Export lager

carton – cardboard box containing 30 cans of beer: *'Give us a carton of bush chook, mate; ta'*

ta – thanks

thongs – flip-flops

stubby holder – neoprene holder for your bevvy; essential road-trip accessory

footy – Australian Rules football

7 Iconic Eats

Perth's lunchtime favourite is the humble conti (short for continental) roll packed with cured meats, cheese and various pickled vegetables. Italian migrants started the trend in the 1950s.

The WA marron is a delectable freshwater crayfish that's not dissimilar to the East Coast yabbie.

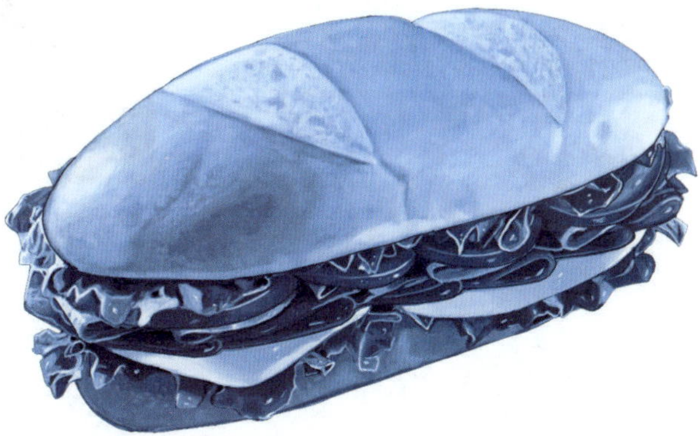

Read, Listen, Watch & Follow

READ

Welcome to Country (Marcia Langton; 2019) Travel guide to Indigenous Australia, with sections on West Coast Australia.

The Shepherd's Hut (Tim Winton; 2019) Nobody describes the WA landscape like the West's living legend.

True West (David Whish-Wilson; 2019) Crime thriller set among the badlands of Perth's freeways.

WA Naturally Pocket-sized natural history guides covering WA's flora, fauna and geology by region.

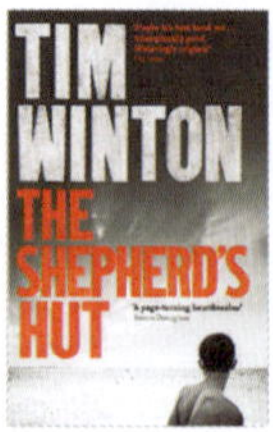

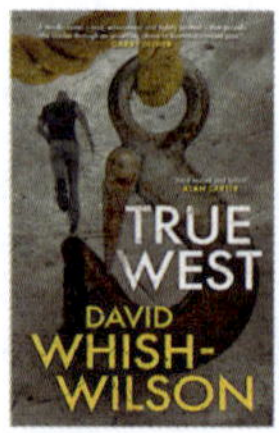

LISTEN

Waringarri Radio (693AM; 102.1FM) This rocking, mob-run East Kimberley station is the perfect accompaniment to the long drive.

Sounds of the Kimberley (WAM; 2020) Compilation album of the best new Kimberley musicians you've probably never heard of.

Bent Trees & Swanny Deez (Ratsalad; 2024) A hardcore Gero three-piece that take no prisoners with their high-energy, riff-laden rock.

Wrong Skin (Richard Baker; 2018) Gripping true-crime podcast investigating an Aboriginal couple's disappearance in the Kimberley.

DANIEL KNIGHTON/GETTY IMAGES

The West Live (thewest.com.au/the-west-live) Podcast on Western Australian life with a focus on Perth.

The Slow Rush (Tame Impala; 2020) Award-winning fourth album by psychedelic indie-rock group from Perth (pictured).

WATCH

Mystery Road (2018–25; pictured top) Series following Indigenous detective Jay Swann across the Kimberley, Goldfields and South West.

Reckless (2025) Fast-paced comedy-crime drama series set in Fremantle.

Dirt Music (2019) Film of Tim Winton's bestseller showcasing the WA landscape.

Run (2026) High-octane drama series loosely based on WA's infamous 'Postcard Bandit' bank robber.

Outback Truckers (2012–; pictured right) Reality TV show giving viewers an idea of outback WA roads, conditions and people.

TOP: CONTRIBUTOR:TCD/PROD.DB/ALAMY, BOTTOM: IAN GEORGESON/ALAMY

FOLLOW

Perth Blogs *(destinationperth.com.au/blog)* Attractions and festivals.

National Indigenous Times *(nit.com.au)* WA news from an Indigenous viewpoint.

Hello Perth *(helloperth.com.au/blog)* City life.

WA Museum *(visit.museum.wa.gov.au/learn/news-stories)* History and culture around WA.

Environs Kimberley *(environskimberley.org.au)* The Kimberley's premier environmental group.

PERTH

BEACHES | OUTDOORS | CITY LIFE

RESEARCHED BY ROSAMUND BRENNAN

PAULO HENRIQUE PIGOZZI/SHUTTERSTOCK

- **Jazz Up Your Evening** (p46)
- **Fremantle Nooks & Crannies** (p48)
- **Perth's Ambitious Restoration Projects** (p50)
- **The Picnic Spots Locals Love** (p52)
- **Sculpture-Gaze at First Light** (p54)
- **A Local's Take on Leederville** (p56)
- **Street Art Tour** (p60)
- **Best Free Spots for a Barbecue** (p62)
- **WA's Weird & Wonderful Wildflowers** (p64)
- **Under-the-Radar Perth Beaches** (p66)
- **The Boab Transplant** (p70)
- **Savouring Indigenous Flavours** (p72)
- **A Mystery Tour of Maylands** (p74)
- **Play the Day Away** (p76)
- **Listings** (p78)

0 — 5 km
0 — 2.5 miles

Seek out the subterranean, 1920s-inspired **Jazz Cellar** (p46)
15min from Perth City Station

INDIAN OCEAN

Take an open-air **street art walk** through the city (p60)
central Perth

Admire a 750-year-old tree in **Kings Park** (p70)
6min from central Perth

Rottnest Island

Find a secluded picnic spot at **Coombe Reserve** (p53)
20min from central Perth

PERTH
Trip Builder

Basking in ridiculously good weather, Perth has a sunny disposition that's shared by its lifestyle-oriented locals. People love to hit the beach, picnic in leafy parks and, after dark, enjoy small bars and upbeat jazz haunts. Welcome to the good life.

FROM LEFT: *SUGAR GLIDER* BY AMOK ISLAND,PHOTO BY BEWLEY SHAYLOR, COURTESY OF FORM; MICHAEL MAJOR/SHUTTERSTOCK; BMPHOTOGRAPHER/SHUTTERSTOCK

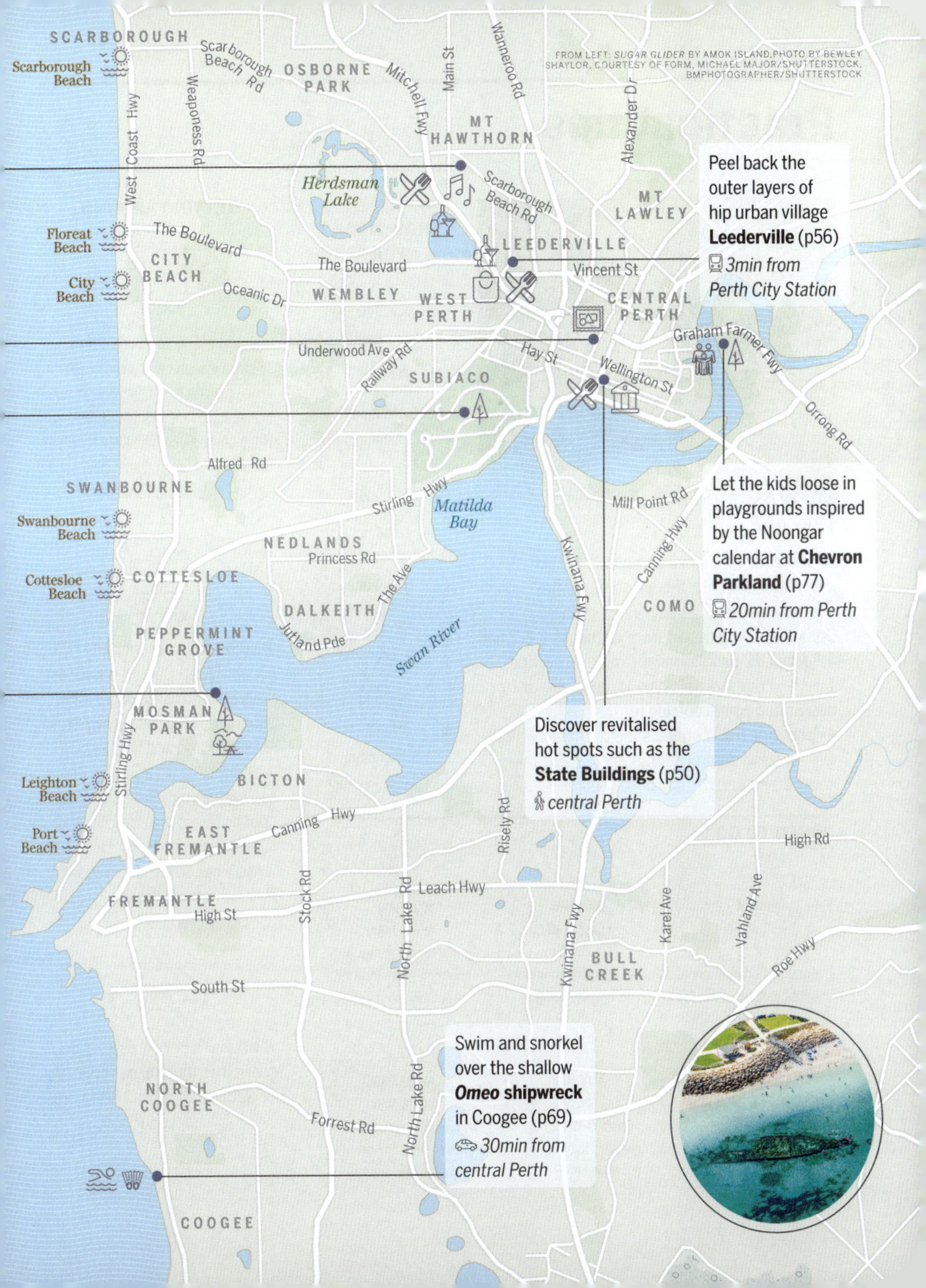

Practicalities

JAMESTEOHART/SHUTTERSTOCK

ARRIVING

Perth Airport Terminal 1 handles most international flights, though some Qantas international services also use Terminal 3. Domestic flights depart from Terminals 1, 2, 3 and 4; Terminal 2 handles mostly regional services. Taxis and rideshare pickups are available at designated points outside terminal exits. The Airport Line train connects the terminals with the city centre in around 20 minutes. Driving takes about 25 minutes, traffic permitting.

HOW MUCH FOR A

Cold beer
$11

Burger
$25

Ice cream
$7 (per scoop)

WHEN TO GO

BIRAK
DEC & JAN
The start of summer's cloudless skies, when the coast beckons.

BUNURU
FEB & MAR
Hot, dry, sun-drenched days made for beach-going.

DJERAN
APR & MAY
A shift to milder days and cooler evenings ideal for outdoor pursuits.

MAKURU
JUN & JUL
Rains fall, arctic winds blow and temperatures drop for winter.

DJILBA
AUG & SEP
Crisp, clear nights give way to sunshine and showers.

KAMBARANG
OCT & NOV
Mother Nature reawakens with warmer airflow and wildflower carpets.

GETTING AROUND

Train Many of Perth's train stations are still a distance from points of interest, but the Fremantle line will whisk you to most places you're likely to want to see, and from there it's most enjoyable to walk.

Bus Perth's free inner-city CAT (Central Area Transit) buses are marked with a black cat logo. Joondalup also has its own free CAT network, and the Surf CAT operates from Stirling Station to Scarborough Beach. Regular public buses are complicated unless you're staying close to the inner city and can avoid connections.

Taxi and Uber Fares from an inner-city suburb like Leederville or Subiaco to central Perth are about $15.

EATING & DRINKING

Perth's food is influenced by its location: as it's isolated from Australia's East Coast, it looks more to neighbouring Asia. You'll discover an inventiveness to its modern-fusion fare, which is often spiked with authentic Asian flavours. In recent years native and indigenous ingredients have had a moment. Marron (freshwater crayfish; pictured right) is a regular on upmarket menus, perhaps garnished with the citrus twang of Geraldton wax, while kangaroo, served rare for its leanness, may be dusted with pepperberry or quandong (native peach) powder.

Best Negroni cocktail
Darling Darling (p49)

Must-try marron
Wildflower (p73)

TOP: MAKSIM FESENKO/SHUTTERSTOCK
BOTTOM: SAM JEFFS/SHUTTERSTOCK

CONNECT & FIND YOUR WAY

Wi-fi Central Perth and nearby Leederville offer free public wi-fi, and many cafes and cultural institutions offer free hot spots. It's simplest to buy a prepaid SIM or eSIM so you can connect on the go.

Navigation Perth is split by the Swan River (Derbarl Yerrigan) and edges the Indian Ocean. Most places you'll visit will be on or between the two.

CYCLING

Many hotels now offer free bikes; Perth's bike paths have been well developed in recent years, with good lighting and safety.

WHERE TO STAY

Perth is a relatively affordable city, but accommodation can be pricey. Staying centrally means more hotels and easier public transport; if hiring a car, go suburban.

Area	Pros/Cons
Central Perth	New, flashy, overlooks the river. Shopping, nightlife and dining pockets. Easy transiting.
Northbridge	Nightlife, small-bar buzz, Chinatown. Some trashy streets. Fast access to cultural hubs and transit links. Neighbours Perth CBD.
Leederville	Cafe strip, hip neighbourhood, street art. Walkable.
Subiaco	European vibes, leafy streets. Quiet with some nighttime activity. Inner city.
Cottesloe	Beach frontage, posh-casual, cafes. Car required.
Fremantle	Port town offering everything from chic boutique hotels to backpacker hostels. Historic streets and beaches galore.

MONEY

Almost anything in Perth can be purchased by contactless card payment, but carry some cash for emergencies and small items. Many parking zones offer the first hour free with ticket.

01 Jazz Up Your EVENING

MUSIC | CULTURE | DISCOVERY

Hidden off a quiet suburban street, out the back of a car park, the Jazz Cellar is an underground – literally – institution that, despite 20 years of fun, has remained a closely kept secret. Embark on a musical exploration of it and its contemporaries; there are three excellent options dotted around the city.

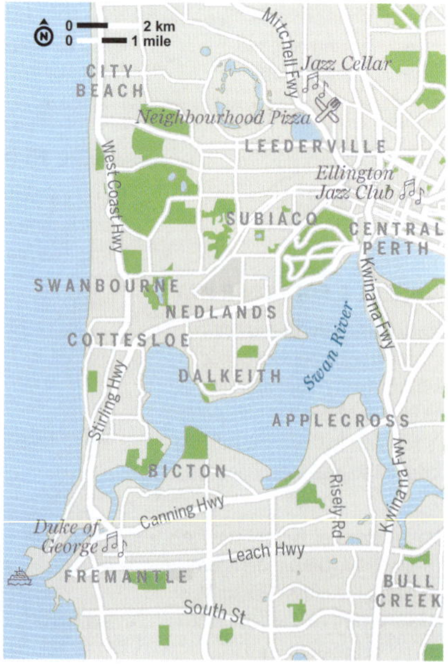

How to

Getting here From the city, take bus 15 to Mt Hawthorn and get off outside the IGA. It's a 10- to 15-minute walk to Jazz Cellar from there. Uber to the other jazz clubs.

Tickets Book at least two weeks ahead at jazzcellar.net.au. This secures your spot, but you'll still need to pay $30 in cash at the door.

When to go Doors open at the Jazz Cellar at 5.45pm and the band starts at 7pm; the night wraps up around 10pm.

Enter through the red phone box Every Friday night the Corner House Jazz Band fires up a tiny stage with hard-driving traditional jazz. Established in the 1980s and a Friday-night mainstay at the **Jazz Cellar** (pictured) for more than 20 years, the band plays swing and vintage styles with snap and swagger. There's room for around 100 people at a squeeze; the atmosphere is electric, and dancing is all but inevitable.

Tracking down the entry is half the fun. Find the Salvation Army opportunity shop on Buxton St and look to the right of the building, where you'll see an open gate leading to a rear car park. Walk in and enter the red phone box, go down narrow stairs and discover a small, windowless cavern decked out with vintage posters and signs – you have arrived.

Rub shoulders with the best Head to the **Ellington Jazz Club** for far more serious, seated viewing. This is where Perth's jazz aficionados mingle with lecturers and students from the highly regarded

JAZZ CELLAR

Western Australian Academy of Performing Arts – it has turned out globally esteemed jazz artists including Jamie Oehlers. Expect low lighting, small, round tables and minimal chatter.

Try a two-fer For dinner and a show, try the **Duke of George** in East Fremantle. This basement haunt in a former broom factory offers a revolving lineup of styles, performed as multicourse meals are delivered to your table. While the jazz is top notch, there's a lighthearted feel to this venue; we can't promise anything, but there may be dancing in the aisles, depending on the night's vibe.

Hot Tips

The Jazz Cellar allows BYO (bring your own) food and drinks, making for an affordable night.

Rather than ordering pizza at the convenient hole-in-the-wall a half-block away, grab takeaway from **Neighbourhood Pizza**, an alleyway warehouse off the bustling Scarborough Beach Rd strip. Find it down light-strung Anvil Lane, between the Vinnies store and Tsukaya restaurant; it's just 10 minutes on foot from the Jazz Cellar.

For libations, hit **The Mezz**, a shopping centre with a Woolworths supermarket and a BWS liquor store. If pizza ain't your thing, there are good takeaway options in the leafy courtyard here.

Above Jazz Cellar

02 Fremantle Nooks & CRANNIES

SECRET SPOTS | LOCAL PICKS | ENTERTAINMENT

Freo, as it's affectionately referred to by locals, is Perth's characterful port town and a well-trodden traveller fave, but there are still a few secret spots. Let us lead you to a hidden-in-plain-sight rooftop bar, a tiny drinking den that evokes 1800s-era seafaring and the place for the tastiest 'cheap cut' of fish you may ever try.

RUBEN M RAMOS/SHUTTERSTOCK

How to

Getting here If you're not already staying in Fremantle, take the Fremantle train line in. The station is close to everything.

When to go To avoid extreme heat or rainy days, visit March to June or September to December. Weekends are twice as busy as weekdays; from day to night, families give way to evening revellers.

Good to know Freo is a hot spot for buskers, especially around the Fremantle Markets, so keep a few coins handy.

CERINCOK/SHUTTERSTOCK

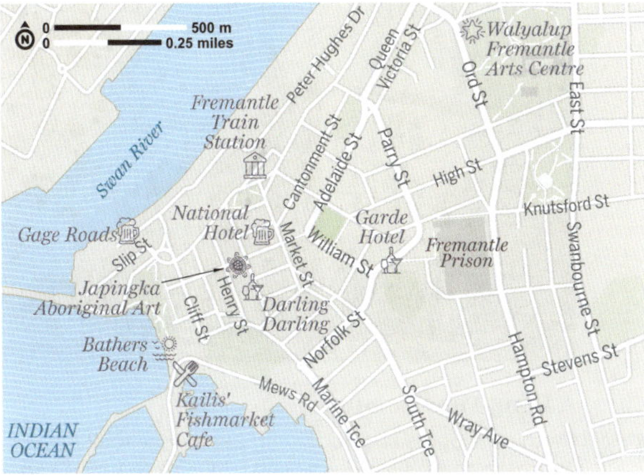

A rooftop secret You'll hear the **National Hotel** before you see it. The multilevel Federation-era pub usually has live music playing in the main bar, but don't stop there. Go in the narrow side entrance and up the stairs. Take them slowly, not only so you don't puff but also so you'll have time to take in the gallery of art the owners have curated on the colourful walls. Reaching the top, you'll walk out onto a sun-drenched deck with clusters of couches and tables. Locals converge here to take in Fremantle's rooftop, ocean and working port views.

A merchant vessel on land As the sun goes down, slip in to the 25-seat **Darling Darling** and be transported to another time. The bijou bar (walk-ins only) seems to breathe low-lit, mahogany-hued history from every surface, but it's all a carefully created illusion. Marvel at the weathered ropes, the wooden ship wheels, the barrels topped with free, crack-'em-open peanuts and the chainlink light fittings. There's atmosphere in spades. Expect a queue at weekends.

A cheap feed For the best-value bites in Freo, head directly to **Kailis' Fishmarket Cafe** on the pretty harbourfront and order the $16 fish wings. Forget any ideas you have about fillets – this is better. A wing is a cut from around the fish fin, and it's one of the tenderest, sweetest parts you can savour. Trust us, you'll never go back.

Left National Hotel
Below Kailis' Fishmarket Cafe

Tips from a Freo Fan

Gage Roads Brew Co This brewery faces onto Fremantle Harbour; you can watch tugboats and cargo ships pass by.

Japingka Aboriginal Art Support Aboriginal artists at this High St gallery.

Walyalup Fremantle Arts Centre Catch a free outdoor concert on Sunday in the warmer months.

Garde Hotel This central Fremantle precinct combines the heritage Warders Hotel (p51), set in former prison-guard cottages, with the contemporary Garde development. Stay overnight, sip wine at micro-bar Gimlet or dine at Emily Taylor restaurant, all in one place.

Bathers Beach Take a dip where the first European settlers of the Swan River colony came ashore in August 1829.

Recommendations by

Ryan Mossny
Tour guide with Two Feet & a Heartbeat walking tours @twofeetperth

Perth's Ambitious Restoration Projects

IF ONLY THE WALLS COULD SPEAK

Once a city prone to knocking heritage buildings down to rebuild in glass and steel, Perth has been reimagining its historic bones over the past 20 years or so, dusting off old haunts and creating them anew. Get to know the hotels, bars and restaurants that now flourish inside vintage structures.

Left State Buildings
Centre Rechabite Hall
Right Fremantle Markets (p48)

JASON KNOTT/ALAMY

A Long Time Coming

Perth developers and decision-makers once took the approach that only new was good. In the late 1960s and '70s in particular, a slew of Perth's architectural beauties were demolished, from tall Gothic masterpieces to grand gold-rush-era hotels. Notably, the State Heritage Act only became law in 1999. It helped to preserve some examples of late- 19th- and early- 20th-century architecture that poke between the skyscrapers and marked the dawning of a new appreciation of historic buildings' value. The adaptation of existing structures also had practical merits: as Perth's population surged, there was a need to increase density and rein in urban sprawl. More recently, arguments for greater sustainability in the built environment – for social and environmental reasons – have also weighed in.

From Dust to Darling

The majestic Treasury building, dating back to 1874, is one of Perth's most awarded conversions. It lay dormant for nearly two decades before one of the founding members of the Little Creatures brewing empire (p81) – today a property developer – embarked on its multimillion-dollar reinvention. Before reopening in 2015 as the State Buildings, it housed the WA capital's original General Post Office, its treasury and government offices and a police cellblock. An impressive 95% of the original buildings were retained; they're now filled with a chic collection of bars, restaurants (p80) and boutiques and a five-star hotel.

DOMONABIKE/ALAMY

EQROY/SHUTTERSTOCK

Secret Society Space

In nearby Northbridge, the looming, whitewashed Rechabite was the headquarters for a secret society known as the Independent Order of Rechabites. Over its 100-year lifespan it was used for church services and school productions and as an election polling station before becoming Perth's most popular dance hall. For decades it fell into disuse, but then its sweeping wooden staircase, lofty ceilings and ornate tile floors were thoroughly resuscitated. Reopened in 2019, it's now a neon-lit performance space with a mess-hall-style restaurant and basement and rooftop bars. (Ironically, the Rechabites were firmly focused on fighting the influence of liquor.) Take the glass elevator up through the four floors and appreciate the layers of construction left deliberately exposed.

> The State Heritage Act only became law in 1999.

Ghosts Make Way

At the port end of the city, Warders Hotel has shrugged off its former life as housing for guards at nearby Fremantle Prison. The 1851 limestone row has been transformed into 11 hotel rooms. Opened in 2020, the hotel has the city's smallest bar, Gimlet, and alfresco Asian restaurant Emily Taylor, named after a spice trading ship that came to grief off Fremantle in 1830. Nearby, on High St, the long-shuttered P&O Hotel has found new life: its street-front bar is now Ode to Sirens, a buzzy, vinyl-spinning hangout celebrating music, art and good times. There are plans to revive the landmark as a hotel.

Heritage Conversions

Freo's West End precinct contains more than 250 heritage buildings, many from the late-19th-century gold boom. **PS Art Space** is a contemporary art space in a converted shipping warehouse. Across the road is the **Republic of Fremantle**, a boutique distillery and cocktail bar. Nearby is the excellent **Bread in Common**, one of the most architecturally awarded heritage conversions in WA. Pop into **Paperbird**, a children's bookshop where hand-picked picture books, artful gifts and small-press treasures line the shelves. Upstairs, a light-filled gallery celebrates illustration and storytelling, hosting exhibitions, workshops and events that blur the line between bookshop, studio and cultural space.

Marcus Canning
Founder of Fringe World, Rooftop Movies and the man behind Rechabite's reinvention; @therechabitehall

03 The Picnic Spots LOCALS LOVE

OUTDOORS | LOCAL SECRETS | LEISURE

Perth is blessed with more sunny days than any other Australian capital, so it's no surprise that picnicking is a popular pastime. Read on for three places that in-the-know locals love best.

PAUL KANE/GETTY IMAGES

How to

Getting here These three destinations are best reached by car or Uber.

When to go Perth sees cloudless blue skies for most of the year, so anytime is picnic time – even some winter days. During hot spells, go around 10am or just before sunset.

Top tip Kids will love the lush gardens of Cottesloe Civic Centre. Down the southern steps, a grassy playground is shaded by a canopy of trees.

JASON KNOTT/ALAMY

Left Playing cricket, Matilda Bay
Below Bayside Kitchen

Family fun Mention **Matilda Bay** to any local and their eyes will light up, but few visitors are aware of this little sandy beach along the Swan River that's shaded by native gums. Groups of picnickers, families in particular, flock here on weekends with boogie boards, lilos and coolers in tow. It's not uncommon for them to spend the entire day dipping in and out of the water, doing bombs off the twin platform jetties, observing the (harmless) jellyfish, watching for dolphins and resting on rugs and deck chairs under the trees. For those who don't have picnic gear, there's a nice cafe at the water's edge called **Bayside Kitchen**.

Your own private Idaho For a far more secluded picnic spot, drive further around the river to the **Coombe Reserve**, which is found at the toes of Perth real estate's most expensive street (Saunders St) – glimpsing the multimillion-dollar mansions alone justifies the trip. Venture beyond the immediate grassy park to the tiny beach beyond. So long as there's not a wedding in play, you'll likely have this quiet nook all to yourself.

Grassy enclave Finally, the gardens of **Cottesloe Civic Centre** are an underrated oasis, eclipsed by the suburb's famous sweep of sand. Walk into the free-to-visit, estate-like grounds and find a place on the west-facing lawn beneath the pines. The ocean views are gorgeous – it's almost criminal that barely another soul will be there.

Be Sun Smart

The Australian sun is very harsh. Before you head outdoors, you'll need to follow the local mantra of 'slip, slop, slap'. It stands for 'slip on a shirt, slop on some sunscreen and slap on a hat.'

The saying comes from the Cancer Council's 1981 sun smart campaign, using a board-short-wearing, tap-dancing cartoon seagull named Sid. The rise in public awareness around the skin cancer risk was so successful you'll frequently hear Aussies rolling out the saying some four decades later. Take the advice and avoid being out in the heat of the day, or seek a shady tree to picnic under. Happily, many of Perth's playgrounds are shaded.

04 Sculpture-Gaze at FIRST LIGHT

OUTDOOR SPACES | ART | BEACH

Perth's most popular and iconic strip of sand, Cottesloe Beach, gets more packed than normal in March, when dozens of huge artworks take up residence on the sand. Here's how to beat the crowds and stroll peacefully around the state's biggest outdoor exhibition, Sculpture by the Sea, before wending your way to some great eats nearby.

JARROD TAYLOR *STRUCTURAL WAVE* SCULPTURE BY THE SEA, COTTESLOE 2021; PHOTO: RICHARD WATSON

How to

Getting here Take the Fremantle train line from Perth to Cottesloe. In summer a free beach bus departs from near the station. Otherwise, it's a 15-minute walk to the coast.

When to go Cottesloe is lovely at any time of the day, but arrive at sunrise to view the sculptures minus the masses.

Top tip Walk to the end of the rock groyne (breakwater), where there's always an interesting sculpture. On the return journey you'll notice artworks that can only be seen from that angle.

MERLE TOPSI DAVIS, *SEA ANOMALIES 3*, SCULPTURE BY THE SEA, COTTESLOE 2022. PHOTO: MARTINE PERRET

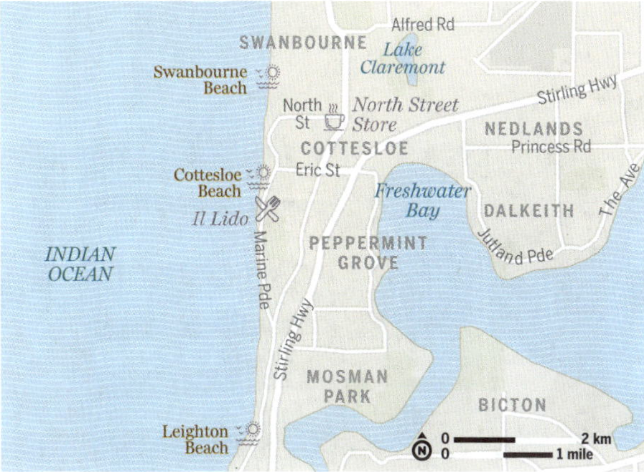

Left *Structural Wave* by Jarrod Taylor, Sculpture by the Sea 2021
Below *Sea Anomalies 3* by Merle Topsi Davis, Sculpture by the Sea 2022

Artfully dodge the crowds Cottesloe Beach is always (and deservedly) busy, but during **Sculpture by the Sea** beachcomber numbers swell by tens of thousands. It's one the largest free-to-the-public sculpture exhibitions in the world, showing works by international and local artists. The sculptures, often standing several metres tall, run along the sea wall, up grassy terraces and under Norfolk pines. To view the art without a dozen smartphones held up in front of you, set the alarm and go at the time locals believe is the most beautiful part of the day: dawn.

Breakfast with views Give yourself an hour to roam around the sculptures, which are sprinkled over a fair distance. Consider jumping in for a swim – the beach has a shark-proof net. Afterwards, climb 20m up the hill for breakfast at **Il Lido** cantina; try the Shark Bay prawn omelette, a menu mainstay. The cantina has an alfresco dining square from which you can gaze over the Indian Ocean. Afterwards, join the conga line of fitness-loving locals as they power walk along the beachfront path.

Worth the walk Head north until you reach North St, then puff up the hill and past a couple of roundabouts until you reach the far end of the road. There you'll see the unflaggingly popular **North Street Store**, usually identifiable by its wraparound queues. The only place to sit is on the verge outside, yet people happily do it because the baked goods here are addictively delicious. Fit in a burger or the speciality cinnamon scroll if you possibly can.

Public Art Fund

In a city sometimes teased for its lack of art and culture, it's perhaps surprising that in 1989 the Western Australian government introduced a Percent for Art Scheme to embed creativity into the built environment. Today major state-funded projects – typically those with a budget over $2 million – must allocate up to 1% of construction costs to public art.

The result is a growing collection of sculptures, murals, street patterning and artistic lighting scattered across Perth. Keep your eyes peeled and you'll spot plenty to admire.

05 A Local's Take on LEEDERVILLE

URBAN | NEIGHBOURHOOD | CULTURE

Inner-city Leederville is one of Perth's most idiosyncratic neighbourhoods, loved for its eclectic mix of boutiques and bars, its approachable but distinctive restaurants and its light-strung laneways and street art. Here's our insider's guide to this hip part of town.

FLEUR BAINGER/LONELY PLANET

How to

Getting here From Perth centre, take the Joondalup train line (often named as Butler on live signs) one stop to Leederville, or catch bus 15; both will drop you on Leederville's main cafe strip, Oxford St.

When to go Leederville is fun year-round. During the day it's all about shopping and people watching; at night the bars, big pubs and restaurants bustle.

Top tip If you're driving, there's a large public car park just behind Oxford St; access is via side streets near the Good Grocer.

BIG STATE IMAGES/ALAMY

At first glance, Leederville looks like an easy-to-read, eclectic inner-city suburb. Its streetscape is dotted with stripy red-and-white umbrellas, alfresco dining nudges out into car-parking spaces and every shopfront is individual. But there's even more to it than that. In fact, peeking behind the facade is exactly how to get to know Leederville's authentic heart.

Take **Babylon Cafe**, a narrow coffee house that's found down a side street and behind a rug shop. Its sign gives nothing away, saying simply 'Babylon'. But walk past the forest of potted plants and mismatched garden chairs and duck your head under the low, vintage brick doorway and you find a buzzing den scented with caffeine. Many claim it does the area's best coffee – but as there's plenty of competition, that's a debate for another day.

Electric Lane

A disused Leederville laneway has been reimagined as a social thoroughfare, branching off to bars, businesses and office buildings. Named in 2021, Electric Lane honours the Leederville Hotel's distinction as the area's first business to get electric lights – they lit up in 1905.

FLEUR BAINGER/LONELY PLANET

Above left Urban Records (p58)
Above Train heading towards Joondalup
Left Oxford St

A short wander away is one of main drag Oxford St's long-timers. **Urban Records** does what it says on the label: it sells racks and racks of vinyl, with the odd stack of discounted CDs slotted in. There are street clothes, watches and record players, which all seems pretty standard. But edge further down the aisles and you'll find **Urban Depot**, a shop within a shop. It's a haven of the unlikely, with mind-tickling books by the School of Life sitting alongside joke ice trays, risqué greeting cards and chic women's fashion. If you need a gift, this is your place. The laid-back owner, Paul, has been selling curiosities for decades and is always ready to hand out local tips.

If you're fascinated by fresh seafood – with its enormous coastline, Western Australia has an abundance of it – stop in at **Kailis Bros Fish Market**. If you ask, staff will join you at the open tank and carefully pick up one of the state's freshwater crayfish, known as marron,

Leedy's Must-Dos

Luna Leederville An iconic cinema, showcasing international and Australian films in nostalgic surrounds. It even has an outdoor rooftop cinema!

Bunn Mee A foodie escape to Vietnam, via authentic banh mi and Vietnamese ice coffees. You can smell the grilled pork belly from 50m away and you'll be well fed for $10 to $20.

Roberts on Oxford A quaint, small bar that is homey yet upmarket. Rob, the owner, built the bar himself.

Galup Just beyond Leederville in Wembley, Galup is a stunning urban lake edged by walking paths and wide lawns. Long valued by Noongar people as a meeting place, it's a popular spot for sunset walks and birdlife, minutes from Oxford St.

Recommendations by Jenny Lam *Former MasterChef contestant and the whiz behind Bunn Mee and Phat Lon in Leederville @jennylamau*

Left Luna Leederville
Below Leederville Hotel

for you to get a closer look. Occasionally they'll offer up the tongs, so if you're game, have a try.

From there, cross the street to the sprawling landmark **Leederville Hotel**, which had a makeover in 2021. Bypass the main bar as well as the main restaurant and instead order a craft brew from the beer bar, **Sandgropers** (it's the name of a local dune-loving insect and also what Western Australians affectionately call themselves). Every month a different small-batch brewery takes over the taps, so you never know what you'll get to try.

Head to the back of the Leederville Hotel to find **Servo**, an energetic new restaurant that edges the rear laneway. Its food is perhaps the most adventurous around, with dishes such as mussels with fennel pollen on squid ink baguette. It also has a secret weapon: just outside the glass doors and off the outdoor dining zone is a garage space complete with cubby house, chalkboard wall and plastic building blocks. The kids are happy, and the parents can devote a bit more attention to dining and chatting. Smiles all around.

FAR LEFT: RANDOM LIGHTS PHOTOGRAPHY/ALAMY
LEFT: SALLY ROBERTSON/ALAMY

06 Street Art TOUR

ART | WALKING TOUR | DISCOVERY

Fancy a walk on the wild side? Perth's street art has been thoughtfully curated, giving it an urban gallery vibe. Follow this route that sneaks behind bars and edges down alleys to glimpse some of the hidden masterpieces.

SHAKEY - ART BY JACOB BUTLER

Once Upon a Time in Wolf Lane by Shakey

How to

Getting here The walk kicks off in the city centre, so take a train or bus to Perth Central Station and go from there.

When to go Spring and autumn offer the most comfortable walking conditions. By day you'll see more detail in the art, but by night the bars are open – while on Nicks Lane you'll see people in search of a secret bar, Toots (p81).

Cost It costs nothing to view this street art, but budget for a few drinks and nibbles at some of the bars or eateries en route.

↑ Look up!

Some of Perth's more dynamic pieces of public art hang high above sight lines. At night in Perth's Cultural Centre, look up along the alley adjacent to the Alex Hotel to see Joshua Webb's neon *Blue Sun* illuminating the path to hidden watering holes.

Tabitha McMullan *runs nonprofit cultural body FORM @formwa*

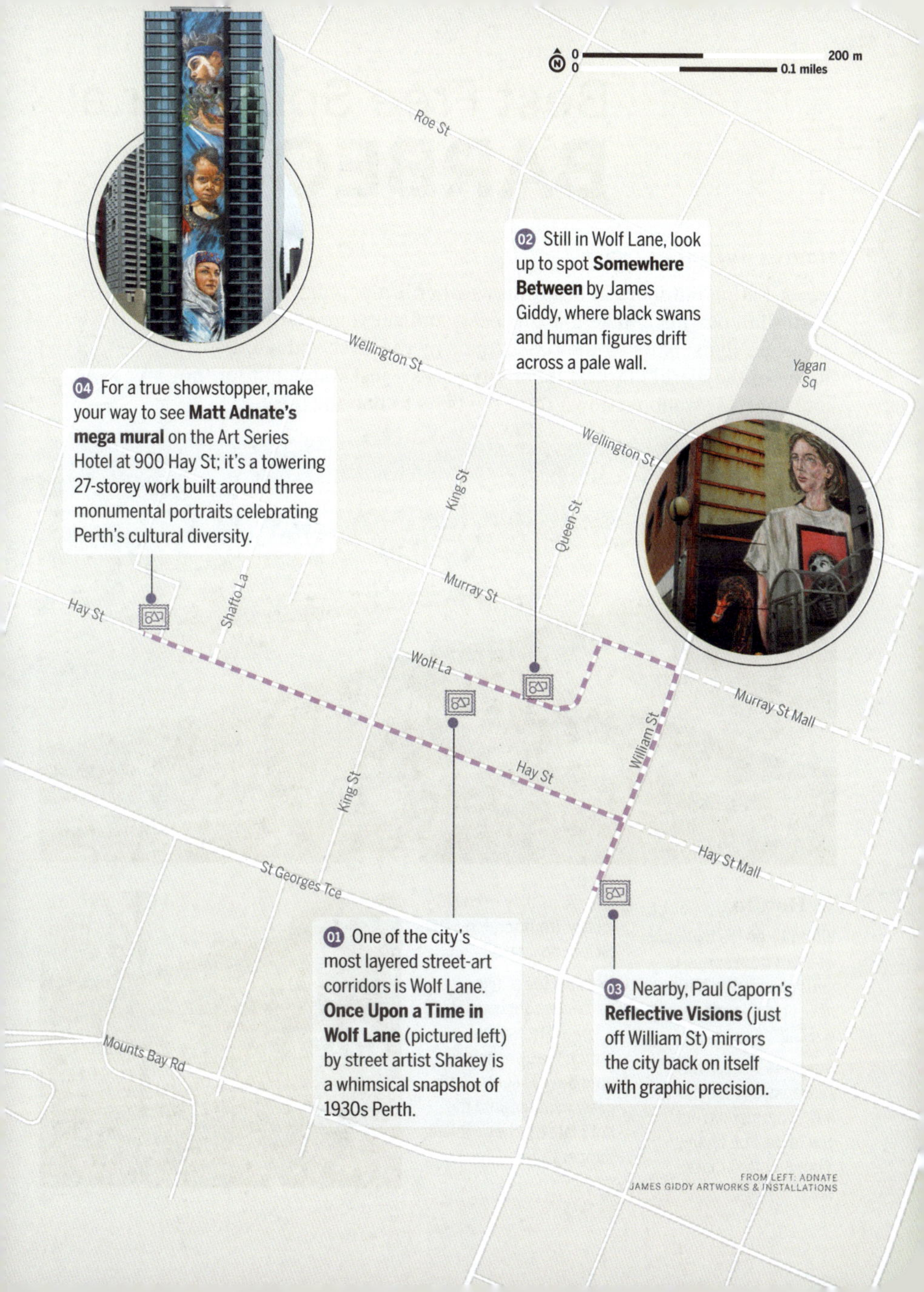

01 One of the city's most layered street-art corridors is Wolf Lane. **Once Upon a Time in Wolf Lane** (pictured left) by street artist Shakey is a whimsical snapshot of 1930s Perth.

02 Still in Wolf Lane, look up to spot **Somewhere Between** by James Giddy, where black swans and human figures drift across a pale wall.

03 Nearby, Paul Caporn's **Reflective Visions** (just off William St) mirrors the city back on itself with graphic precision.

04 For a true showstopper, make your way to see **Matt Adnate's mega mural** on the Art Series Hotel at 900 Hay St; it's a towering 27-storey work built around three monumental portraits celebrating Perth's cultural diversity.

FROM LEFT: ADNATE
JAMES GIDDY ARTWORKS & INSTALLATIONS

07 Best Free Spots for a BARBECUE

PICNIC | OUTDOORS | FREE

Eating outdoors in beautiful weather is a popular Western Australian pastime. Make like the locals and get yourself to these free barbecue spots: one's by the beach, one's by the river and another is in one of the world's largest inner-city parks – just watch out for the kookaburras swooping down from the trees to nab the meat.

DAVID STEELE/SHUTTERSTOCK

How to

When to go It's barbecue weather from spring to autumn in Perth; if it's not raining, locals are sizzling.

Supplies You can buy sausages and meat from any supermarket, but you're best off finding a butcher that makes 'snags,' as they're called locally, from scratch. BYO oil for cooking.

How to Free public barbecues are usually operated by a push button that you hold in until the gas lights. Wait a few minutes until the hot plate reaches cooking temperature.

BJP7IMAGES/SHUTTERSTOCK

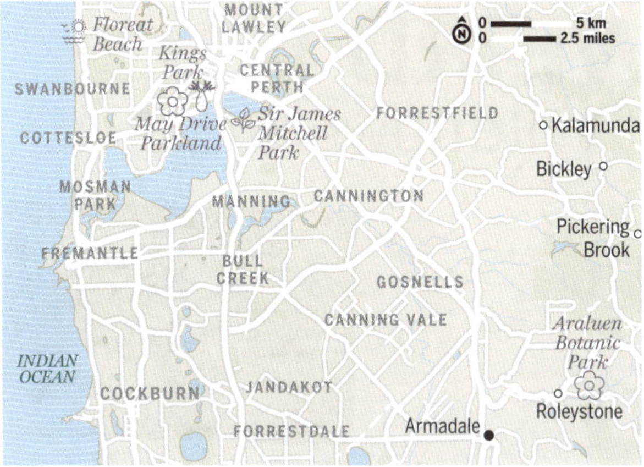

Ocean views Groups of extended families and friends come to **Floreat Beach** for the ocean-view barbecues that lie to the left of the Kiosk cafe. They face a lush lawn and an excellent playground in the form of a sprawling octopus made from soft wood; kids can scramble up, then slide down the slippery dip into sand. Duck to the ocean for a dip or lean on the viewing platform that looks over the water. Happily, the seagulls aren't too much of a bother here.

Park barbecues Most travellers only make it to the city-view section of Kings Park (p70). Drive into its heart and find the **May Drive Parkland** (on the park's western side off Saw Ave or Poole Ave), where there are huge replicas of WA megafauna, an island playground with misting plant sculptures and lakeside barbecues. Beware the winged wildlife when you're cooking – kookaburras, whose call sounds like a cackle, are particularly good at stealing sausages. Alternatively, the entry fee to **Araluen Botanic Park** in Roleystone is well worth it; the 59-hectare valley garden, which is carpeted in tulips from August to October, also has electric and wood-fired barbecues.

Local etiquette If all barbecues are in use, don't worry: it's customary to say hello and ask if you can share the hot plate. If there's room, Australians are generally very happy to share and will often help you cook if you're a novice or forget your tongs. You're expected to clean up after yourself so the hot plate is gleaming and ready for the next person.

Left Floreat Beach
Below Araluen Botanic Park

Sir James Mitchell Park

For the best view of the Perth city skyline, take the commuter ferry across the Swan Valley to Sir James Mitchell Park, a huge green space that edges the foreshore in South Perth.

The first thing you'll see are two enormous canopy sculptures of Australian wildlife: a 10m-high frill-necked lizard and a numbat – WA's mammal emblem – in yellow and orange perforated steel.

Look out for the smaller sculpture of an emu and its chicks. From there, head in an easterly direction to spot the free barbecues; they're close to the playgrounds and surrounded by shady trees.

WA'S WEIRD &
Wonderful Wildflowers

01

02

03

04

01 Sexual predator
This carousel spider orchid *(Caladenia arenicola)* impersonates native wasps so convincingly – pheromones and all – that male insects try to mate with them.

02 Scented blossom
The *Eucalyptus kingsmillii* can be seen in Kings Park (p70) in Perth, as can all the flowers here. Australia has loads of perfumed, flowering trees.

03 Spider flower
There are hundreds of types of *grevillea variifolia*, known as the spider flower. This drought-hardy shrub grows happily in the sand and gravel along the Ningaloo Coast.

04 Sun worshipper
The scented sun orchid *(Thelymitra macrophylla)* pops up everywhere during wildflower season, which runs from June (in the mid-north) to late October (in the south).

05

06

07

08

05 Bug beater
The wily triggerplant *(Stylidium araeophyllum)* dusts visiting insects with pollen by smacking them with a hidden swat that's triggered by the touch of tiny legs.

06 Fringed lily
The edges of the leafless fringed lily are like the fine lace used in haute couture. Its delicate purple petals open at dawn and are closed by the afternoon, like a shy beauty.

07 Donkey orchid
Let's be honest, the donkey orchid looks like an ass. As its name suggests, its perky petals resemble a donkey's ears. Its flowers are delightful – and with their bright colours, easy – to spot.

08 Firewood banksia
This is a firewood banksia *(Banksia menziesii)*. The woodland species seems dry and scratchy until its intricate details are seen up close.

01 ANNE-TIPODEES/SHUTTERSTOCK, **02** BLICKWINKEL/ALAMY, **03** ROB DAVIS/LONELY PLANET, **04** ROB DAVIS/LONELY PLANET, **05** ROB DAVIS /LONELY PLANET, **06** ROB DAVIS/LONELY PLANET, **07** ROB DAVIS/LONELY PLANET, **08** CHRIS DE BLANK/SHUTTERSTOCK

08 Under-the-Radar Perth BEACHES

BEACH | OUTDOORS | SHIPWRECK

Once you see a Perth beach, you'll be forever ruined for other city beaches. But it's not only silky white sand and crystal-clear waters you'll find here. Rock pools, dusk swims and fire twirlers are also part of the allure.

MICHAEL WILLIS/ALAMY

How to

Getting here These beaches are most conveniently accessed by car. A bike route also links most destinations along the coast.

When to go Perth beach lovers hit the sand from October to June. Only the truly dedicated make it into the water all the way through the winter months.

Top tip Hit the coast before 10am for the best water clarity and the calmest waters before the 'Fremantle Doctor' (p37) blows in.

FAITHIE/SHUTTERSTOCK

The privacy-lovers' beach If gazing into rock pools and sheltering in eroded rock caverns sounds like your kind of adventure, make your way to **Bennion Beach** in Perth's north. The tiny stretch is wedged between popular Trigg Beach and Mettams Pool, the latter a much-loved snorkelling and annual abalone-diving spot. Go exploring to find your own private nook facing a soft reef and calm, shallow waters. This beach is open to dogs; it can be great fun watching joyful pooches bound about. Those in the know come here for the tranquillity – it pays to bring a good book.

The hippy haven What **South Beach** lacks in pristine sand (it's a mix of caramel and black grains) it makes up for in eye-catching entertainment. By day there's a grassy park for picnics and a playground shaded by Norfolk pines leading to calm water

STEPHEN DOREY/ALAMY

Beach Etiquette

Perth beachgoers are accustomed to having plenty of sand to themselves, so be careful not to sit too close or set up directly in front of your fellow sun worshippers – it won't be appreciated. Beach thefts are rare; be relaxed about your belongings, but keep them within sight.

Above left Bennion Beach
Above City Beach (p68)
Left South Beach

that seems knee-deep forever – perfect for paddling. As dark approaches, out come fire twirlers, hacky-sack players, buskers and all manner of eccentric visitors. It's busy in a laid-back kind of way. In the warmer months, a floating pontoon just offshore draws swimmers and sun seekers, while just south of the rock groyne a dedicated dog beach becomes a joyous free-for-all of paws and waves. Adding to the ritual, a pop-up beach sauna nearby offers a steamy contrast to ocean dips.

The sunset spot Closest to Perth's centre, **City Beach** is one of few stretches of sand to be floodlit at night, allowing for delightful dusk swims on steamy evenings. It's also a prime sunset-watching spot; join the groups of friends and families sharing hot fish and chips from the nearby **Clancy's Fish Pub** beach cafe as the giant orb plunges below the ruled line of horizon. Seaside sunsets are something of a WA speciality.

CY O'Connor Beach

Mix beauty with history with a visit to CY O'Connor Beach in North Coogee.

The vast ruins of the 1950s South Fremantle Power Station loom in the sand dunes, providing a dramatic backdrop.

Look out for the statue of CY by WA artist Tony Jones out in the ocean. Most visible at low tide, it marks the site where the state's hugely impactful chief civil engineer rode his horse into the ocean and shot himself in 1902, in despair that his Goldfields water pipeline wasn't going to work. In fact the pipeline did work, and it's celebrated today as one of the great engineering feats of the early 20th century.

Marcus Canning
artist and explorer
@therechabitehall

The submerged shipwreck The newly developed coastal suburb of **Coogee** is in Perth's far south, and when you see its glass-clear waters and blindingly white sand, you'll wonder why it took so long for the estate builders to come. Off a nondescript street, look for a steel staircase that descends over a rock groyne into the shallow ocean.

Just beyond it is the **wreck of the *Omeo***, a cargo steamer that ran aground here in 1905 and has since become a snorkeller's exploration site. If you have kids or aren't a confident swimmer, check the tides before you come and arrive at low tide, when part of the wreck is accessible by wading in on foot, in just over a metre or so of water. Otherwise, splash in and consider following the **Coogee Maritime Trail**, an underwater snorkelling route that runs from 2m to 7m deep. Look out for the golden sea lion sculpture – its nose peeks above the waterline.

Left CY O'Connor statue
Above Wreck of the *Omeo*

The Boab Transplant

HOW A BEGUILING BOAB STOPPED TRAFFIC IN WA

One of the largest inner-city parks in the world, Kings Park also has the distinction of being home to a sacred tree that can live for up to 1500 years. The story of its fraught journey south from the state's far north is as fascinating as its stately presence.

STEPHEN DOREY/ALAMY

Left Gija Jumulu, Kings Park
Centre Gija Jumulu moving to Kings Park
Right Kings Park

A Global Feat

A police escort, the removal of multiple traffic lights and 3200km of travel: shifting the Kings Park boab, known as Gija Jumulu, was an almighty effort – and one much greater than first imagined. It all began with a phone call to the Botanic Gardens & Parks Authority in 2008. The boab, sacred to the Gija people of the East Kimberley and only found in the state's tropical north, had to be moved to make way for a significant new motorway near the community of Warmun, and its Traditional Custodians wanted to know how to transplant it. A decision was made to send it to Kings Park, launching a world-first translocation that same year. Never before had a mature tree such as this been transported across such a distance, on land. When uprooted, it was estimated to be 750 years old. Before it departed, the Gija performed a cultural farewell ceremony.

Touch & Go

The first hurdle came when, on moving day, it was discovered that the tree trunk and root ball were dramatically larger and heavier than calculated. A new truck trailer had to be sourced within a day or two if all the pre-arranged road blocks across the entire length of the state were to be accessed. Stress levels rose, but at the 11th hour, a new trailer capable of transporting the 36-tonne specimen was volunteered. Next began six days of travelling through outback and regional Australia. As word spread, entire town communities came out to wave and honk as the boab passed through.

MICHAEL WILLIS/ALAMY

RONAN O'CONNELL/LONELY PLANET

Quite the Spectacle

Wide and rounded like a tall bottle, sprouting green tufts and tangled branches from its top, the tree measured 14m from top to bottom. Its trunk spanned 2.5m and its branches reached 8m wide – after pruning. It took up two lanes of the highways it travelled on, and when it arrived in Perth, parked cars had to be moved and traffic lights uprooted to allow it to fit down city roads. After a long, slow journey through the city complete with news helicopters buzzing overhead, it arrived in Kings Park to cheers and applause. A huge crane lifted it into its new home, in a climate far cooler than what it had been used to. No one was sure if it would survive, but eventually – triumphantly – green shoots began to emerge.

> Never before had a mature tree such as this been transported across such a distance, on land.

The year 2021 marked a decade since the boab was planted in Kings Park. The tree continues to bloom, standing regally at the Two Rivers Lookout where the Swan and Canning Rivers meet. It has the best views in town. The tree acts as a signpost to the plants and flowerbeds of the Botanic Garden, each representing the environment of different parts of the vast state of Western Australia. The garden's plant collection is most breathtaking in spring when the wildflowers bloom, heralding the Kings Park festival each September.

How the Regal Park Became

For at least 40,000 years, the land where Kings Park now stands was a significant space for the Noongar people. They called it Mooro Katta or Kaarta Gar-up. European settlement in 1829 saw that change. John Septimus Roe, the first surveyor general of the Swan River colony, protected the wooded area two years after the land was forcibly seized from Aboriginal people. Its preservation was overturned by Perth's early inhabitants only six years later, and they used the area for logging. The timber mill continued for 36 years until a large tract of bush was successfully preserved. By 1890 the parkland had been extended and soon after it was officially opened. It was called Kings Park in 1901 to mark Edward VII's ascension to the British throne.

09 Savouring Indigenous FLAVOURS

ABORIGINAL | CULTURE | FOOD

From time with an Aboriginal Elder to a cocktail using spirits made from indigenous plants, here are some of the ways to taste bush flavours found only in Australia. Wrap your mouth around ingredients that might include lemon myrtle, lilly-pilly, tree ants and more as you dive deeper into WA's culinary diversity.

JONNEI/SHUTTERSTOCK

How to

Getting around Uber or walk your way around the city.

When to go Each season delivers new flavours and fresh ingredients. Look up the six-season Noongar calendar and decide which one is for you.

Top tip Native ingredients aren't necessarily singled out on menus, so ask your waitstaff to tell you which ones they are, where they were sourced and what they taste like.

THE RITZ-CARLTON, PERTH

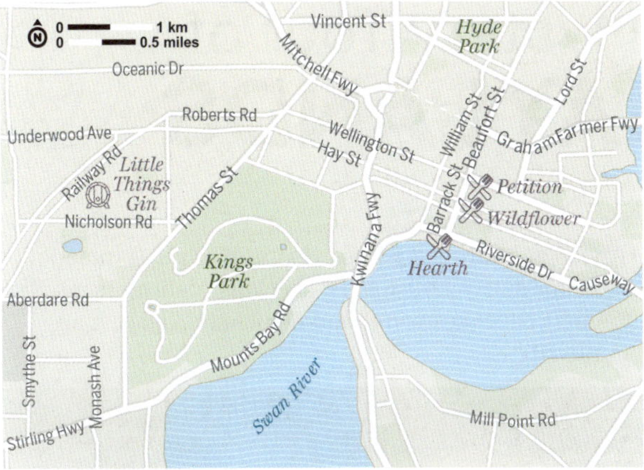

Perth's most innovative chefs are increasingly centring their menus on native foods that have long been overlooked in professional kitchens. Australia's endemic bounty has always been valued by WA's Aboriginal peoples, and now everyone with a curious palate is diving into these fresh, unique flavours. Savour the mineral twang of crisped saltbush, the zing of lemon aspen and the crunch of beach spinach at some of Perth's most refined restaurants.

Fine-dining twists Go all out at **Wildflower**, the city's classiest fine diner, which sits in a glass box atop Como the Treasury boutique hotel. Its multicourse tasting menus change in harmony with the Noongar people's six-season calendar, reflecting the indigenous ingredients available in each period. Marron, a local delicacy only found in WA, is almost always featured. Wildflower's opening chef Jed Gerrard took his ethos to **Hearth**, the flagship restaurant at the nearby Ritz-Carlton. Although he's since moved on to Margaret River winery restaurant Wills Domain (p115), his approach continues to permeate the carte in a more subtle way, much as it does at chic, energetic **Petition**, inside the State Buildings. Look out for pipis, an endemic shellfish, and native spinach.

Small-batch gin Native flavours are also increasingly infused into locally distilled sprits. At **Little Things Gin**, lemon myrtle, native river mint and Australian thyme make up the botanical mix, best savoured in its distillery bar. Elsewhere, look out for Giniversity's Australian Native Gin, made from Geraldton wax (which tastes similar to makrut lime leaf), lemon myrtle and emu plum.

Left Kakadu plum
Below Hearth

A Dining Experience

Perhaps more than any other player in WA's cooking scene, pop-up dining company **Fervor** engages deeply with Indigenous Australian ingredients and knowledge. Chef and founder Paul Iskov goes foraging with Aboriginal people before each degustation-style dining event, working the finds into the night's always surprising menu. Expect the likes of green tree ants, desert lime, bunya nuts, boab tubers and an A to Z of other ingredients likely to be new to you. Most of Fervor's events are held in remote destinations around WA, but occasionally it brings its talents to Perth. Check the website events calendar and book well ahead.

10 A Mystery Tour of MAYLANDS

URBAN | DISCOVERY | BARS

Meet Maylands, a gritty neighbourhood whose visitor drawcards include alleys decked with street art, community-centric bars, specialist delicatessens, hidden-gem op shops and the best cupcakes you'll find anywhere – all just an eight-minute train ride from the city.

BOGDANBLENDEA/SHUTTERSTOCK

How to

Getting here The Midland train line handily drops you opposite Maylands' cafe strip on Whatley Cres. From there, it's best to make your way on foot.

When to go Maylands buzzes most in the late afternoon and evening on Friday and Saturday. Come hungry and allocate more time than you expect to spend here: there are plenty of treasures.

Top tip There are good op shops to be found in the neighbourhood, if you go searching.

A Maylands Microbrewery

Most of Maylands' finds run along Whatley Cres, but if you venture to traffic-jammed Guildford Rd you'll discover the **Seasonal Brewing Co**, which opened in 2019. Powered by renewable energy, composting all its waste and recycling water, this craft-beer haven is as authentic as the former mechanic's garage it inhabits.

01 On Whatley Cres, look at the pavement to spot the yellow brick road leading to the curio-filled **Vintage Emporium**. Snaffle unique costume jewellery, draped clothing and quirky ceramics.

02 It's impossible to resist the treats at **Sherbet Bake Shop**, inspired by the super-cute cupcake bakeries of New York City.

03 **Volare** brings a European aperitivo spirit to Maylands, with knockout martinis, a concise wine list and a deli-style menu of small plates designed for sharing.

04 Books, board games and community events define **Rabble Books & Games** (pictured above), a warm independent bookshop on Eighth Ave with thoughtfully curated reads for kids and adults alike.

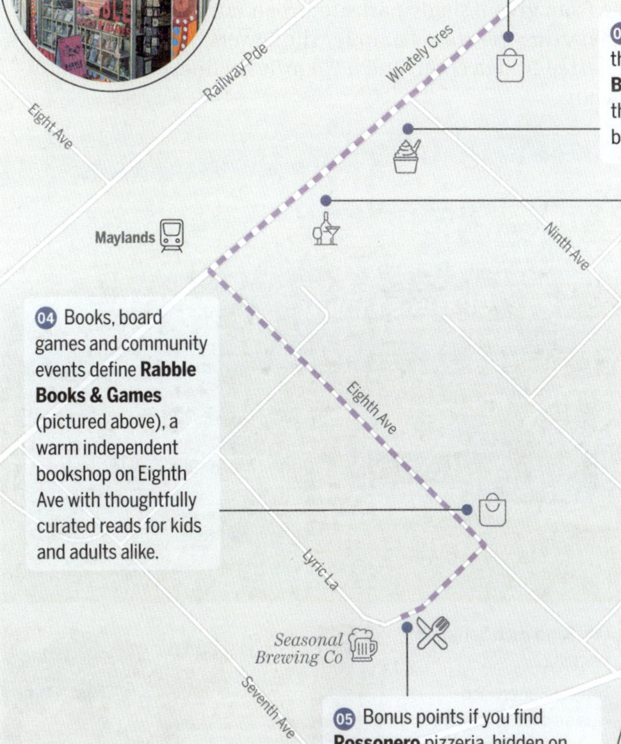

05 Bonus points if you find **Rossonero** pizzeria, hidden on Lyric Lane beside the eponymous Lyric's Bar with its beer garden and underground jazz cellar. Go late for live music and comedy.

FROM TOP: RABBLE BOOKS & GAMES, RONAN O'CONNELL/LONELY PLANET

11 Play the DAY AWAY

FAMILY | ADVENTURE | OUTDOORS

A great place to visit for those travelling with kids, Perth has loads of outdoor spaces ranging from green, shady parks to urban farms, markets and vast playgrounds incorporating the state's unique wildflowers. Find all of those options, as well as a 314-step bridge climb and a 75km/h zip line, on this gently paced walk around the city.

POMINPERTH/SHUTTERSTOCK

How to

Getting here To reach Perth City Farm, where this adventure begins, drive, take a train to Claisebrook Station or jump aboard the free yellow CAT bus.

When to go A farmers market is held at Perth City Farm each Saturday morning.

Top tip Supervised kids are free to explore the whole of Perth City Farm; venture behind the buildings to discover chooks and crops of leafy greens.

LUKE RILEY CREATIVE

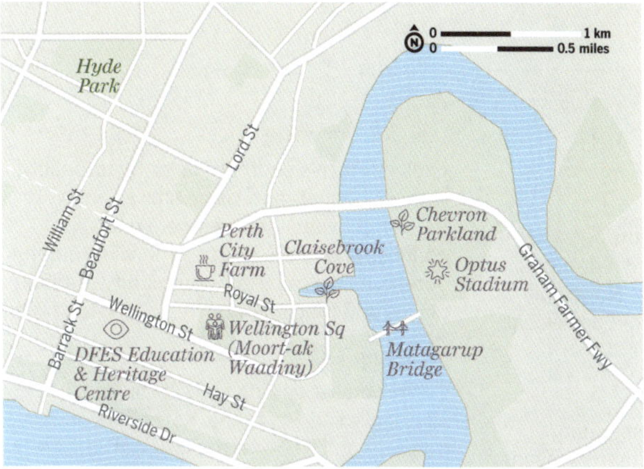

Start at **Perth City Farm**, a rustic slice of green among train lines, a student campus and assisted accommodation flats. It's free entry; say hello to any volunteers you see as you roam the veggie patches and watch the chooks. There's a good cafe on-site with raised sandpits filled with toy trucks for the kids. Opened in early 2021, the $17.5-million playground in **Wellington Square (Moort-ak Waadiny)** is a five-minute walk away. It has landscaped bush, water fountains and parkour zones. Kids love climbing up towers shaped like banksias, zipping down steel tube slides and jumping on mini trampolines.

Stroll to Royal St for lunch and follow the duck-dotted waterway leading to **Claisebrook Cove**, where kids can run across the footbridge and roam around Victoria Gardens. Towards the river is a steep hill ideal for body rolls. Walk another 10 minutes to **Matagarup Bridge**, designed to look like swans, and Perth's **Optus Stadium**, judged the world's most beautiful sports facility in 2019. Consider harnessing up for the bridge climb, which reaches the 72m-high, glass-bottom SkyView Deck. It's open to kids aged eight and up who bring their 'big person' along. The zip line here is for 10-year-olds and above.

Follow the river to **Chevron Parkland**, home to six nature playground zones (ignore the playground near the bridge). It was created with the Whadjuk community and connects to the six seasons recognised by WA's Noongar people. Kids can scale towers modelled on quandong trees, run through numbat burrows, find hatching emu eggs and build stick cubbies. There are free barbecue facilities here, too.

Left Optus Stadium
Below Perth City Farm

A Mini Firefighter's Dream

The Department of Fire and Emergency Services (DFES) Education & Heritage Centre is housed in the original Perth Central Fire Station and grants free entry to those keen to try on firefighting uniforms, don hard hats and hoist themselves up into a fire truck. There's also a firefighter's pole to swing on as well as a relics gallery (the latter is more for big kids). The centre is part of Hibernian Pl, a cluster of restaurants edging a public lawn.

Listings

BEST OF THE REST

In the Open Air

Somerville Auditorium

Encircled by pine trees, this outdoor cinema on the beautiful University of WA grounds shows international films from November to April. Bring a cushion to avoid deck-chair bot-rot and order on-site pizza.

Rooftop Movies

Over summer an unlikely scene emerges atop a six-storey car park: vintage caravans, palm trees and bean bags facing a screen suspended on shipping containers. Food trucks provide sustenance.

Esplanade Park

This big green space opposite Fremantle Port has a rope-climbing pyramid, a tall slippery dip, an all-ages skate park and a parkour activity zone. You'll be there for hours.

Hyde Park

Encircling a tranquil lake, this large, leafy square has paths overhung by Moreton Bay fig trees. Spot native turtles in the lake.

The World's Oldest Living Culture

Go Cultural

As you walk through Elizabeth Quay, your Noongar guide will share the meeting places, hunting areas and gathering spaces once frequented by Aboriginal people.

Nyungar Tours

Kings Park is an important ceremonial and Dreaming site for WA's Aboriginal people. A Noongar woman will guide you over the park's treetop bridge and through its bush gardens while telling rarely heard Whadjuk Yorga (women-focused) stories.

Djurandi Dreaming

Explore Perth's southern lakes by torchlight with a Noongar man, as he shares how these freshwater sources were once vital connections to the ocean for local Aboriginal people, as well as tribal community meeting places and food sources.

In Culture Tours

On immersive walking tours through sites including Fremantle, Kings Park and Rockingham, Noongar man Steven Jacobs shares First Nations stories of the land with heart and humour.

The Great Outdoors

Heirrison Island

Ride, walk or drive to Heirrison Island, facing the city, where a small group of roos lives in a fenced sanctuary. If you go around dawn or dusk, you're almost guaranteed to spot them.

Whale Watching

The world's longest whale migration passes Perth's coastline from September to November. Several companies run whale-watching expeditions.

Hyde Park

Hike Collective

Eco-minded guided hikes focus on connecting with nature. Explore Rottnest Island's lakes and bays or wander through the landscaped gardens at Araluen Botanic Park.

GoGo Active Tour

Discover secret cliff hideaways even locals don't know are there with a guided kayak along the Swan River. Journeys explore waterbird habitats, limestone caves and even visit a winery.

Perth Waterbike Adventures

Pedal along the Swan River past city dolphins while drinking in the best view of Perth's skyline. Ecofriendly, near-impossible to capsize and far easier than pushbikes, aquatic bikes let you paddle at your own pace, alone or on a tour.

Family Fun

Scitech

Kids love this hands-on science centre topped with a planetarium dome. See fluoro material travel through wind tunnels in the dark, race water boats and control electronic arms.

Elizabeth Quay Water Park

Opposite the Elizabeth Quay station, kids love running through jets of water as they rise and fall and, at dusk, marvelling at the colourful lighting display.

Perth Zoo

Visit rarely seen cassowaries and tree kangaroos as well as a reptile enclosure full of venomous snakes and a nocturnal house home to bilbies and quokkas.

Caffeine Hit

Telegram Coffee

Join the queue at this petite cafe within a wooden box – it opens its eucalyptus panels via a hand-powered pulley system each

Koala, Perth Zoo

morning. Find it inside the heritage-listed State Buildings.

Lil' Toastface

Arguably Perth's tiniest cafe, this literal hole-in-the-wall pumps out excellent coffees and great toasties. Pull up a chair or milk crate and watch Northbridge's personalities go by.

Pixel Coffee Brewers

At this hip spot north of Leederville's cafe strip, the interior sage-and-white subway tiles and greenery are lovely, but the 'parklet', an upcycled seating space taking up a car space out the front, is where it's at.

Breakfast of Champions

Odyssea $$

Overlook the ocean as you sip fresh juice or get stuck into smashed avocado with chorizo and poached eggs.

Hylin $$

With lots of seating under the trees beside the road, this cute, narrow cafe does filling breakfasts and excellent coffee. The brisket Benny is a highlight. Note that parking inspectors are scrupulous around here.

Moore & Moore $$

This popular breakfast and brunch spot with an art gallery and garden seating is a Fremantle icon in the historic West End. They use a hot plate to cook everything, so they only do poached or fried eggs – never scrambled.

Dining Out after 9pm

Vincent Wine $$

With an impressive wine list, this very European corner wine bar serves French classics until late. Perch at the brass bar or sit on the deck.

Bar Rogue $$

It's walk-ins only and snack-focused at this Highgate wine bar, opened in 2021. Flavourful choices include cold fried chicken on waffles, or a miso-glazed pork-belly skewer.

Tiny's $$

Tucked back from the road in the city's west, Tiny's has a cult following for its rotisserie chicken, house-made gravy and duck fat potatoes.

Cheap Eats

Chu Bakery $

After just one bite of the flaky *kaya* (coconut jam) croissant, you'll have forgotten the 15-minute wait in the queue outside. Grab a sourdough loaf while you're there.

Le Vietnam $

Asian herbs, pâté and sliced pork fill the crusty white baguettes here, where the banh mi are renowned.

The Best in Chinatown

Viet Hoa $

Here's where to fill up on a steaming bowl of *pho* (noodle soup) in Northbridge. Go traditional and get the raw beef, with fresh mint and crisp bean sprouts on the side.

Good Fortune Duck House $

The boneless roast duck is next level, with its only competition the Peking duck pancakes. Get some green beans with chilli pork mince on the side.

Tak Chee House $

The home of tasty, authentic Hainan chicken rice, this Malaysian eatery has cheap and cheerful interior decor. Service can be brash.

Dragon Palace $$

Always packed with lovers of yum cha, this enormous, bustling restaurant floor can feel overwhelming, but those Shanghai soup dumplings are worth it.

Natural Wine Hubs

Wines of While $$

A wine-loving doctor opened this 50-seat wine store and bar in Northbridge with the aim of sharing his passion for chemical-free wines.

Casa $$$

This hip but friendly bar opened in Mt Hawthorn in 2021 with a long list of minimal-intervention wines. Arrive late afternoon and sit at the sidewalk tables or lean on the narrow bar out the back.

EA GIVEN/SHUTTERSTOCK

Elizabeth Quay Water Park (p79)

Nieuw Ruin $$

With 300 wines on the list and a penchant for the unusual, this cottage-feel Fremantle bar charms with its drinks savvy and its welcoming atmosphere.

Sip & Fizz

Republic of Fremantle

Gin is the speciality at this warehouse-feel distillery with a bustling bar, fun outside seating and excellent eats. Hear how the base spirit is batch-stilled from local grapes.

Little Creatures

Once a microbrewery, now a global name; the original harbourside tank sheds form the backdrop for a hectic kitchen (try the roo skewers or prawn pizza), long sampling bar and lively beer garden.

Gage Roads Brewery

Picture a 100m-long beach-shack-style brewpub in a former cargo shed perched on a working port. Views include Rottnest ferries wrapped in quokka imagery.

Running with Thieves

This cavernous shed opposite South Beach pumps out creative seasonal, often limited-edition beers. You might sip chocolate-orange stout, an oats-and-cream ale or passionfruit cosmopolitan seltzer.

Secret Bars

Toots

All '70s mirror balls and pastel hues, Toots is within another secret bar in Chinatown, for which you'll need a password to gain entry on Friday and Saturday nights.

Sneaky Tony's

This low-lit rum den of exposed brick, Cuban beats and serious cocktails looks from without like an anonymous Chinatown doorway. Those in the know whisper a password to get inside.

Little Creatures

Astral Weeks

Dedicated to a high-quality listening experience, this 2022 opening in a former Chinese herbalist's shop is fitted with a Line Magnetic sound system. Lo-fi wines are served. Note there's no sign.

Ripper Rooftops

QT Hotel

From the pinnacle of QT Hotel the city stretches out around you in all directions. The view's best seen at night with a cocktail in hand.

Songbird

Shoot up to this flash, open-air, open-to-all bar on the 1st level of the Ritz – it's not exactly a rooftop, but it feels like one. Nab a seat on the balcony overlooking Elizabeth Quay.

Mechanics Institute

Down a laneway and up some stairs, this hipster-vibe 2nd-floor bar is loved for its open deck, slick cocktails and edgy staff. Bonus: they'll deliver burgers from the ground-level diner.

PERTH REGION

NATURE | ADVENTURE | OUTDOORS

RESEARCHED BY ROSAMUND BRENNAN

- **Surprises in the Swan Valley** (p86)
- **The Pinnacles at Sunset** (p88)
- **Oddities & Curiosities of Katter Kich** (p90)
- **Dawn 'til Dusk in the Avon Valley** (p94)
- **Overnighting on Rottnest** (p96)
- **Beyond the Quokkas** (p98)
- **Easy-Access Roo Spotting** (p100)
- **Driving Perth's Valleys** (p102)
- **Eco Eats, Unicorns & Waterfalls** (p104)
- **Listings** (p106)

GUNNERCHU/SHUTTERSTOCK

PERTH REGION
Trip Builder

Treasures lie right at Perth's fingertips: quokka-filled Rottnest Island is 19km across the water, and the Perth Hills townships are only 30 minutes' drive away. Slightly further afield are the surreal rock formations of the Pinnacles and Katter Kich (Wave Rock).

FROM LEFT: FARRIS NOORZALI/SHUTTERSTOCK
TSL/SHUTTERSTOCK

Practicalities

ARRIVING

Perth Airport Most visitors arrive at Perth Airport, from where it's a quick drive to the Swan Valley or Perth's centre. Car rental companies are located near Terminals 1 and 2.

CONNECT

Reliable close to Perth, internet service can be patchy in the bush and between towns. Limited free public wi-fi and hot spots.

MONEY

Contactless payment is common, but internet-based systems are often down. Always carry cash; ATMs are few in rural towns.

WHERE TO STAY

Place	Pros/Cons
Rottnest Island	Cottages, hotel rooms, self-contained tents and BYO camp sites.
Swan Valley	Quiet and family run, with farmstays, B&Bs and a few sophisticated options.
Perth Hills	Tranquil at night. Some lovely B&Bs on produce properties, plus retreats and spas.
Cervantes	Mostly camp sites or beach houses. RAC Cervantes Holiday Park ticks many boxes.

GETTING AROUND

Car By far the easiest way to get off the beaten track and explore properly.

Coach tours These visit the most popular destinations but tend to stick to the key sights.

Train The Transwa AvonLink train travels from Perth to Northam, passing through the picturesque Avon Valley.

TOP: IAN GERAINT JONES/SHUTTERSTOCK
BOTTOM: SHAM CLICKS/SHUTTERSTOCK

EATING & DRINKING

Vast country-pub meals are seen as a throwback to when Western Australia was more of a frontier state. Winery regions are largely more highbrow; expect the likes of confit duck with mixed grain salad. Always try the local vino, or join the locals in a pint of WA beer.

Best winery lunch
Millbrook (p105)

Must-try chicken parmigiana
Sandpiper Tavern (p89)

BIRAK	BUNURU	DJERAN	MAKURU	DJILBA	KAMBARANG
DEC & JAN	FEB & MAR	APR & MAY	JUN & JUL	AUG & SEP	OCT & NOV
Hot, dry easterlies bring inland heat; coastal breezes offer relief.	Fierce inland temperatures and afternoon coastal winds.	Cooling days and light rains; dewy mornings and calmer conditions.	Cold fronts bring heavy rains, grey skies and storms.	Rain and clear, cold days; wildflowers bloom.	Warming temps and lighter winds; vibrant wildflowers.

12 SURPRISES in the Swan Valley

WINE | MARKETS | CURIOSITIES

Rows of grapevines stripe the landscape in the Swan Valley, only a 30-minute drive from Perth, in a scene that has greeted visitors for more than 180 years. European migrants kicked off winemaking in these parts, and their descendants have continued the tradition. What makes the Swan Valley particularly special is you can bypass big-name wineries for rustic, family-run options.

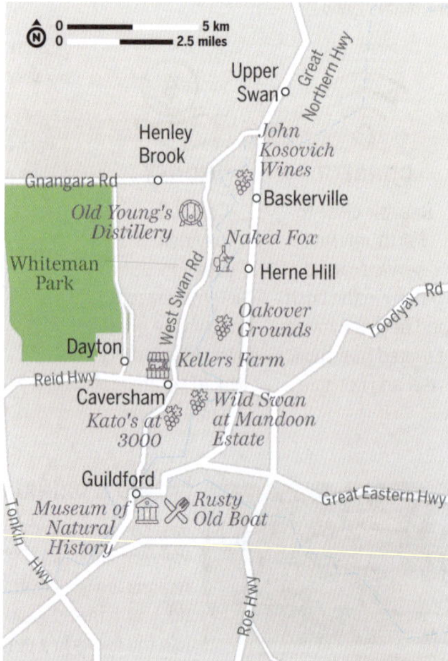

How to

Getting around Join a tour, or self-drive; the pleasant 32km Swan Valley Food & Wine Trail loop drive passes most attractions.

When to go Anytime works; spring's **Entwined in the Valley** *(entwinedinthevalley.com.au)* is held each October.

Something different At Sandalford Wines, try SupaGolf, a scaled-down take on golf that lets you sip wine between swings. Or do a tasting tour via river cruise or kayak (try GoGo Active Tours).

Digging up hidden gems Opened early in 2022, the **Naked Fox** wine bar is run by a young couple who threw in their day jobs to pursue their love of local wine. The menu features 280 bottles sourced from independent WA vineyards. Beyond the bar, there are picnic rugs ready to be rolled out on the grass beneath old trees, metres from the vines that the pair use to make their own blends under their Beneath the Vines label.

Farm-gate trails Fresh produce stalls are dotted along the valley's roadsides. Source table grapes from **Kato's at 3000**, where the family grows 15 varieties, harvesting from January to late March. In Dayton, **Kellers Farm** sets up a weekend street market selling seasonal produce, preserves and free-range eggs as chickens and goats

mill about. Swiss-born Philipp Keller bakes Swiss chocolate bread, while his wife, Marija, of Croatian heritage, wood-fires an incredible cheddar and jalapeño sourdough.

Local eats Treat yourself to 'fancy' fish and chips at Guildford's **Rusty Old Boat**, a maritime-themed diner with a wine and cocktail list to pair with sustainably caught fish, or linger over a long lunch at **Wild Swan at Mandoon Estate**, where hyper-seasonal Western Australian produce shapes a refined menu designed to pair with estate wines in a light-filled riverside setting.

Explore Further

John Kosovich Wines (Baskerville) This winery celebrated 100 years of sensational family winemaking in 2022. Some of my earliest memories are running around in the cellar. I love the bottle-aged chenin and the MPV – but do not, on any account, miss tasting the rare muscat.

Oakover Grounds (Middle Swan) There's wine, cider and coffee tasting as well as a marketplace full of local and imported gourmet treats. Jump on the free paddle boats for a potter around the lake.

Museum of Natural History (Guildford) A 1920s theatre now houses a cornucopia of taxidermied curiosities. You'll find emus, armadillos, dinosaurs and dolphins.

Recommendations by

James Young
Distiller and CEO at Old Young's Distillery
@oldyoungsdistillery

Above Naked Fox

13 The Pinnacles AT SUNSET

GEOLOGY | NATURE | NATIONAL PARK

Rising from the desert sand like thousands of knobbly fingers, the Pinnacles are like nowhere else in Australia. Yet many visitors see them at times when they're far from their best. If you possibly can, choose to tour these limestone formations at sunset, when they beam and glow before being silhouetted against the pink and purple sky.

BENNY MARTY/SHUTTERSTOCK

How to

Getting there The Pinnacles are a two-hour drive north of Perth. Cervantes and Jurien Bay are the nearest towns.

Know the wind Plan activities in harmony with the wind's direction and strength. Light winds from an easterly direction are prime for the beach and boating. When the wind switches to a southerly in the afternoon, go caving.

Good to know The Pinnacles Desert Discovery Centre is open until 4.30pm. Entry to Nambung National Park costs $17 per vehicle.

AM PHOTO CO/SHUTTERSTOCK

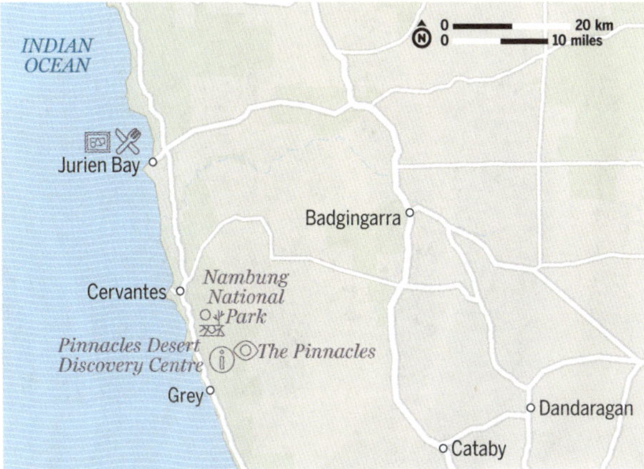

Left The Pinnacles
Below Jurien Bay

The best time of day Most visitors drive through the 25,000- to 30,000-year-old, space-like limestone spires known as the **Pinnacles** during the day, on their way to somewhere else. They turn off Indian Ocean Dr, roll slowly through the karst formations on the loop route and head off again. Don't make the same mistake. Timing your visit for golden hour, when the setting sun drenches the landscape in warm yellow hues, makes for an incomparable experience. It's also likely to be a much cooler one, with the heat of the midday sun softened, allowing you to follow walking trails through native bush and to boardwalk lookouts rather than just touring in your car. The tallest columns are 5m high and about 1m wide – it's worth getting out to study them up close. There's another bonus, too: if you stay late enough, the region's dark skies deliver sharp, bright stargazing.

Once you're done, head to the nearby rock lobster fishing town of Jurien Bay and grab a feed at the **Sandpiper Tavern** (just bear in mind, the kitchen closes at 8pm, as do most country eateries). It's within walking distance of a rather unusual art gallery. Glow-in-the-dark **Sea Spray Art** only opens for short windows during the week and on select evenings, so it's worth checking its hours before you go.

Local Knowledge

A lot of the best experiences in this region are advertised locally on the Jurien Bay Community Chat page on Facebook. Through it, you'll know when the sound healing group or the astro photography group will be holding occasional sessions at the Pinnacles. The site is an incredibly spiritual place even after sunset.

Check the Jurien Bay Crayz Facebook page to see when a local rock lobster fishing boat is selling live crays to the public.

Kiera Wuillemin
Artist and gallerist at Sea Spray Art
@sea_spray_art

14 Oddities & Curiosities of KATTER KICH

OUTBACK | ADVENTURE | ROCK FORMATIONS

Imagine a monster wave poised just as it's about to crash. That's the scene that greets you at Katter Kich (Wave Rock), a 15m-high, 2.7-billion-year-old slab of granite that stretches 110m long. Here's how best to visit it.

MARCO TOMASINI/SHUTTERSTOCK

How to

Getting here Katter Kich is a four-hour drive inland from Perth. Coach tours are possible, but for ease of exploration it's best to drive.

Stop-offs Visit historic York, the quirky Tin Horse Hwy, the 182m-long community waterslide at Kulin and Corrigin's poignant dog cemetery.

When to go Avoid summer, when temperatures soar.

Top tip Park by Wave Rock village to avoid pricey parking in bays closer to the rock.

ALEISHA ORR/SHUTTERSTOCK

Some 300km east of Perth, surrounded by scrub and dry, sunbaked earth flushed the shade of sienna, is **Katter Kich (Wave Rock)**. The formation, naturally eroded by wind and water that has hollowed out its softer underside, achieved global fame in the 1960s when *National Geographic* magazine published a photograph of it. It's vertically striped in a rainbow of earthy stains, the result of rain flushing iron oxide and carbonates down its curved surface.

Most visitors come during the day, when piercing light mutes the rock's colours. Instead, go at sunset. As the bruising sunlight softens, the wave's scale becomes more apparent and it's vastly more enjoyable to walk around. Edge along the base (be sure to snap a playful pic of you 'surfing' the wave) and carefully across the peak, where you're gifted endless views of bush and farmland.

MINO SURKALA/SHUTTERSTOCK ©

Tin Horse Highway

Detour 15 minutes from the main road to take in the Tin Horse Hwy. With their tongues in their cheeks, local farmers have welded and painted more than 70 characterful horses from bits of tin and metal, dotting them along a 15km stretch. Most are on the Gorge Rock–Lake Grace Rd.

Above left Katter Kich
Above Waterslide, Kulin
Left Tin Horse Highway

The Curiosity: Float like an Astronaut

Only 800m away is the **Lake Magic Swimming Pool**, with water so saline you bob about weightlessly, as though you have zero gravity. Take the steps gingerly – they can be slippery – and expect squishiness underfoot. Limestone cabanas with hammocks and showers have been built around the perimeter, adding a desert day-spa vibe. It's part of the Wave Rock Resort site, but the pool is open to anyone. The water comes from **Lake Magic**, a gypsum-rich expanse next door that provides beautiful reflections at dusk.

Hippo's Yawn

Another rock formation, Hippo's Yawn stands almost 13m tall and is reached via a 1.7km loop walking trail from the Katter Kich car park. You can crawl to the back of the gaping 'jaw' and scramble up a tumble of boulders. It really does look like a hippo yawning. Kids bound through the gaps, whereas for adults it's more of a twist and slide.

WA's Most Inland Winery

About an hour's drive south of Katter Kich (a small distance in these parts) is **Walkers Hill Vineyard**.

Any wine buff knows it shouldn't be possible to grow grapevines this far east, but the owners of this establishment are not wine people. The former truckie and hairdresser were desperate to buy land; this piece came with a vineyard. The wine tastes of its terroir – flinty, dusty ironstone – but they do the best food for miles (bookings essential). Tip: the owners hold a community grape pick each February/March. Anyone can join in. Exact dates are announced on Facebook, with about a week's notice.

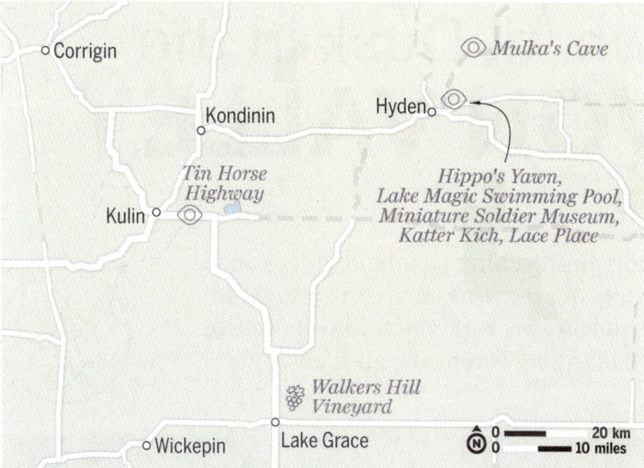

Left Red wine grapes
Below Noongar paintings, Mulka's Cave

Mulka's Cave

This site holds the largest collection of Noongar paintings in southwestern WA, yet few have even heard of it. While most other sites have fewer than 20 works, Mulka's Cave is home to more than 450 pieces on its cool, dark walls. Look carefully and you'll see hundreds of Aboriginal handprints captured with ochre spray, plus other art motifs depicted in seven colours. It's worth taking the 18km graded dirt road out – drive carefully.

The Oddities: Niche Collections

Now for a couple of things you'd never expect to find in the outback. The **Miniature Soldier Museum**, only metres from Katter Kich, features at least 10,000 army characters assembled in detailed war scenes, alongside large ships made from sardine tins, Spam cans and bottle tops. Both world wars are represented, along with others including the Napoleonic and American Civil Wars. Under the same roof, the **Lace Place** houses a vast collection of delicate creations under protective low light. Each 2.5cm of lace represents an hour of embroidery. As you exit into the adjoining cafe, gaze upwards or you'll miss the huge, butterfly-shaped dried flower creations the owner made in the 1980s, to act as insulation.

15 Dawn 'til Dusk in the AVON VALLEY

CULTURE | HISTORY | NATURE

Scrubby bush and horizon-reaching farmland greet you in the Avon Valley, dotted with historic towns encircling grand old pubs. Stop in at convivial, cafe-strewn York and follow its source, the Avon River (Wagyl, in Ballardong Noongar), all the way to Northam.

RIC JACYNO/SHUTTERSTOCK

The Stolen Generation

Many Aboriginal people living today are part of what are called the stolen generations, whereby children were forcibly removed from their families by the state and federal governments between 1910 and 1970.

Northam's **Bilya Koort Boodja Centre** (pictured) has an important 'sorry space' dedicated to healing through sharing this traumatic history, the impact of which continues to linger.

How to

Getting around The AvonLink train travels from Perth to Northam, but you'll need a car to explore properly. In town, park and follow the Dorntj Koorliny Track, a looping walking path along the Avon River. The track's name is Noongar for 'walking together', and it was laid by volunteers. The mix-and-match pavers made the community project affordable.

When to go Flowering canola fields illuminate the landscape from mid-August to September.

RIGHT: MYWEATHERTOP/SHUTTERSTOCK
BELOW: RIC JACYNO/SHUTTERSTOCK

01 **Hot-air ballooning** just out of Northam is a standout experience. Coast at low elevation above the region's submarine-yellow canola fields before rising above the clouds for an eagle-eye view.

05 Walk or drive along Northam–Toodyay Rd to see the **Northam Silo Art**, a striking large-scale mural painted across the town's grain silos. It transforms this industrial landmark into a bold piece of public art.

02 Wander thoughtfully through **Bilya Koort Boodja Centre for Nyoongar Culture and Environmental Knowledge**, where you may meet and learn from Aboriginal people.

03 At 117m-long, Northam's pedestrian **suspension bridge** is the longest in Australia. Look for the town's imported white swans on the Avon below. WA's native swans are black.

04 Take a look at two 1970s **Brutalist buildings** designed by lauded architect Iwan Iwanoff in the town centre. One is the town **library**, where artistically placed concrete blocks cast patterns in the sunlight.

Goonmalling Rd
Northam–Toodyay Rd
Fitzgerald St
0 1 km
0 0.5 miles

16 Overnighting on ROTTNEST

ISLAND | WILDLIFE | BEACH

Keen to understand the living creature behind the thousands of grinning selfies with celebrities? Rottnest Island's quokkas are known for their photogenic poses, but a simple snap sells them short. Experience the transformative nature of spending a night – or three – in Perth's holiday haven, surrounded by curious wildlife, peaceful coves and oodles of natural beauty.

MARTY/SHUTTERSTOCK

How to

Getting here Rottnest-bound ferries depart from Perth's city centre, Fremantle and Hillarys Boat Harbour. There are also lightplane and helicopter options.

Getting around Most people hire bicycles. You can also get about on foot or by e-bike, take the shuttle, or buy a ticket for the hop-on, hop-off bus that loops around the 11km-long island.

When to go The days are warm and skies are blue from September to May.

TRABANTOS/SHUTTERSTOCK

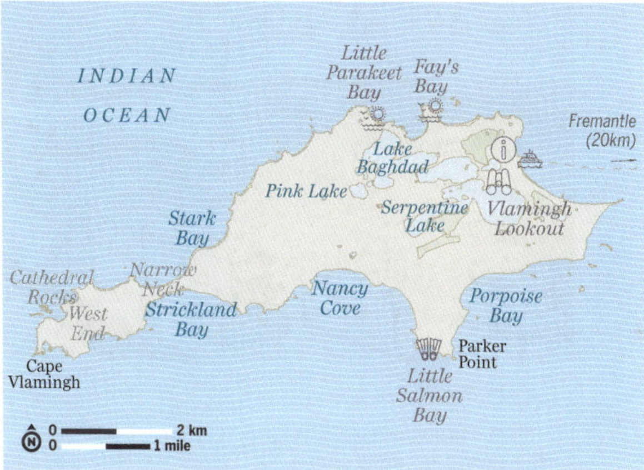

Gone are the crowds With many day-trippers departing on the 6pm ferry, tens of thousands of visitors to Rottnest Island never see it at its best – as the sun softens, the bustle calms and the marsupials emerge. They leave with quokka selfies, a slick of sunscreen and the crunch of salt in their hair. It's fun, sure, but you can do better. Those who stay overnight have an entirely different experience. As night nears, quokkas – which are nocturnal – come out in droves. In the dark they're most active, bouncing across walking paths and around anyone wandering by. They scramble up trees, tussle with one another and nibble on grasses. It's a significant contrast from daytime, when they barely move, appear stunned or lazily scavenge. These quokkas are only there because of people – and that's why feeding them is a no-no. If you see a quokka sleeping during the day – they curl up while seated and rest their heads on their tails – don't bother them; they need their shut-eye.

Relax into 'Rotto' pace While you're here explore beyond the main settlement to follow little-used hiking trails and boardwalks and have enchanting beaches all to yourself. Paradisiacal **Little Parakeet Bay** is flanked by eroded limestone formations and faces an ocean pool. At **Fay's Bay**, a curving, flat beach gives way to craggy rocks with leafy seagrasses and rock pools at their base; it's an ideal spot for children to explore and amateur fishers to drop a line. At sheltered **Little Salmon Bay**, an excellent snorkel trail is dotted with underwater panels.

Left Narrow Neck
Below Quokkas

A Few Fun Quokka Facts

When 17th-century Dutch sailors explored the craggy limestone island, they mistook its resident fur balls for large rats. The quokkas' presence resulted in the island's name, Rottnest, which means 'rat's nest' in Dutch.

Quokkas get most of the hydration they need from eating native greenery, such as grasses, succulents and seedlings, so they rarely drink water.

Quokka joeys poke their little heads out of their mothers' pouches each September, and the island holds a public, weekend-long Quokka birthday party for all the newborns. They're ultra cute but should never be touched.

Beyond the Quokkas

ROTTNEST ISLAND'S LAYERED AND COMPLEX BACKSTORY

Rottnest Island – called Wadjemup by the Whadjuk Noongar – is outshone by its famous quokkas. But look beyond the cuteness and you'll find an isle of living history, where heritage buildings tell stories of lonely colonial settlement, world war efforts and hard-knocks farming.

Left Thomson Bay
Centre Vlamingh Lookout
Right The Quod

JON ARNOLD IMAGES LTD/ALAMY

Early Origins

Perth's playground, winking 19km across the Indian Ocean, wasn't always an island. Some 7000 years ago, Rottnest Island formed part of the WA mainland. Artefacts found, such as a 27,000-year-old cutting tool made of chert, suggest Rottnest's Traditional Custodians, the Whadjuk Noongar people, walked across the land bridge well before sea levels rose, using it as a meeting place and ceremonial site.

It was far more recently, in 1831, that Rottnest's first European residents set up here. Robert Thomson is believed to be the first person to live on Rottnest Island, along with his wife and children. Along with other settlers, they farmed everything from livestock to grains, tobacco and fruit, as well as harvesting salt from central saline lakes. Rottnest's main settlement, Thomson Bay, is named after the family.

Parts of the Thomson homestead and water well – possibly the oldest human-made structures on Rottnest – can still be viewed. A 4km walking trail weaves through the area that the Thomsons farmed. Follow it from hilltop Vlamingh Lookout down to a boardwalk with pink-hued salt lakes and samphire carpets on either side that leads to Little Parakeet Bay (p97).

A Hidden History

The Thomson family was the last to privately own land on Rottnest – in 1839 private ownership was prohibited. The island became an Aboriginal penal colony, and over the next century nearly 4000 men and boys were imprisoned here.

Prisoners undertook brutally hard labour, quarrying stone and constructing most of the colonial buildings still standing in Thomson Bay. Tragically, at least 373 Aboriginal men and boys are believed to have died and been buried here, making

ME.KRIS/SHUTTERSTOCK

ALEISHA ORR/SHUTTERSTOCK

this the largest known site of Aboriginal deaths in custody in Australia. The burial ground remained unknown to the public until the 1980s. The prison, known as the Quod, was closed in 1904; the last inmates left in the 1930s. The many Aboriginal lives lost on Wadjemup means the island holds special significance for WA's Aboriginal peoples.

A New Era Dawns

In the decades that followed, Wadjemup was steadily repurposed towards holidaymaking. Once washed with white lime that reflected harshly in the lucid light, its small workers cottages were slapped with a peach ochre that remains synonymous with the island today. The two world wars pressed pause on tourism, with Rottnest used as a prisoner-of-war camp and military defence base. After the wars, the canons and army barracks became tourist attractions, the Boys' Reformatory was turned into accommodation, and the governor's summer residence was converted into a pub.

> The only people allowed to live on the island are long-serving staff members.

Private ownership remains banned, with only long-serving staff allowed to live on the island. While the settlement's holiday houses have been gently upgraded over time, they retain a deliberately simple feel. More recently, rising visitor numbers have brought new accommodation, including Samphire Rottnest, the Lodge Wadjemup and Pinky's Rottnest Island. While these additions have prompted debate, Rottnest's sandy-footed, car-free simplicity remains central to its appeal, with a careful balance continually struck between old and new.

The Wadjemup Project

Launched in 2022, the Wadjemup Project is an Aboriginal-led initiative reshaping how Rottnest Island is understood and experienced today. Developed with Whadjuk Noongar Elders and communities across WA, it focuses on truth-telling, ceremony and memorialisation. Conservation works are underway at the Quod, the island's former prison and most visible symbol of this history, following major state funding announced in 2023. As part of the project, Traditional Custodians have led Wadjemup Wirin Bidi, a spirit trail ceremony that acknowledges the spirits of Aboriginal men and boys imprisoned on the island. Planning is also underway for a permanent memorial at the Wadjemup Aboriginal Burial Ground.

17 Easy-Access Roo SPOTTING

WILDLIFE | NATURE | OUTDOORS

The thrill of seeing your first kangaroo bound effortlessly through tall grasses, illuminated by the day's last light, is hard to beat. Here's where to find creatures in the wild, with the help of a little patience and local know-how. Mix in a bit of luck and you'll also spot echidnas and bandicoots, plus a colony of koalas.

IMAGEVIXEN/SHUTTERSTOCK

How to

Getting around Public transport is tricky in these semi-rural areas, so it's simplest to drive yourself.

When to go Australian wildlife is most active at dawn and dusk.

A caveat Go just before these times to minimise driving during risky periods, when creatures may bounce and run unexpectedly from roadsides. Be mindful as you head back in the dark.

ANASTAS_STYLES/SHUTTERSTOCK

Left Kangaroos, Yanchep National Park
Below John Forrest National Park

Wildlife hot spot Depending on the day, there might be less than a handful, or huge groups of relatively tame, yet wild, roos at **John Forrest National Park** in the Perth Hills. You'll see western grey kangaroos, kookaburras, and '28s', a local parrot with vibrant green colours, close to the park's paved walkways, near the car park area. In September and October prolific native wildflowers bloom – look closely at the bush to spot their astonishing details.

Backyard stickybeaking Drive around the semi-rural fields surrounding the townships of **Darlington** and **Kalamunda** and park on the roadside. You'll spot roos naturally grazing in open paddocks, in vineyards (like Darlington Estate Winery) or in bush inside **Kalamunda National Park** – where there are also echidnas, bandicoots and native birds.

Dusk and dawn discoveries To explore on foot, consider camping at the Perth Hills Discovery Centre inside **Beelu National Park**. Take any of the bushwalking trails and keep an eye – and an ear – out for wildlife.

Easy viewing Big packs of smaller roos are reliably seen nibbling on the lawn near the pub within **Yanchep National Park**, in Perth's north. There's also a wheelchair-accessible boardwalk through a thicket of trees where a group of koalas live. You won't see them in the wild, though – koalas are not native to Western Australia. This colony was first started in 1938, for residents' enjoyment.

Getting up Close

There's a certain excitement about observing wild creatures, and actually holding one is a guaranteed heart-melter. Given that most of Australia's wildlife is nocturnal, the **Kanyana Wildlife Rehabilitation Centre** in the Perth Hills district of Lesmurdie runs all-ages night tours as well as daytime discovery programs that include intimate, hands-on encounters. In all, it looks after more than 3000 displaced, injured and orphaned creatures at its **Wildlife Hospital** each year. You might see echidnas, bilbies, red-tailed black cockatoos, possums and a range of other wildlife. The not-for-profit organisation also breeds threatened species that you'd struggle to see otherwise.

18 DRIVING Perth's Valleys

FOOD | HIKING | NATURE

Go fruit picking, discover one of the smallest cellar doors in WA and hike along beautiful bush trails. The artsy townships of the Perth Hills are an easy jaunt from the city, offering a delightful switch from urban to rural.

BMPHOTOGRAPHER/SHUTTERSTOCK

How to

Getting around Public transport is limited; it's best to drive.

When to go Spring and autumn are best for dramatic colours and blooms.

Bush magic There are dozens of excellent bushwalks to explore, from the **Kalamunda Railway Heritage Trail** to the **Carmel Walk** and **Victoria Reservoir Trail**.

Insider Intel

Kookaburra Cinema (Mundaring) Fantastic movies under the stars.

Kishi (Kalamunda) A 20-seat Japanese restaurant with great fish.

Lions Lookout (Korung National Park) A 4km loop walk with city views and the Travelling Snack food truck Friday to Sunday. Best at sunset.

Recommendations by

Nicolas Smeets
Owner of the Travelling Snack food truck
@travellingsnackrestaurant

01 Book in to pick-your-own fruit block at **Carmel Cherry Farm**. The small local orchard grows delicious exotic fruit from cherries to lychees. Other orchards may take drop-ins.

02 On Carmel's forested slopes, settle in at **Hainault @ Carmel** for Perth Hills wine tastings and generous share platters in a relaxed cellar-door setting.

03 Locals describe the **Whistlepipe Gully hike** as like being in a magical fairy playground. The 3.5km return trail is relatively easy, with a few rocky climbs.

04 Follow the trail to the platform lookouts at **Lesmurdie Falls**, then descend into the bush and arrive at the waterfall's feet.

05 The fruit tree blossoms at **Core Cider** in Pickering Brook from September to November are so prolific they look like snow. Join a tractor tour, then grab a tasting paddle.

19 Eco Eats, Unicorns & WATERFALLS

FOOD | SUSTAINABILITY | WINERY

Welcome to a wonderful local secret. A thoughtfully run winery restaurant in Jarrahdale offers what is perhaps Perth dining's best deal, for so many reasons. Tuck into a genuinely sustainable, hyper-seasonal, multicourse lunch on No Waste Mondays – they're arguably the best leftovers you'll ever eat. Afterwards, soak up the serenity and admire the bird life of adjacent Serpentine National Park.

RIC JACYNO/SHUTTERSTOCK

How to

Getting here A car is the only way to go. It'll take about one hour from Perth city centre.

When to go Anytime of year is great, but the changing colours of the grapevine leaves and European trees in autumn makes for great eye candy.

Top tip Remember, the food served is strictly governed by the seasons, so if you love stonefruits and fresh herbs, go in summer, whereas in winter you'll see more root vegetables on the menu.

VAIVIRGA/SHUTTERSTOCK

Not many restaurants book out on a Monday – and not many use up the entire week's leftovers with one banging-value lunch sitting. Enter **No Waste Mondays** at **Millbrook Winery** in semi-rural Jarrahdale, where the eco-minded chef-gardener goes off-menu to leverage every bit of produce in his kitchen before closing on Tuesday and Wednesday. He and his team fashion multicourse creations that often differ from table to table, delivering an environmentally friendly, bespoke dining experience.

The chef, who lives locally, tends an extraordinary kitchen garden and farm. There are fresh honey, free-range eggs, olives, orchard fruit and more than 100 varieties of **heirloom vegetables**. So while he creates dishes from odds and ends, they're no less exceptional. He's a restaurant industry unicorn, reaching the holy grail of zero waste (something, happily, many more are now striving for). You might expect to pay a pretty penny for this, but it's only $60 (wine is extra), one of many reasons it books out weeks in advance despite still being an in-the-know experience.

Follow your glorious lunch with a hike through **Serpentine National Park**, part of the Darling Scarp, where waterfalls spill over sheer, jet-black rocks. Go beyond the main attraction and hike up the steep hill to discover rock pools and serene clusters of native bush, often with no one else around. While hopping wildlife is rarely seen during the day, there are some 70 species of bird twittering in the trees – look out for western rosellas, black cockatoos and yellow robins.

Left Serpentine National Park
Below Heirloom tomatoes

Do the Darling Range Like a Local

Mundijong Markets Hit the market on the first and third Wednesday of each month. There's heaps of random junk, but I always score at least one great rare find in the auction.

Langford Park I love the mountain bike track here. Don't fall off too badly, though – it's a long drive to the nearest hospital.

Jarrahdale Tavern Sip a perfectly poured pint of Guinness. The tavern's history dates back to 1894.

Scarp Road Go bush bashing through Scarp Rd. At the top of the hill you can look back over the valley and see the farmhouse where I live at Millbrook.

Recommendations by

Guy Jeffreys
Executive Chef at Millbrook Winery in Jarrahdale; @veg_guy

Listings

BEST OF THE REST

Wine Time

Mandoon Estate

The options are copious at this sprawling Swan Valley property: choose from pizzas and pub grub at the Homestead Brewery, go fancy at Wild Swan restaurant or keep it simple with a bought-on-site picnic on the Lawn, where there's an art gallery for adults and a playground for kids. Head indoors to the cellar door to sample Mandoon's wines.

Upper Reach Winery

A new TreeHouse Bar, wine appreciation classes, a restaurant facing the vines and even a behind-the-scenes vineyard and winery tour chased with a wine tasting and two-course lunch... There isn't much that you won't want to do at Upper Reach, a charming, family-run estate in the Swan Valley where the emphasis is on inclusion and education rather than wine snobbery.

Plume Estate Vineyard

Expect boutique wine, designed-to-share seasonal dishes and views over a gently sloping valley at this intimate Perth Hills estate.

Lancaster Wines

The tin tasting shed is cleverly positioned in the middle of the vineyard, making for a very scenic but also very approachable cheese and wine tasting. Lancaster has some of the oldest vines in the Swan Valley. Bonus: it's opposite a chocolate factory.

Pick-Your-Own Farms

Bickley Valley Asparagus Farm

Green, purple and white asparagus picking happens each spring, usually August to November, at this bucolic Perth Hills property with valley views. It's best you stay overnight at the on-site B&B cottage – if you want to join the harvest, it starts early. Otherwise drop in to the farm shed and pick up some snap-fresh organic produce.

Orchard Perth

Citrus is on offer nearly year-round at this farm in the pretty Chittering Valley, a 45-minute drive from Perth. Besides picking oranges and mandarins, you can jump aboard a tractor tour, take part in occasional stargazing nights with pizza and live music or even have a private picnic complete with freshly squeezed juices. Kids love feeding the farm animals.

S&R Orchard

You get two bites here: from roughly December to March you can pluck apples from the trees, whereas in September the branches blossom and the orchard rows become selfie heaven. S&R runs tractor tours and has an animal farm, and there's usually a food truck on site and ice cream for sale, so you can make a day of it.

Strawberry picking

Hoang Le's Strawberries

Stock up on sweet, sun-ripened berries at this family-run grower in Wanneroo, just north of Perth. Pick-your-own usually opens in late spring – check the Facebook page for updates. Expect to get sticky and dirty.

Charming Drives

Yalgorup National Park

Unexpectedly beautiful lakes, woodlands and billabongs peel off the road that winds though Yalgorup National Park, which holds wetlands of international importance. Watch for waterbirds as you follow marked nature trails through the scrub.

Lake Clifton

Take the Old Coast Rd from Mandurah (rather than the newer, faster Forrest Hwy) and stop at Lake Clifton, where there's a boardwalk allowing glimpses of rarely seen early life forms known as thrombolites. They're not particularly pretty, but they are fascinating, and this is the largest living thrombolite reef in the southern hemisphere.

Destination Dining

Lontara $$$

Spiky Asian flavours ripple through the menu at Samphire resort's signature restaurant, overlooking the ocean on Rottnest Island. Always check the chilli factor with the staff, just in case.

Oscar's in the Valley $$

A Swan Valley classic set above the Avon River, this elegant restaurant draws diners for refined modern Australian cooking and tranquil water views. Come for a long lunch on the deck, when the setting really shines.

Luxe Island Seafood Cruise $$$

Savour a surprisingly good-value seafood degustation aboard a private vessel with Rottnest Cruises. Before your white-

Lake Clifton

tablecloth, wine-matched lunch begins, try to catch a coveted Western rock lobster in the boat's pots – are you game to pick one up?

Pies, Hot Dogs & Burgers

Alfred's Kitchen $

Outdoor fire pits, rustic red bricks and old-school burgers have delivered Alfred's serious longevity. Located in Guildford, it's the city's longest-running roadside burger kitchen, with everything cooked on the grill until late.

Joey's Swan Valley Diner $

This cute pink-and-white eatery doubles as a drive-through hot dog and burger joint. That's a fun option, but most prefer to park the car and sit at the picnic tables to dig in while the food is hot. It does breakfast, too.

Miami Bakehouse $

A popular pit stop on the Forrest Hwy, this bakery is loved for its award-winning pies, coffee and treats like raw raspberry and chocolate slice. Dozens of life-size painted kangaroo sculptures decorate the alfresco area.

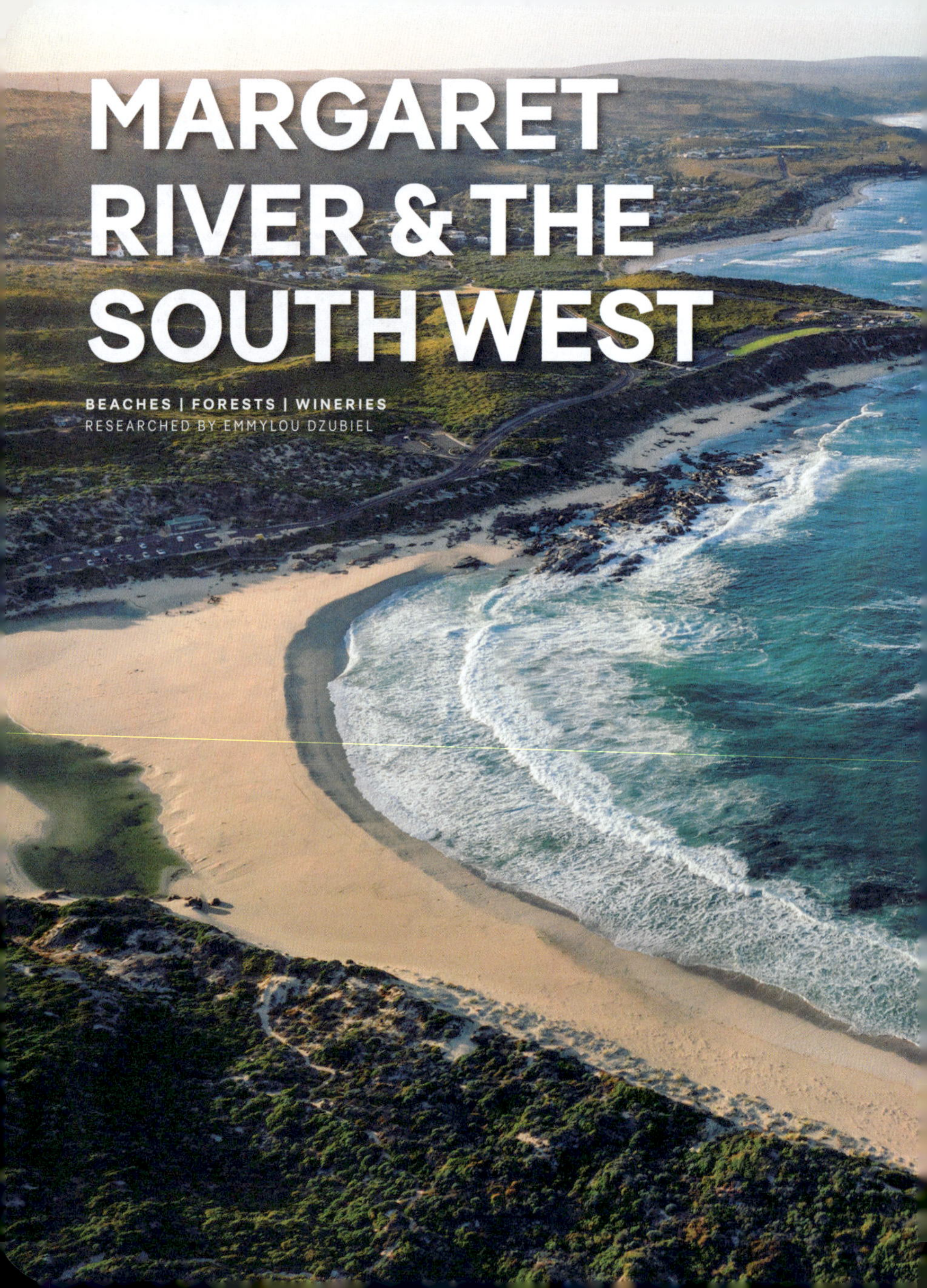

MARGARET RIVER & THE SOUTH WEST

BEACHES | FORESTS | WINERIES

RESEARCHED BY EMMYLOU DZUBIEL

- **A Margaret River Taster** (p112)
- **Farm-to-Table Trail** (p114)
- **The Biggest, Tallest & Quirkiest** (p116)
- **Go Forest Bathing** (p118)
- **An Almighty Coast** (p120)
- **Living on Country** (p124)
- **Fun for all Ages in Busselton** (p126)
- **Explore the Valleys** (p128)
- **The South West's Artistic Side** (p130)
- **Margaret River's Underworld** (p132)
- **Up the Adrenaline Level** (p134)
- **Listings** (p136)

MATT DEAKIN/SHUTTERSTOCK

MARGARET RIVER & THE SOUTH WEST

Trip Builder

Pristine white beaches, thrilling surf breaks, gorgeous swathes of unique eucalyptus forests, epic hiking and biking trails, glittering underground caves and charming rural villages – this foodie and nature lovers' heaven is known worldwide for good reason.

Discover more than 40 large-scale murals around the revitalised port city of **Bunbury/ Goombarup** (p131)
2hr from Perth

Find a foodie paradise in the rolling green hills of **Ferguson Valley** (p128)
2hr from Perth

Be blown away by world-class surf in **Yallingup**, literally 'the place of holes' (p135)
30min from Margaret River

Base yourself in **Busselton/ Undalup** for a lively foreshore, white beaches and fun for the whole family (p126)
45min from Margaret River

Satisfy your senses around **Margaret River/Wooditchup**, the epicentre of a world-famous gourmet food and wine industry (p112)
3hr from Perth

Witness the annual northward migration of whales at **Flinders Bay** in Augusta as they pass along the coast (p122)
30min from Margaret River

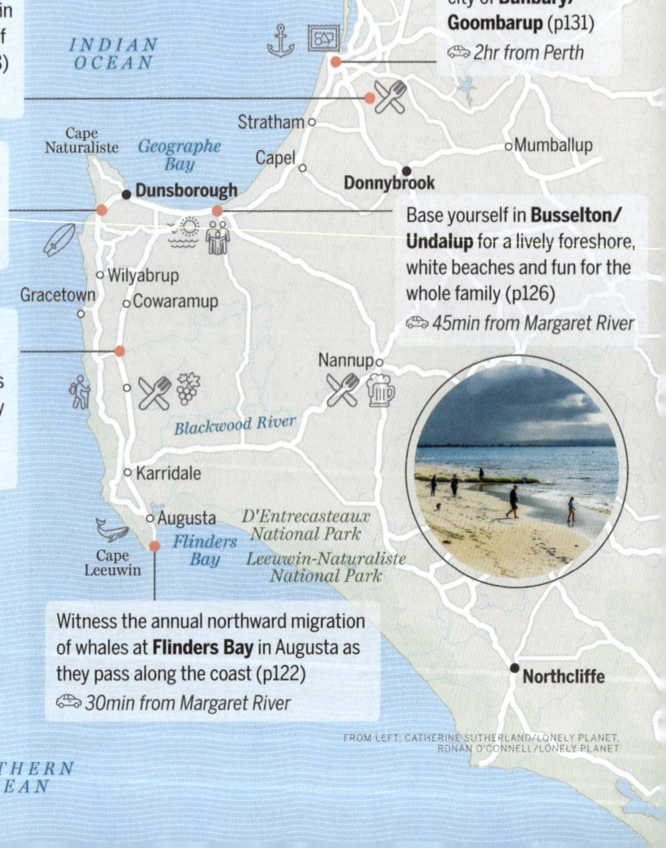

FROM LEFT: CATHERINE SUTHERLAND/LONELY PLANET, RONAN O'CONNELL/LONELY PLANET

Practicalities

ARRIVING

Busselton Jetstar has direct flights from Melbourne to Busselton Margaret River Airport. Hire a car at the airport or join a tour.

Bunbury Coaches run daily from East Perth to Bunbury and onwards to destinations such as Margaret River and Augusta.

FIND YOUR WAY

Reliable maps are available at visitor centres; never travel without one, and don't rely on phone reception or GPS in remote areas.

MONEY

Card payment is common, especially in major centres, but carry some cash for out-of-the-way places and roadside stalls.

WHERE TO STAY

Place	Pros/Cons
Busselton	Luxury resorts, pet-friendly caravan parks and family spots. Short drive from Margaret River's attractions.
Yallingup	Exclusive luxury spas and spectacular private views through to rustic camping and glamping options.
Bridgetown/ Balingup	Glamping, farmstays and forest retreats in the rolling hills of the South West.
Pemberton	Cute forest cottages and lakes edged by elegant eucalyptus.

GETTING AROUND

Car Your best bet is to drive; if you're a confident driver, hire a 4WD and experience divine secret spots.

Bus Public-transport is reliable but limited by infrequent schedules; buses connect most towns.

Tours Options, from wineries to canoeing can give you unique insights.

TOP: HAIREENA/SHUTTERSTOCK
BOTTOM: PALMOLIVEZ/SHUTTERSTOCK

EATING & DRINKING

Famous for its food and wine scene, Margaret River is home to gourmet restaurants, wineries, craft breweries, innovative distilleries and artisanal providores selling chocolate (pictured above left), cheese, lavender ice cream, olive oil and more. Caves Rd, running from Cape Naturaliste to Cape Leeuwin, is dotted with tempting culinary stops.

Best farm experience
Forage Safaris (p113)

Must-try unique flavour
Lavender ice cream (pictured), Cape Lavender Teahouse (p137)

BIRAK	BUNURU	DJERAN	MAKURU	DJILBA	KAMBARANG
DEC & JAN	FEB & MAR	APR & MAY	JUN & JUL	AUG & SEP	OCT & NOV
Busiest time of year, warming up, great for outdoors.	The hottest season and best time to get wet.	Clear days and crisp nights; best for whale watching.	Cool, wet and wild, exhilarating storms.	Windy but getting warmer.	Spring wildflowers in full bloom.

20 A Margaret River TASTER

FOOD | WINERIES | TOURS

As a leading Australian winegrowing region, you can be fairly certain you'll taste some exquisite wines, from cabernet sauvignon to chardonnay, and gourmet food while in the Margaret River/Wooditchup area. But don't miss out on getting your hands dirty – learn how food is grown and made, follow an organic wine trail or join an innovative tour to get up to date on lo-fi winemaking.

MICHELLE MORRISON PHOTOGRAPHY ©

How to

Getting around Pick a designated driver when visiting the wineries and breweries, and if no one's willing to put their hand up, join a bus tour.

Farm-gate food Roadside stalls around Manjimup offer the freshest produce – look out for seasonal stone fruit, berries, apples, asparagus and avocados.

Top tip Buy directly from the farmers themselves every Saturday morning at the **Margaret River Farmers Market**. Fresh and delish!

PHIL HILL/ALAMY STOCK PHOTO ©

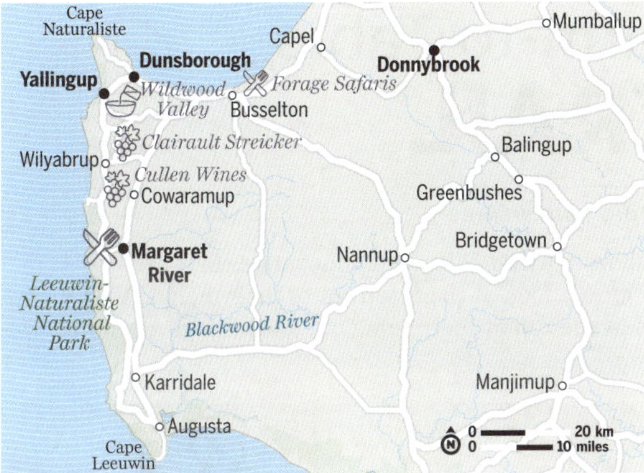

Get hands on with local produce Forage your way through quality farms of the South West, including avocado, apple and chestnut, with **Forage Safaris**. Customisable tours delve into the intricacies of farming with tastings of the unbeatable produce this region has to offer. In the quiet serenity of Yallingup, the **Wildwood Valley** cooking school, run by a trained chef, offers classes that highlight fresh, local produce inspired by an interesting mix of Tuscan and Thai flavours.

Wineries With over 200 wineries in the region, there's certainly a lot of choice. **Cullen Wines** in Wilyabrup is known for impeccable organic and biodynamic wines, including the cabernet-based red Diana Madeline and chardonnay Kevin John wines. At **Clairault Streicker**, create your own cabernet sauvignon or shiraz blend using real-deal equipment and under the expert guidance of a winemaker; you'll expand your knowledge of wine blending, learn what makes your palate zing and then take your creation home. You even get to name your own drop.

Foodie festival The hugely popular **Western Australia Gourmet Escape** *(gourmetescape.com.au)*, held in late November, combines the Margaret River region's pristine landscapes with an extravaganza of fresh, innovative food. It's considered the premium showcase of Western Australia's food and wine, and the star-studded guest list usually includes some of the biggest international and Australian names in the foodie world. It's not just for the elite gastronome but for people who simply love great food.

Left Wildwood Valley cooking school
Below Cullen Wines

The Best Winery & Cultural Tours

Koomal Dreaming Learn about the native ingredients used by many chefs in the Margaret River region on a tour led by Wadandi custodian Josh Whiteland. You'll forage for native bush foods, discover their cultural uses and then gather around the campfire for a seasonal lunch – dishes might include kangaroo, emu, abalone, coastal herbs or quandong.

Margaret River Discovery Tour A handpicked winery and gourmet experience, plus exciting 4WD and canoeing adventures, led by tour guide Sean Blocksidge – and all in a day.

Walk Talk Taste Meet locals working in the food and beverage scene and hear about the produce that inspires them on an intimate evening tour of Margaret River town.

21 Farm-to-Table TRAIL

SUSTAINABILITY | FINE DINING | BREWERIES

In and around Dunsborough and Yallingup, innovative chefs are putting seasonable, locally grown food at the forefront of their menus. Visit a few fine-dining restaurants at the top of their game but keep things grounded with some casual brews.

JESSICA WYLD

How to

Getting around If you're not joining a tour, having a car is the best way to experience this trail – you never know what might take your fancy as you travel along.

When to go Many restaurants and wineries have grassy areas for soaking up the outdoors while kids burn energy on the playground. Many also have cosy wood fires and make for a great winter escape. If you want to visit farms, March, April, October and November are comfortable, dry months.

What's up?

In southern WA, many place names end with -up, which, in the Bibbulmun language, means 'place of'. '

One of the biggest misconceptions is that Yallingup is the place of lovers because historic Caves House (pictured) was once popular with honeymooners. Yallingup is in fact the place of caves and holes, which makes sense given it's above the limestone ridge.'

Iszaac Webb
Wadandi Cultural Custodian & Knowledgeholder
@undalup.com

01 At **Eagle Bay Brewing Co** near Dunsborough, enjoy preservative-free brews, ridiculous views and a hearty modern Australian menu using ingredients direct from the kitchen garden.

02 Book a table at **Yarri** in Dunsborough for a modern Australian small-plates or fine-dining menu inspired by local growers and paired with wines from Snake + Herring.

03 Settle in with a tasting paddle and a few share plates at family-friendly **Wild Hop Brewing Company** in the Yallingup Hills. On summer Sundays, there's live music.

04 Sustainable and wild-harvested food is the focus of head chef Jed Gerrard's fine-dining degustation at award-winning **Wills Domain** in Yallingup – and the recipe is working. The wine's not bad either.

05 The team at **Beerfarm** keep a close eye on their Black Angus cattle, fed a mix of grass and spent grain from brewing, resulting in spectacular local beef.

The Biggest, Tallest **& QUIRKIEST**

01

03

02

04

05

01 Longest jetty
Busselton's wooden jetty stretches for a whopping 1.8km, making it the longest wooden jetty in the southern hemisphere and the second longest in the world.

02 Quirkiest
Yes, it's true: there's a town here completely populated by garden gnomes. Gnomesville (p129) has got to be seen to be believed.

03 Delicate wonder
With over 350 terrestrial orchid species in the South West, keep an eye out for the delicate spider orchid genus: the widespread *Caladenia* or the bright-yellow cowslip *Caladenia flava.*

04 Snorkelling joy
The natural pool known as the Aquarium (p121) off Smiths Beach Rd is good for snorkelling.

05 Tallest trees
Reaching up to 90m, the cream-barked karri *(Eucalyptus diversicolor)* is the fifth tallest eucalypt and king of the South West forests.

06

07

08

09

06 The most south-westerly point
Cape Leeuwin Lighthouse (p132) stands where the Southern and Indian Oceans meet, a powerful blustery spot where you feel the might of the ocean.

07 Falling leaves
The Golden Valley Tree Park in Balingup is the largest arboretum in the state and comes alive with amazing colours when the weather turns cool.

08 White wonder
In October, Donnybrook is surrounded by trees awash with magnificent pink and white apple fruit blossom.

09 Natural rush
Injidup Natural Spa (p121) is created when waves crash over the rocks into a natural pool.

22 Go Forest BATHING

FORESTS | WATERFALLS | HIKING

When you visit the South West region you'll discover endless forests – unique, remote and pristine – making this the perfect spot for forest bathing, plus canoeing, fishing and bushwalking. Enter the forest and match the pace of the slow-moving rivers that wind through this region, taking in even the smallest details as you go.

RINI KOOLS/SHUTTERSTOCK

How to

Getting around Having your own wheels is a wonderful way to explore.

Pack for the weather Cool and often enshrouded in a veil of mist, the Southern Forests grow here due to an especially wet climate; even in summer, prepare for cool nights and frequent rain, especially from June to September.

Tours If you're short of time or want to get off-road, **Margaret River Exposed** can help maximise your time. For environmentally aware adventure tours, check out **Pemberton Discovery Tours**.

LKONYA/SHUTTERSTOCK ©

Get grounded, be mindful The idea of forest bathing, a Japanese concept that emerged in the 1980s, encourages you to tune in to all of your senses when you go into the forest. And what better place to get a taste of forest bathing – or indeed just to appreciate the beauty of tall trees – than in the vast expanses of karri, marri and jarrah forest in the South West. Listen to the harmonious sound of waterfalls and birdsong and fill up your lungs with the rich, earthy aroma of petrichor after a good rain – it's a welcome recalibration from busy modern life.

Zen-like beauty There are plenty of walks for forest bathing – just choose a spot and go. The **Beedelup Falls** in the Greater Beedelup National Park are spectacular in winter and the suspension bridge adds to the adventure. The Zen-like beauty of **Boranup Karri Forest**, with its tall, elegant, pale-pink karri trees, is an earthly balance to the other attractions of the Margaret River region. The even size and symmetry of the karris is, ironically, due to logging here 100 years ago. Boranup Dr is a wonderful experience for people of all abilities.

All aboard! The charming and rickety **Pemberton Tramway** meanders through spectacular karri forest, crossing rickety trestle bridges until you arrive at the gorgeous Cascades in Gloucester National Park. This is a romantic and fun way to experience the Southern Forests, especially for those with limited mobility and for kids, who love the ride. From Pemberton you can also take the 86km **Karri Forest Explorer Drive**, which offers many chances to get out and smell the rich forest, including the 12km Heartbreak Trail.

Left Gloucester Tree
Below Beedelup Falls

Fire Look-out Trees

In the 1950s fire lookout towers were installed in the tallest trees to provide an early warning system for spotting smoke in the dry summers. As the fifth-tallest eucalypt species, the karri towers over the forest canopy, providing a truly bird's-eye view. The network of lookout towers has long been replaced by spotter planes, but you can still climb the metal rungs of the **Dave Evans Bicentennial Tree** in Warren National Park to get incredible views across the forest. Be warned: most people have pretty sore legs the next day. Or zip around the now closed **Gloucester Tree** with **Aerial Adventure** in Gloucester National Park.

23 An Almighty COAST

BEACHES | SURFING | MARINE LIFE

From incredible rock formations to natural spas, unique wines and ocean creatures of all kinds, it's impossible to visit this region without spending time on the coast. While the area is known for its world-class surf and famous championships, there's plenty to experience if surfing isn't your style.

EMMA JONES/SHUTTERSTOCK

How to

Getting around All the places listed here are accessible with 2WD, but be aware that these are narrow and winding country roads, so watch out for wildlife. Always drive to the conditions.

When to visit Between June and December whales pass along this coast during their annual migration north to warmer waters.

Swim safe The ocean here is powerful and dangerous; observe warnings and be careful at all times, especially on rocky coastal areas. If a sign says 'No Swimming', then this is what it means.

NEXXT FRAME PHOTOGRAPHY/SHUTTERSTOCK

Rockin' Rocks & Natural Havens

The unique rock formations of the Leeuwin-Naturaliste coast are the result of granite gneiss rocks being weathered over eons by the powerful movement of the waves. Some of the more notable are **Canal Rocks** near Yallingup and **Sugarloaf Rock** at Cape Naturaliste (also an incredible spot to watch the sunset).

A short drive from Sugarloaf Rock, to the other side of the cape, is **Meelup Beach**, with clear aquamarine waters and pure white sand – it's perfect for a tranquil swim. If a bit more froth has you bubbling, then **Injidup Natural Spa** is a hidden rock pool where waves crash over the rocks to create a spa-like sensation. For protected snorkelling, head to the **Aquarium** near Smiths Beach.

AGENT WOLF/SHUTTERSTOCK

Seaside Winery

Home to the state's most unique winery, the coast of Augusta offers the chance to sip wines that have been aged in an underwater process at **Subsea Estate**. Utilising the natural sway, low light, and consistent temperature and pressure of the Southern Ocean gives the wines a distinctive flavour profile.

Above left Injidup Natural Spa
Above Sugarloaf Rock
Left Canal Rocks

Short Coastal Walks

There's nothing more invigorating than short walks to appreciate this coast. An easy and fully accessible option is the 4km walk from Cape Naturaliste Lighthouse (p132) to Sugarloaf Rock, while the 4km return hike to **Quinninup Falls** from Moses Rock car park takes you along part of the Cape to Cape Track (p136) for a true wilderness experience.

Hiking is best from September through November when wildflowers dot the coastal heath and you might spot the thrilling sprays of whales as they migrate northward. Also, it shouldn't be too hot, though keep a lookout for snakes.

Spotting Graceful Rays

Beautiful **Hamelin Bay**, to the south of Margaret River, is another beachside getaway. It's best known for its frequent

The Whale Highway

Flinders Bay in Augusta is where humpback, southern right and blue whales first reach land after crossing the ocean from Antarctica. Between June and August, whale-watching cruises here enable you to get a close, though respectful, look.

From September to November you can also take whale-watching trips from Dunsborough as the whales and calves make their way back south after the calves are born in the warmer waters of the north.

The **lighthouses** at Cape Naturaliste and Cape Leeuwin both provide great vantage points for whale watchers, as does Sugarloaf Rock.

FAR LEFT: NICO FARAMAZ/SHUTTERSTOCK, LEFT: ADWO/SHUTTERSTOCK

visitors, three species of wild sea creature: smooth stingrays, black stingrays and eagle rays. On calm mornings these locals can be seen around the picturesque old Hamelin Bay jetty and along the shallows of the beach. Remember that these are wild creatures – keep a safe distance, don't touch them and definitely don't feed them.

4WD Adventures

The pristine **Yeagarup Dunes** form one of the largest land-locked dune systems in the world. Driving along the top of the dunes, with karri forest on one side and pure sand on the other, is awe-inspiring. Equally incredible are the towering hexagonal basalt columns of **Black Point**, formed 135 million years ago, as is nearby **Lake Jasper**, the largest natural freshwater lake in WA. These are true adventures for experienced 4WDers. Alternatively, contact **Pemberton Discovery Tours** for their unique options.

Left Humpback whale
Above Sting rays and seagulls, Hamelin Bay

■ **Iszaac Webb**
Wadandi Cultural Custodian & Knowledgeholder
@undalup.com

Living on Country

TREAD SOFTLY WHEN YOU VISIT, LEAVING ONLY FOOTPRINTS

Iszaac 'Zac' Webb is filled with an incredible passion and energy for sharing his culture and the traditions of the Wadandi people. Not only does he teach the significance of – and respect for – the Traditional Custodians of the land, he also partners with community and government organisations to increase knowledge and understanding.

Left Ceremony performance by Undalup Mob Wadandi people
Centre *Gnuraren* (western ringtail possum)
Right Spring-flowering willow myrtle

MATT DUNBAR/GETTY IMAGES

A Common Creation Story

Zac is a Wadandi Pibulmun man. His forefathers, the Wadandi (Saltwater People), lived on the land from Bunbury/Goombarup in the north, over the Capes area and through to the Blackwood River/Goribilyup. His grandmother is from the Pibulmun (the people of plenty where the forest meets the sea), whose family lived on the southern side of the river through to Nannup/Nanninup.

There are 14 clans that make up the larger Bibbulmun tribe, which loosely covers the area from Jurien Bay in the north to Esperance in the south. They share a common creation story: the people were camped around Lake Jasper/Yoondadadup. The basalt rock at Black Point/Bohlganup was a volcano, emitting gases that made the old people fall asleep. The earth shook, and when they woke they split into the different clan groups, who went in separate directions, eventually speaking distinct dialects though sharing similar customs and the same beliefs.

Teaching Traditional Ways

Zac works on multiple projects through the Undalup Association, all with the goals of reigniting knowledge of traditional ways, demystifying his culture and teaching the importance of *boodja* (Country).

At the heart of one of these projects is working with local businesses, scientists and government organisa-tions to upskill young Aboriginal people. Through this

JACOBLOYACANO/SHUTTERSTOCK

ALYBABA/SHUTTERSTOCK

program, students gain conventional certifications as well as a valuable additional layer of cultural knowledge. For example, they might learn about the peppermint tree, but with Zac and his team they also learn it is the *wannang*, from which women can make a *wanna* (digging stick).

'When the Elders tell us off, they are teaching it – we shouldn't take it personally; we should take it on board.'

'*Gnuraren* (western ringtail possum) will eat the new leaves and build their *drey* (nest) in a symbiotic relationship. The existing model of education teaches that the tree grows in *silicous* (sandy) soil; with cultural education, we teach to look at the plants around it for context. In the most practical sense,' Zac says, 'having their classes on Country keeps young people more engaged and, most of all, proud of who they are.'

There are always some challenges. 'People don't know the right steps; they are scared of making mistakes. We all make mistakes; this is how we learn. When the Elders tell us off, they are teaching it – we shouldn't take it personally; we should take it on board.'

Zac's hope for the future is that we can all work hand in hand as custodians of the land, find a deeper connection to Country and reach an understanding that we are all connected.

Everything is Connected

Kaya Nala Maat Kaya Noonduk (Hello our family welcomes you) to Wadandi *boodja* (Saltwater People's Country).

We are the Country, and Country is us. Everything is connected – every tree, rock or stone. When we visit the ocean, we greet it, we say hello. When we arrive at fresh water, we take a mouthful of water and hope to create a rainbow spray, and in doing so, pay homage to the rainbow serpent of the fresh water.

You don't have to call out greetings to the ocean or freshwater spirits like we do. Instead, you can give quiet gratitude in your head. You can pay respect silently; you can be present in the Country. This is what we would like visitors to do.

24 Fun for all Ages in BUSSELTON

FAMILY-FRIENDLY | ADVENTURE | PLAYGROUNDS

With family-oriented resorts and a lively foreshore, Busselton/Undalup is a solid option for your first visit to the South West. In fact, the whole region is extremely child-friendly – plan on making day trips along the coast, including to Dunsborough or Margaret River, and be confident that everyone will be happy.

ARIANA SVENSON/LONELY PLANET

How to

Getting around Set yourself up in Busselton and then make day trips with a car.

Where to stay Busselton is the quintessential family resort town; accommodation options feature waterslides, bouncing pillows and endless pools. Alternatively, farmstays and forest retreats often include playgrounds and animal feeding.

Make lots of stops In Myalup, the **Crooked Carrot** has a fun playground and restored vintage Melbourne trams, while the **Old Coast Road Brewery** has a WA-themed mini-golf course.

KAI EGAN/SHUTTERSTOCK

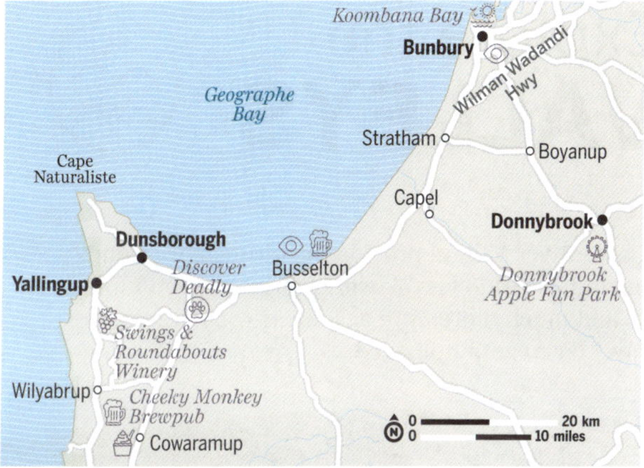

Busselton jetty and foreshore Kids of all ages will love taking the cute solar-powered train out to the end of the 1.8km-long Busselton jetty, where the underwater observatory enraptures with a glimpse of what lies below. Back on land, there's an awesome playground, a seasonal fairground and the **Shelter Brewery Company** on the foreshore. At sunset, take an easy walk, salt in your hair, ice cream in your hand, and there's really nothing quite like it. This place is pure family fun.

Kid-friendly wineries and breweries At most dining establishments you'll find children's menus and kid-friendly playgrounds. A good choice is **Swings & Roundabouts Winery** in Yallingup, a 30-minute drive west of Busselton; everyone loves the yummy pizzas and, yes, swings here. Just 10 minutes further south along Caves Rd, the **Cheeky Monkey Brewpub** in Wilyabrup has an awesome family atmosphere and pours top brews with lake views.

The biggest there is Around 60km east of Busselton is the revamped **Donnybrook Apple Fun Park**, the long-time holder of 'the biggest free fun park in Australia' title. Combine your trip here with some fruit picking in season and Donnybrook makes a great day out.

Detour to Cowtown Cowaramup gets its name from the Aboriginal word *cowara*, meaning purple-crowned lorikeet – but at some point it was dubbed 'Cowtown' due to the area's thriving dairy industry. The town's main street features 42 life-size black-and-white Friesian cows. Get your sweet fix at the **Candy Cow** lolly shop or grab a scoop or two at **Millers Ice Creamery**.

Left Donnybrook Apple Fun Park
Below Fish beneath Busselton jetty

Fun & Adrenaline in the South West

A Maze'n (Margaret River) One of the largest hedge mazes in Australia.

Discover Deadly (Carbunup River) An interesting introduction to snakes and other reptiles.

Koombana Bay (Bunbury) Extremely cool foreshore playground. Next door the **Bunbury Dolphin Discovery Centre** has a state-of-the-art interpretation centre and tours that get you up close to the dolphins that come to the bay most mornings in the warmer months (October to April).

Manjimup Timber Park Rad adventure playground with a mega slide that can be combined with the interactive Power Up Electricity Museum.

25 Explore the VALLEYS

BIKING | FORESTS | MURALS

The Ferguson and Collie River Valleys provide the ultimate weekend getaways, with rolling green hills, world-class artworks, pristine jarrah forest, adrenaline-filled adventure and much more. And as long as you're in the know, you don't have to travel far to get unplugged.

ALTER MANN/SHUTTERSTOCK

How to

Getting around The Collie River Valley is to the northeast of Bunbury, while the Ferguson Valley is to the southeast. You're best off exploring the region with your own car.

Where to stay The area is dotted with cute farmstays, forest cottages and lakeside retreats. For camping head to Potters Gorge or Lake Kepwari.

Where to eat Locals refer to the Fergie Valley as a foodie's dream – it has a dozen boutique wineries, two craft breweries and many passionate chefs.

ARIANA SVENSON/LONELY PLANET

Left Wellington Dam
Below Honeymoon Pool

The world's biggest dam mural You literally can't miss the 8000-sq-metre mural along the **Wellington Dam** wall, just a short drive west of the small town of Collie. When artist Guido van Helten applied for the job he didn't submit a design but instead proposed meeting with the people of the Collie River Valley. The final result, completed in 2021, is a mural that depicts their lives on the water. Follow the fantastic **Collie Mural Trail** to discover 40 murals in the area, including works by local Aboriginal people.

Ancient forest The massive expanse of the jarrah, marri and yarri forests of **Wellington National Park** forms the lungs of this beautiful area and is heaven for hikers, bikers and birdwatchers. Year-round, the Collie River has spots for swimming, canoeing and fishing – or simply a moment of meditation alongside the slow-moving river. The gloriously named **Honeymoon Pool** is an essential stop, but also, make sure to wander along Lennard Rd for a refreshing dip at serene swimming holes like **Long Pool**. From September to October the park comes alive with wildflowers.

Gnomesville This just might be the quirkiest place you'll visit on your trip here. Some years ago a collection of garden gnomes congregated on a random roundabout 15km from Dardanup in the Ferguson Valley. Word got out and the community, well, grew and grew... At last count, there were over 10,000 gnomes. It's a lot of fun to take a look around. Be part of the story and bring your own gnome.

Mountain Biking in the Valley

Mt Lennard Mountain Bike Trail This trail at Pile Rd in Wellington National Park is considered one of WA's best. The organic nature of the trail means plenty of fresh air and trees, while the jump area at the bottom gives riders a place to go all-out.

Arklow Mountain bike trails Nearby in Collie, these trails are a combination of old forestry tracks and railway formations for those with beginner and intermediate skills. There are multiple log rides, big jumps and fast roller-coaster descents. These are part of the broader Wambenger Trails network, named for the threatened carnivorous marsupial that's native to these parts.

Hire bikes at the **Kiosk at the Dam** or an e-bike through Adventure Connections.

26 The South West's ARTISTIC SIDE

ART | GALLERIES | FESTIVALS

The dramatic South West landscape, with its pristine forests and rugged coastlines, is the ultimate inspiration for generations of artists, writers and those who make gourmet masterpieces and creations for the oenophile.

PHOTOGRAPHER: PETER KOVACSY © 2022 'BLUE BIG SKY' BY PETER KOVACSY

Literary Festival

Held in May, the **Margaret River Readers & Writers Festival**, the biggest literary event in regional WA, brings together emerging and established storytellers from WA and further afield. This thought-provoking event provides artistic interaction with the incredible surrounding environment and is both inspiring and intriguing.

How to

When to go Immerse yourself in this creative, meandering itinerary at any time of the year.

Support local artists There's nothing better than meeting the maker of your chosen piece. Check if **Margaret River Region Open Studios** aligns with your visit, when over 100 artists open their studio doors.

Go even further Extend your road trip further south to Northcliffe where the 1.2km **Understory & Art Nature Trail** shows an incredible collection of artworks that grow symbiotically out of the forest.

01 With more than 40 murals around the port city, especially off Victoria St, Bunbury is a must stop for art lovers. Don't miss the **Bunbury Regional Art Gallery**.

02 Indigenous fine art gallery **Yallingup Aboriginal Art** has a fantastic range of contemporary Aboriginal artworks, including prints, jewellery, crockery and more, by local Noongar artists.

03 One of Australia's most creative jewellers, **John Miller Design** in Yallingup creates meaningful pieces using the native flora, fauna and landscape for inspiration.

04 Margaret River is a wealth of artistic endeavour. Visit **Melting Pot Glass Studio** to learn more about glassmaking and **REDSEA Gallery** for exceptional local, interstate and international pieces.

05 For those looking for a unique memory, make a visit to **Peter Kovacsy Studio** (pictured p130) in Pemberton. A well-known artist, Peter specialises in glass, timber and metal sculptures.

BUNBURY REGIONAL ART GALLERY

27 Margaret River's UNDERWORLD

CAVES | HISTORY | LIGHTHOUSES

Not all of Margaret River's treasures are visible at first glance. In fact, the entire Cape to Cape area, between the lighthouses of Cape Naturaliste and Cape Leeuwin, features caves eroded from the sandstone Leeuwin-Naturaliste Ridge. The result is a bejewelled network of 150 caves to explore along the aptly named Caves Rd and breathtaking lighthouses standing sentinel on a wilderness coast.

IAN WOOLCOCK/SHUTTERSTOCK ©

How to

Getting around It's about a 1½-hour drive from cape to cape on Caves Rd, along which is a wealth of caves, tranquil forest and places to eat and drink. Reduce driving time by focusing on the northern or southern cape – don't try to do them all in one day.

When to go The caves all share the same slightly humid atmosphere, which makes them great to visit year-round.

Some fitness required Both lighthouses and all of the caves have a lot of steps; you'll need reasonable physical fitness.

The Cape Lighthouses

Both still operational, the **Cape Naturaliste** and **Cape Leeuwin Lighthouses**, are a perfect juxtaposition with the darkness of the caves. Soak up wild views, turbulent oceans and the feel of the salty wind in your hair. Cape Leeuwin Lighthouse (pictured), the tallest mainland lighthouse in Australia, stands at the most southwesterly tip of the country.

01 After a short guided tour through **Ngilgi Cave**, the most northerly of the caves, near Yallingup, take in the bright colours, stalagmites and stalactites in your own time.

02 The self-guided **Mammoth Cave**, near Margaret River town, provides universal access for the first section and is a good choice if you have little kids.

03 The remarkable **Lake Cave** is named for its beautiful lake and reflections, but it's just as memorable for its karri-framed entry (and lots of steps).

04 For a more adventurous caving experience, head to the 86m-deep **Giants Cave**. Get in contact with Margaret River Climbing Co for caving and abseiling tours.

05 The most southerly cave is considered by many to be the most beautiful: **Jewel Cave**, 8km northwest of Augusta, has three massive, crystal-encrusted chambers.

FROM LEFT: NICKICHEN/SHUTTERSTOCK, MICHAEL HERITAGE/SHUTTERSTOCK.

28 Up the Adrenaline LEVEL

ADVENTURE | ZIP LINES | WATER SPORTS

Seen it all before? Then up the ante with some fun-fuelled adventures on the land, on the water or up in the trees. From zip-lining, ropes courses and horse riding to coasteering and kayaking, each adrenaline-filled activity will highlight the beauty of this region in a unique and unforgettable way.

TIM CAMPBELL

How to

Get ready None of these activities is for the faint-hearted – but that's why the rewards are enormous. Always consider whether an activity is right for you, or have a chat with the operator first.

Hitting the surf
Margaret River isn't just for experienced surfers. Several surf schools operate in sheltered beaches and bays so that you can get a taste of this exhilarating sport.

RICHARD JACYNO/GETTY IMAGES

CHAMELEONSEYE/GETTY IMAGES

Far left Zip lining, Forest Adventures Busselton
Below left Surfing, Yallingup
Left Kayaking, Margaret River

Zip lines and ropes course The area has three high rope adventure courses – it's an incredible way to challenge yourself while also getting close to the trees. You can zip through the towering tuart trees at **Forest Adventures** in Busselton, **Next Level Monkey Business** in Dunsborough or further south at **Aerial Adventure Pemberton**.

On a SUP or kayak Options for stand-up paddleboarding (SUP) abound. For white-sand beaches and turquoise waters, try **Stand Up Surfing** at Gnarabup Beach. For kayakers and canoeists, sunset canoe tours on the Margaret River are offered by **Margaret River Discovery Tours**, while a combination of wild food tastings and an exploration of this tranquil waterway is on the menu with **Bushtucker Tours**. For an unplugged kayaking experience, the pristine Blackwood River is southwestern Australia's largest river and offers unspoilt stretches of scenery – hire a kayak from **BIG4 Bridgetown Caravan Park** and glide through serene bushland.

Ocean thrills If you're after a buzz without exerting too much energy, check out **Dunsborough Jetski Tours**. You'll jet across the stunning Geographe Bay coastline at thrilling speeds while learning about the history, wildlife and environment of the region. If you'd rather get your kicks with body movement, try out coasteering with **Margaret River Adventure Co**, where you'll (safely) launch your body from rocks into the turquoise waters and ride the swells with guide Jaydn.

Surf Like a Local

The WA surfing scene took hold in the Margaret River region in the early 1950s, with pioneer surfers making the long trek down south in search of waves. Today travellers come from across the globe to learn from hands-on experts, getting even the most beginner surfers confident and coasting along the best waves WA has to offer. Yallingup Main Break can be OK for beginners, but it's better for those with some experience. **Margaret River Surf School** offers lessons at Redgate Beach, while **Yallingup Surf School** runs from several locations around the northern cape.

Listings

BEST OF THE REST

Epic Adventures

Bibbulmun Track

One of the world's great long-distance walking trails, this 1000km track goes from Kalamunda/Calamunnda outside Perth to Albany/Kinjarling on the South Coast. Hiking a short section can be just as rewarding.

Cape to Cape Track

Hike this wonderful 124km track that follows the Leeuwin-Naturaliste Ridge from Cape Naturaliste in the north to Cape Leeuwin in the south. The full trek takes about seven days.

Munda Biddi Trail

Supposedly the longest continuous bike trail in the world, the Munda Biddi Trail covers over 1000km, passing through Collie, Donnybrook, Manjimup and Northcliffe before heading down to the South Coast. Munda Biddi means 'path through the forest'.

Community Connection

Boola Bidi Dreaming

Immerse yourself in Noongar culture through informative walking tours and cultural workshops with the team at Boola Bidi Dreaming in scenic Harvey.

Donnybrook Artisan Hub

Support local artists at the Donnybrook Artisan Hub where a diverse range of arts and crafts are on show. The Manjimup Arts Hub is another good option.

Origins Centre

A weekend retreat at the Origins Centre offers a tranquil setting alongside the charming Balingup Brook, with beautiful gardens and native bush.

Start with Coffee

White Elephant Cafe $$

Top coffee, mouthwatering breakfasts and a choice beachside location overlooking the waves at Gnarabup Beach.

Drift $$

Enjoy a cosy breakfast or brunch made from excellent fresh produce at this Margaret River institution.

Egberts $

Loved by Margaret River locals for the sensational coffee, delicious pastries and smiling staff.

Food for the Soul

Hidden River Estate $$

With stunning views across the vines, Hidden River Estate Pemberton offers tastings and delicious meals. Families love the converted tram carriage that adjoins a cubby house.

Hooked Up Fish n Chips $

Watch the sunset over Surfers Point at Prevelly while munching delicious fish and chips. During the day, watch the surf.

ARIANA SVENSON/LONELY PLANET

Olio Bello

Miki's Open Kitchen $$$

Fresh local produce is used to create unique tastes for the tailor-made Japanese degustation menu at this Margaret River venue.

Park Donnybrook $

In the Goods Shed at Station Sq, Park Donnybrook serves wholesome, local and lovingly prepared cakes and savoury dishes. It makes a great road-trip stop.

Unique Flavours

Cambray Cheese

Sheep are milked on this family-run farm on the outskirts of Nannup, and cows' milk is sourced locally to produce a range of traditionally made, award-winning cheeses.

Tinderbox

Step into this whimsical store and let the aroma of the divine handmade natural beauty products relax your senses.

Cape Lavender Teahouse

A sweet stop for tea, scones and lavender products, Cape Lavender Teahouse in Yallingup is famous for its lavender ice cream.

Olio Bello

Be transported to the Mediterranean at this organic olive farm and tasting room in Cowaramup. The cafe-restaurant serves delicious pasta, and there's a gift shop.

Craft Brews

Beerfarm

Innovative Beerfarm in Metricup offers many intriguing beers, including Calm Ya Farm and Milk Stout. It also has great kids' activities.

Nannup Brewing Company

Head to this Nannup microbrewery, opened in 2021, for relaxed vibes, curated music events, pub food and, of course, great craft beer.

ARIANA SVENSON/LONELY PLANET

Truffle, Manjimup

Cidery

The deliciously tart Pink Lady apple was developed in Manjimup, so the variety was the natural choice for the ciders and juices of the Cidery at nearby Bridgetown.

Local Celebrations

Bridgetown Blues Festival

This November festival attracts some of the best acts from around the world and is a wonderful springboard for Aussie talent – John Butler started on the streets here.

Nannup Garden Festival

Tulips are the centrepiece of the Nannup Garden Festival, held in the second half of August. A record-breaking 20,000 bulbs have been planted in recent years.

Manjimup Cherry Harmony Festival

Each December the town of Manjimup is painted red in celebration of the cherry harvest and the diversity of the local horticultural industry.

Truffle Kerfuffle Festival

The Manjimup area is the southern hemisphere's largest producer of black Périgord truffles. The glorious festival in celebration of these delicacies returns in winter 2026.

SOUTH COAST

BEACHES | WINERIES | FOOD

RESEARCHED BY EMMYLOU DZUBIEL

- **The Power of Wilderness** (p142)
- **A Creative Escape** (p144)
- **Feel Denmark's Vibe** (p146)
- **Southwest Australia's Biodiversity Hotspot** (p148)
- **The South Coast for Foodies** (p150)
- **Outta this World** (p152)
- **For Beach Lovers** (p154)
- **Albany for the History Buff** (p156)
- **Listings** (p158)

JOHN CRUX PHOTOGRAPHY/GETTY IMAGES

SOUTH COAST
Trip Builder

There is no place that captures the breathtaking power of the ocean quite like the South Coast of Western Australia. From isolated windswept beaches through to massive ancient forests, rugged mountain climbs to remote islands, this is a destination for true wilderness lovers. Pair this with some of the freshest air you'll ever breathe, award-winning wineries and a surprisingly innovative food scene and you have paradise in the rough.

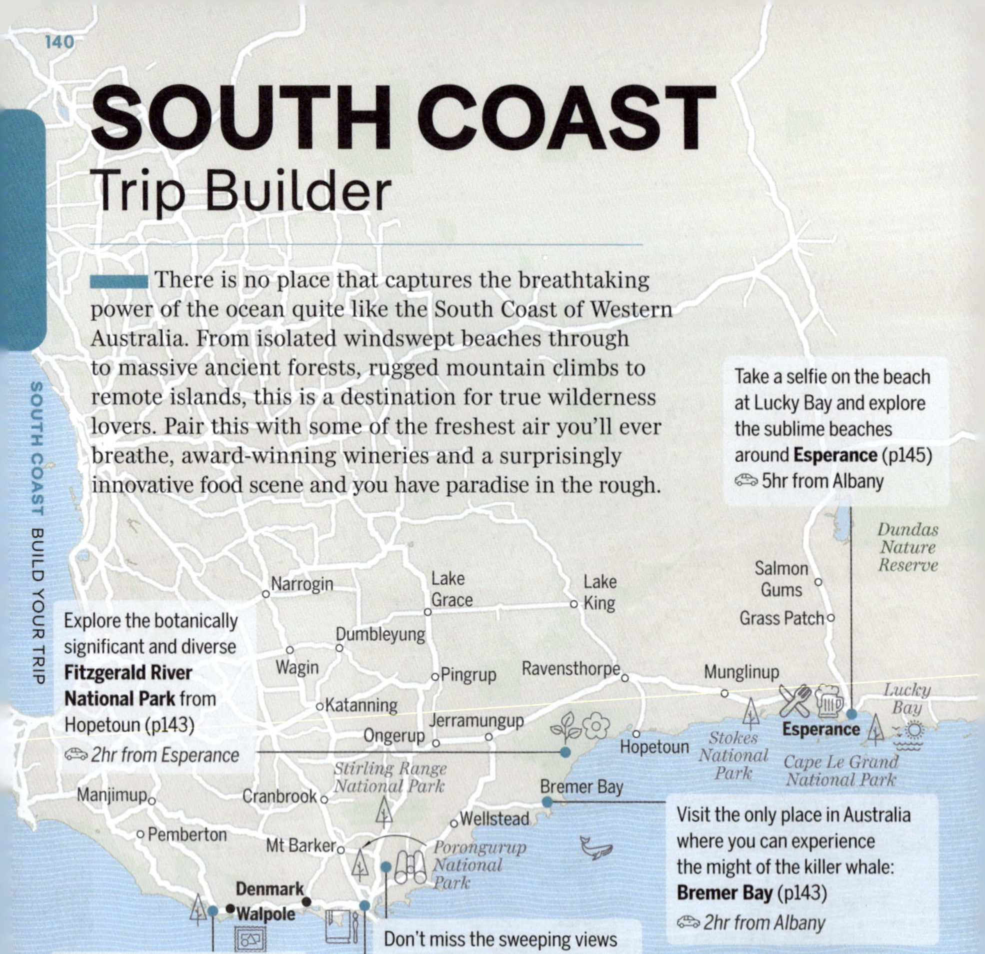

Take a selfie on the beach at Lucky Bay and explore the sublime beaches around **Esperance** (p145)
5hr from Albany

Explore the botanically significant and diverse **Fitzgerald River National Park** from Hopetoun (p143)
2hr from Esperance

Visit the only place in Australia where you can experience the might of the killer whale: **Bremer Bay** (p143)
2hr from Albany

Don't miss the sweeping views from the **Granite Skywalk** at Castle Rock in Porongurup National Park (p143)
45min from Albany

Take in the wild and pristine landscape of the **Walpole Wilderness Area**, with ancient forests and imposing granite peaks (p143)
30min from Denmark

Learn about different aspects of Australia's history in the charming port of **Albany/Kinjarling** (p156)
5hr from Perth

JOHANNA POOL/SHUTTERSTOCK

Practicalities

ARRIVING

Regular flights from Perth arrive in Esperance and Albany, where you can then hire a car.

CONNECT

Reception is pretty good in towns, spotty to nonexistent elsewhere. Visitor centres can offer on-the-spot advice and maps.

MONEY

Card payment is common in major towns; carry some cash for remote areas, farm-gate trails, farmers markets and inevitable internet outages.

WHERE TO STAY

Place	Pros/Cons
Albany	Something for everyone, with access to supplies and delicious food.
Denmark	Boutique and luxury accommodation right through to utilitarian stays by the sea.
Esperance	World-class off-grid camping in Cape Le Grande National Park; the town has options too.
Porongorup Area	A variety of places to stay, many featuring views of the ranges.

GETTING AROUND

Car The best option, especially if you also plan to visit the South West. Many remote spots require a 4WD.

Bus Buses run between Perth, Esperance, Albany and along the South Coast. Service is infrequent (daily, at best).

City tours Explore Albany and surrounds with Albany Tours.

TOP: JONATHON STOKES/LONELY PLANET, BOTTOM: RINI KOOLS/SHUTTERSTOCK

EATING & DRINKING

The fresh produce of this region – oysters (pictured top left), seafood, marron, heirloom vegetables, cheeses, the list goes on – is as exceptional as the wine (pictured bottom left). Trust us, everything tastes sensational on the South Coast.

Must-try marron
Due South (p151)

Best winery
Any in the Great Southern wine region (p151)

BIRAK	BUNURU	DJERAN	MAKURU	DJILBA	KAMBARANG
DEC & JAN	FEB & MAR	APR & MAY	JUN & JUL	AUG & SEP	OCT & NOV
Dry, sunny, long days – great for water sports.	Hot – go fishing.	Colours deepen; perfect mild weather.	Hardy folk won't mind the torrential downpours.	Warm weather arrives – it's time to get outdoors.	Wildflowers dot the coast.

29 The Power of WILDERNESS

NATIONAL PARKS | VIEWPOINTS | HIKING

Everything about the South Coast's magnificent national parks is grand and breathtaking, from the towering red tingle trees and canopy walkway views to the huge botanical diversity. Whether you're doing a gentle walk, tackling a hike or even going kayaking, here you can explore a world rich with Gondwanan relictual species – some are clearly dinosaur sized, and others are not.

PHILIP SCHUBERT/SHUTTERSTOCK

How to

Getting around You'll be best off with your own car here; some national park roads are unsealed but you should manage with a 2WD.

When to visit Wildflower season starts in late September and runs through to November – try not to miss it.

Top tip Save money by investing in a National Parks Pass so you can visit all parks across the state; 5-, 14- or 30-day options and annual passes are available online.

SASIMOTO/SHUTTERSTOCK

Walk with giants The **Walpole-Nornalup National Park** is home to red tingle trees, which are among some of the largest living eucalyptus (reaching up to 45m tall with a girth of around 22m). These fascinating trees grow in a tiny patch of forest that has maintained a special microclimate – not dissimilar to the days of the dinosaurs. Visit the 40m-high, 600m-long **Valley of the Giants Tree Top Walk** – a park highlight.

Stunning views The 670m-high suspended **Granite Skywalk** at Castle Rock takes you through the karri and marri forest of **Porongurup National Park** to scenic lookout points. In nearby **Stirling Range National Park**, **Bluff Knoll** is a popular peak for hiking, with particularly spectacular views at sunrise for early birds. The multiday Stirling Ridge Walk is for the more experienced adventurer. In **Torndirrup National Park** the impressive **Gap** falls 25m into the sea, eroded by the powerful waves of the Southern Ocean. The Natural Bridge and Blowholes are other inspiring natural features here.

A pristine wilderness Finally, don't miss the majesty of **Fitzgerald River National Park**, one of the most diverse botanical regions on earth and a paradise for nature-lovers and adventurers. At the edge of the Southern Ocean, the quartzite peak of **East Mt Barren** provides 360-degree views after a short but challenging climb to the summit (2.6km return), accessed from the Hopetoun side.

Left Granite Skywalk, Castle Rock **Below** Valley of the Giants Tree Top Walk

WOW Wilderness

If you do one tour, then this should be it. Meet passionate ecoguide Gary Muir on a **WOW Wilderness** *(wowwilderness.com.au)* cruise across the pristine Nornalup Inlet to Circus Beach. Gary's passion for the environment – nay, the world – and its history are woven together with his in-depth knowledge of the Walpole Wilderness Area. A gifted orator, comedian and scientist, Gary teaches you about the incredible biodiversity in this beautiful part of the world, as well as the idea that we are all linked – even to Walpole.

30 A Creative ESCAPE

ART | MURALS | STORYTELLING

Discover the talented artists – scattered all over the South Coast – who use this fertile country as inspiration for unique artworks depicting a geographically diverse land.

BRENTON SEE, PUBLIC SILO TRAIL, NEWDEGATE, 2018. PHOTOGRAPHY BY BEWLEY SHAYLOR, COURTESY OF FORM BUILDING A STATE OF CREATIVITY

How to

Getting around Having your own car is going to make exploration of these beautiful artworks a lot easier.

Spring festivals Time your visit with the **Southern Art & Craft Trail** (September), a regional celebration of textiles, jewellery, printmaking and woodcraft; the **Bloom Festival** (mid-September to October), which celebrates the wildflower tapestries across the region; and the **Djilba Wildflower Festival** in Esperance (September).

Heartland Journeys

Immerse yourself in the landscape by visiting the **Heartland Journeys** *(heartlandjourneys.com.au)* website, a valuable project created by Gondwana Link (p149), for thoughtfully constructed self-guided tours, a wealth of information about local places, nature and responsible travel, and many stories from Noongar people about how to maintain *boodja* (Country).

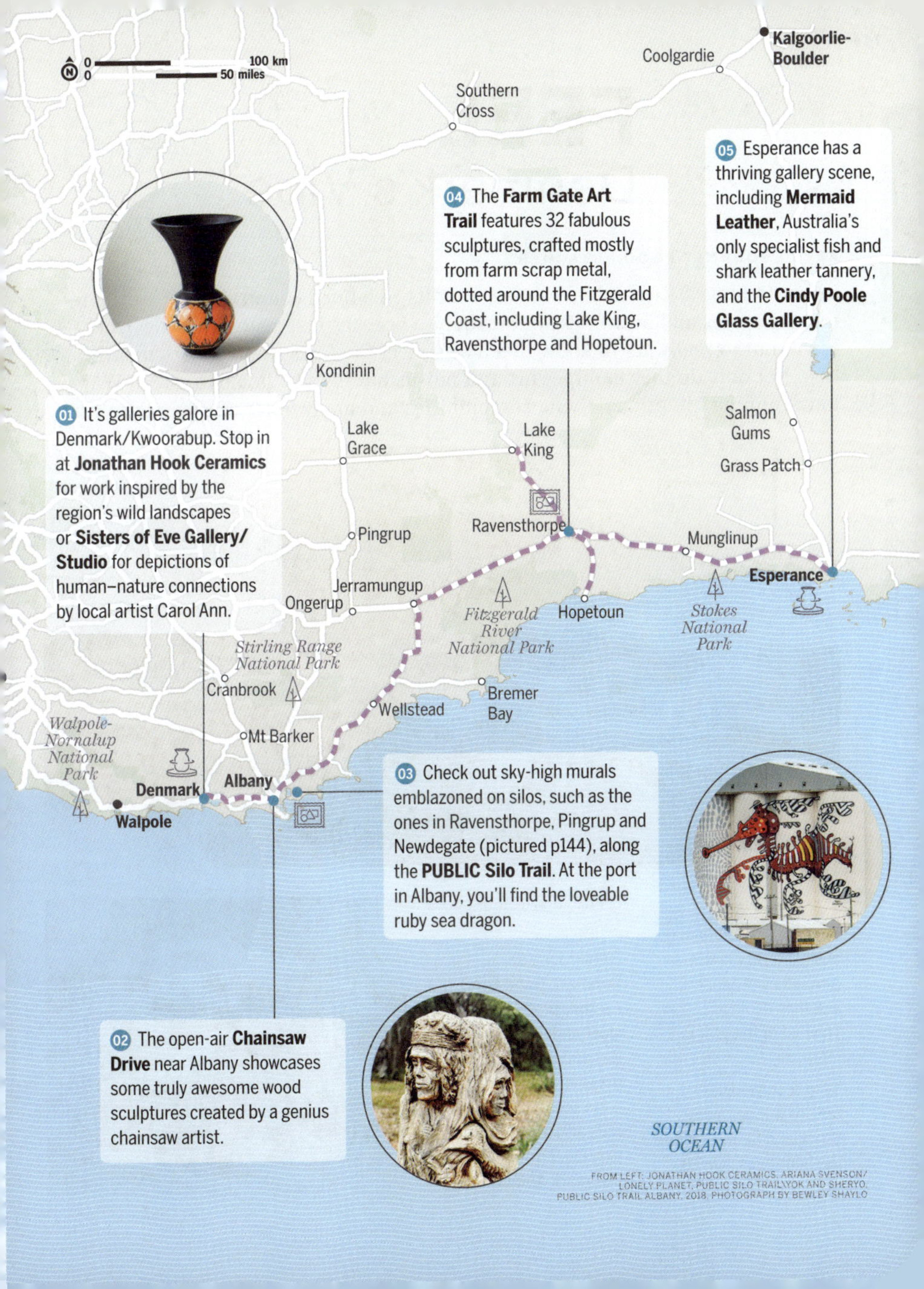

01 It's galleries galore in Denmark/Kwoorabup. Stop in at **Jonathan Hook Ceramics** for work inspired by the region's wild landscapes or **Sisters of Eve Gallery/Studio** for depictions of human–nature connections by local artist Carol Ann.

04 The **Farm Gate Art Trail** features 32 fabulous sculptures, crafted mostly from farm scrap metal, dotted around the Fitzgerald Coast, including Lake King, Ravensthorpe and Hopetoun.

05 Esperance has a thriving gallery scene, including **Mermaid Leather**, Australia's only specialist fish and shark leather tannery, and the **Cindy Poole Glass Gallery**.

03 Check out sky-high murals emblazoned on silos, such as the ones in Ravensthorpe, Pingrup and Newdegate (pictured p144), along the **PUBLIC Silo Trail**. At the port in Albany, you'll find the loveable ruby sea dragon.

02 The open-air **Chainsaw Drive** near Albany showcases some truly awesome wood sculptures created by a genius chainsaw artist.

FROM LEFT: JONATHAN HOOK CERAMICS, ARIANA SVENSON/ LONELY PLANET, PUBLIC SILO TRAIL\YOK AND SHERYO, PUBLIC SILO TRAIL ALBANY, 2018, PHOTOGRAPH BY BEWLEY SHAYLO

31 FEEL Denmark's Vibe

ARTS | GOURMET FOOD | BEACHES

Denmark/Kwoorabup charms with its tree-lined country drives, amazing food, wineries and breweries, and turquoise beaches just a stone's throw from town. But to really get to know this place, meet the folks that make Denmark tick. Not only do they embrace art and music, but it's also home to one of WA's long-running intentional living communities and many other eco-living projects.

DENMARK YOGA CENTRE

How to

When to go Denmark is busiest from Christmas through all of January and then again at Easter. The rest of the year is more chilled.

Take it slow Allow time to wander along Strickland St and explore the boutiques, healing centres and health-food shops.

Family-friendly **Denmark Good Food Factory** produces tasty cider and toffee in William Bay and is home to the massive **Giant Cone** and a fun soccer golf course. Kids also love getting up close to the animals at **Denmark Animal Farm**.

DENMARK FARMHOUSE CHEESE & DUCKETTS MILL WINES

Left Denmark Yoga Centre
Below Platter, Denmark Farmhouse Cheese & Duckett's Mill Wines

Yoga and wellness The amount of natural therapies on offer in Denmark is astounding – options include massage therapy, sound healing, wellness retreats and, of course, yoga. Take a class with a true forest yogi at **Karuna Sanctuary** or explore the teachings at the **Denmark Yoga Centre**. Better yet, base yourself at the Aiyana Forest Retreat, the Cove or any one of the forest cottages on offer (there are many) and then DIY your very own wellness stay. Check out the noticeboards around town for up-to-date classes and therapies. Pure bliss.

Farm-gate trails The best way to introduce yourself to Denmark's diverse food offerings is by taking a drive through the magnificent surrounding countryside and stopping at some of the many wineries, boutique food providers or art galleries (p159). Do a tasting at **Singlefile**, enjoy the magnificent views at the **Lake House** or visit **Rockcliffe Winery** for a glass of shiraz or cabernet sauvignon and live music. Still not satisfied? The unique honey ice cream from **Bartholomews Meadery** or a cheese platter at **Denmark Farmhouse Cheese & Duckett's Mill Wines** might do the trick.

Turquoise water and granite elephants On the edge of **William Bay National Park**, a quick drive southwest of Denmark, **Greens Pool** is a perfect turquoise natural pool fringed by white sands. A short walk around the headland is **Elephant Rocks**, where towering granite boulders look like herds of elephants standing in the water. Both are top selfie spots but also a magnificent introduction to the South Coast. The sheltered water provides calm conditions for swimming and snorkelling; there are also some great short hikes.

Empowering Artists

Denmark is a crucible of artistic endeavour, and **Denmark Arts** (*denmarkarts.com.au*), which organises a number of arts events and festivals, goes a long way to support this.

More than 40 years old, the **Denmark River Arts Markets** showcase the talent of craftspeople, musicians and entertainers.

'I've travelled to markets through the state and nowhere is there a stage that provides such a springboard for artists to find their feet.

The **Festival of Voice**, held in June, celebrates the power and beauty of voice in all its forms. The audience and performers leave deeply touched. In October, **Brave New Works** helps the community bring to life innovative performing projects.'

Kira Schimmelpfennig

Denmark Arts Markets Coordinator
denmarkriverartsmarkets.com.au

Southwest Australia's Biodiversity Hotspot

SOME OF THE MOST BIOLOGICALLY DIVERSE ECOSYSTEMS ON EARTH

The Southwest Australia Biodiversity Hotspot extends over the whole southwestern tip of WA, from Shark Bay in the north to Esperance in the south, loosely corresponding to the land of the Noongar peoples. This is an area of exceptional natural beauty and home to thousands of endemic plants and animals.

Left Fitzgerald River National Park
Centre Numbat (banded anteater)
Right One-sided bottlebrush *(Calothamnus quadrifidus)*

FABRE/SHUTTERSTOCK

Travel to this part of the world and you will find yourself in a place that has the highest concentration of rare and endangered species in Australia. Indeed, so significant are the plants and animals here that the area was recognised as the Southwest Australia Biodiversity Hotspot. It is one of 36 such hot spots in the world and for a long time was the only one in Australia.

The hot spot is home to over 5500 plant species, half of which can't be found anywhere else in the world. These unique plants are, in turn, supported by a vast range of species, including roughly 30 species of native mammal (including the quokka, the numbat and 12 endemic species of bird). There are around 30 species of reptile and close to 20 species of frog endemic to this region.

With research continuing every day, groups of passionate scientists are unravelling the mysteries of such fascinating creatures as jewel beetles and even moths that pollinate plants. While spiders and other invertebrates are not so well known, it is highly likely that their level of endemism is also high.

Due to agriculture and the introduction of foreign species, less than 30% of southwestern Australia's original vegetation remains in pristine condition. But the hot spot designation means that conservation, restoration and protection are today at the forefront of work here.

The Fitzgerald Biosphere

At the heart of the hot spot are the Stirling Range and Fitzgerald River National Parks, where the diversity of landscapes means that, within just 5km, you might find a number of completely different suites of plant species.

KEN GRIFFITHS/SHUTTERSTOCK

SJM51/SHUTTERSTOCK

This is also where you can find the Fitzgerald Biosphere, one of the world's most botanically significant regions and among UNESCO's World Network of Biosphere Reserves. It's special not only because of its pristine state but also for the zone of cooperation around it. This area has been embraced by community groups, who have created opportunities for visitors to learn more. The Yongergnow Australian Malleefowl Centre in Ongerup, for example, provides the chance to see the endangered mallee fowl up close.

> The hot spot designation means that conservation, restoration and protection are at the forefront of work here.

Gondwana Link

Another conservation project is Gondwana Link, which aims to establish a 1000km stretch of healthy, connected wildlife habitat from the wet forests of the southwest to the dry woodlands and mallee of inland Australia. The project is focused on such things as protecting bushland, restoring habitat health as well as connecting small individual projects to the bigger picture. The importance of having people on board with the scientific pursuits – especially visitors – is also key. For this reason, the Heartland Journeys website (p144) was created, through which stories about the important natural values of the area and Aboriginal peoples' management of the land are shared.

Cryptic Bird Puzzles

While the quokka is the cute and slightly brash poster child of the Southwest Australia Biodiversity Hotspot, many of its threatened birds are really cryptic and that's what makes them so exciting.

We were at Cheynes Beach recently, not far from Albany, and we'd spent a bit of time getting our ear accustomed to the different calls. We heard the calls of a noisy scrub bird, western whipbird, western bristlebird and Australasian bittern, and all three species of black cockatoo flew overhead.

The secret to immersing yourself in this wildly diverse landscape is simple: be observant. Stop, look and listen, and you'll uncover a world that is so special it almost brings tears to the eye. Being prepared and knowing what to look for are vital. An excellent guide is *Morcombe's Birds of Australia.*

Sarah Comer
Regional Ecologist, Department of Biodiversity, Parks & Attractions
@exploreparkswa

32 The South Coast FOR FOODIES

AWARD-WINNING CUISINE | DISTILLERIES | REGIONAL SPECIALITIES

While the South Coast's big sister Margaret River/Wooditchup has all the fame, those in the know have a little secret: it's all happening down on the South Coast. The passionate food scene here includes award-winning wines, innovative chefs, cannabis-based gin and the region's answer to crayfish or lobster – the endemic marron.

ZOE VAN ZANTEN

How to

When to go For relaxed lunches, avoid long weekends or public holidays; with fresh food available year-round, you'll discover something new whatever the season.

Food festival Held in March, **Taste Great Southern** is a celebration of regional food and wine, including long table lunches, markets, and music and wine sessions.

Fresh markets The **Albany Farmers Markets** (Collie St) sells fresh seasonal produce direct to the community. Also check out the **Albany Boat Shed Markets**.

ARIANA SVENSON/LONLEY PLANET

Left Dam at Raintree
Below BBQ marron

WA's new foodie capital Yep, we heard Albany described that way! And it all comes down to the growing group of forward-thinking chefs and producers getting together to have conversations about fresh produce and food. Start your foodie adventures here with an unlikely trip to bohemian Paris at award-winning **Liberté**, located within the historic London Hotel. Owner and chef Amy Hamilton has paired the decor perfectly to the French-Vietnamese dishes.

Freshwater crayfish The shell of the marron, which is endemic to southwestern Australia, is normally black or brown but can also be a vibrant cobalt blue. All turn to red when cooked. Whatever you do, don't miss the opportunity to try it. Head to the cavernous **Due South** in Albany for seasonal specials like the Korean chilli crab and marron, or take a drive to the family-run **Marron Tale Cafe & Farm** near Bow Bridge for the marron fettuccine. If you're self-catering, farm-gate fresh marron is sold around the region.

Heady pours Ready for something a bit different? Head to the **Dam at Raintree** *(thedam.raintree.com.au)*, a stunning property just out of Denmark, to sample hemp-distilled spirits in the seltzers and cocktails and an excellent seasonal menu featuring local produce (including marron). You can also tour the on-site **Cannabis Botanical Distillery**, one of the first distilleries in Western Australia that uses cannabis sativa to make its spirit base. Behind this project is innovative farmer Steve Birkbeck.

The Great Southern Wine Region

The picturesque Great Southern region – encompassing Denmark, Albany, Mt Barker, Franklin River and Porongurup – is a rising star in the Australian wine industry and is becoming increasingly well known for producing some high-quality wines. Winemaker Kim Tyrer of Galafrey Wines, located in Mt Barker, 60km northeast of Albany, says it's a region for those in the know. 'In the Great Southern our wines are underestimated but offer excellent quality.

'We have warm days but cool nights here, giving us slow ripening periods. We make some great shiraz and riesling. Each year our wines are well represented in the top 25 rieslings in Australia, including wines from Castle Rock, Dukes, Galafrey and Forest Hill.'

Kim Tyrer
CEO & Winemaker at Galafrey Wines
@galafreywines

Outta this **WORLD**

01

02

03

04

01 Killer whales
From January to March, 150 orcas – the largest congregation in the southern hemisphere – come to feed at Bremer Bay.

02 Top beaches
Making it into Australia's top 10 beaches over the years, Misery Beach and Madfish Bay are well worth a stop.

03 Bluff Knoll
The state's third-highest peak, a great hike (p158) and, famously, the only place it snows in WA.

04 Stonehenge
Yup, you read that right! Visit a full-size replica made of Esperance pink granite.

05 Bald Head
The huge granite headland at the end of a challenging 13km return walk on the Flinders Peninsula.

06 The tassel flower
This flower *(Leucopogon verticillatus)* was the design inspiration for the pylons at the Valley of the Giants Tree Top Walk (p143) near Walpole.

05

06

07

08

09

10

07 Chittic
The pretty orange, red or yellow flower of the *Lambertia inermis* pops out during spring and summer.

08 Royal hakea
Keep an eye out for the extraterrestrial-looking leaves of this endemic plant from June to August; its Noongar name is *tallyongut*.

09 Monumental public art
The PUBLIC Silo mural (p145) by Amok Island in Ravensthorpe showcases the six stages of a flowering *Banksia baxteri*.

10 Resident kangaroos
Lucky Bay near Esperance is so beautiful that even the local kangaroos choose to hang out here.

01 ELSALASS/SHUTTERSTOCK, **02** ANASTAS_STYLES/SHUTTERSTOCK, **03** LEANNE IRWIN/SHUTTERSTOCK, **04** DIANNE WICKENDEN/SHUTTERSTOCK, **05** PHILIP SCHUBERT/SHUTTERSTOCK, **06** INES PORADA/SHUTTERSTOCK, **07** ROBERT WYATT/ALAMY STOCK PHOTO, **08** GERHARDSAUERACKER/GETTY IMAGES, **09** SIX STAGES OF BANKSIA BAXTERI, AMOK ISLAND, PUBLIC SILO TRAIL, RAVENSTHORPE, 2016. PHOTOGRAPH BY BEWLEY SHAYLOR, COURTESY OF FORM BUILDING A STATE OF CREATIVITY, **10** ANEK.SOOWANNAPHOOM/SHUTTERSTOCK

33 For Beach LOVERS

WHITE SAND | SWIMMING | SOLITUDE

The South Coast juxtaposes a wild and powerful coastline with turquoise water, long expanses of white sand and, quite often, blissful seclusion. Whether you're tempted by the remote white swathes found in national parks or the gentle kid-friendly city beaches with waterfront cafes in sight, getting your toes in the sand should be a top priority.

ARIANA SVENSON/LONELY PLANET

How to

Swim safe Don't underestimate the water on the South Coast. Follow the signs and look out for rips, even at popular swimming beaches.

Avoid the crowds Most beaches see few people, except on school and public holidays. To explore off the beaten track, hire a 4WD.

Water sports SUP or snorkel at spots like Peaceful Bay, Twilight Beach in Esperance and Greens Pool. The water can be very cold year-round; consider wearing a wetsuit or shorty.

ARIANA SVENSON/LONELY PLANET

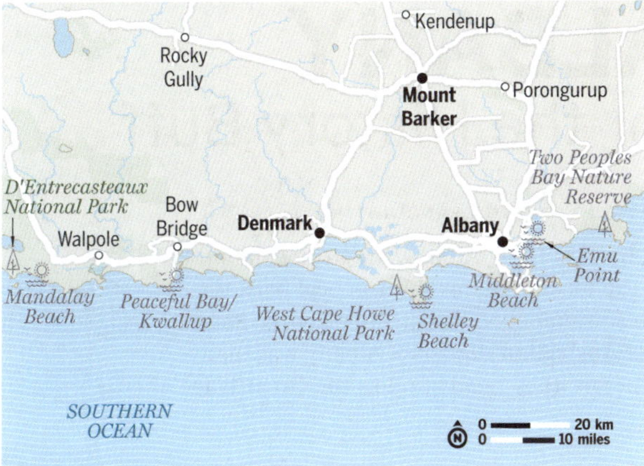

Family-friendly Picturesque **Middleton Beach** and **Emu Point**, both within Albany city, offer the quintessential day at the seaside, with safe swimming enclosures, playgrounds for the kids and excellent cafes such as Three Anchors at Middleton Beach and Emu Point Cafe. Both beaches get bonus points for the excellent walking trails and photo ops.

Easy access The only 2WD accessible spot in West Cape Howe National Park is **Shelley Beach** – and what a spot! This pristine beach is perfect for swimming, camping and fishing, and it's the best place on the South Coast for paragliding – watch as these graceful crafts flip and float on the breeze from a cliff above you.

A peaceful option Between Walpole and Denmark, **Peaceful Bay/Kwallup** is a less popular option than nearby Greens Pool (p147) in William Bay National Park, but this pretty turquoise bay has a sheltered swimming area and a busy boat launch. It's home to a small settlement and caravan park, and families have been holidaying here for generations. There's a real 'step back in time' vibe. Don't miss the delish fish and chips.

True wilderness In the remote D'Entrecasteaux National Park, just 20km west of Walpole, the sublimely beautiful **Mandalay Beach** has views out to Chatham Island. The beach is named for the shipwrecked *Barque Mandalay*, which emerges every few years from the shifting sands and wild surf – you never know, you might just see it. This is a spot for contemplation, not swimming.

Left Middleton Beach
Below Mandalay Beach

Two Peoples Bay Nature Reserve

Popular for its white sand, aquamarine waters and granite rock outcrops, **Two Peoples Bay** and **Little Beach**, both located within the Two Peoples Bay Nature Reserve around 35km east of Albany, have been ranked in the 'best beaches in Australia' – yet their real treasures lie deeper.

Regional Ecologist Sarah Comer says, 'Take the 4.6km Heritage Trail from the Two Peoples Bay Visitor Centre to the beach, and you are in a truly extraordinary landscape of animal diversity. Both quendas and quokkas can be seen on the trail. Keep your ear attuned to the call of the noisy scrub bird, which was rediscovered here after it was thought to be extinct. You might also see a seal basking on the rocks or whales in the bay.'

Sarah Comer
Regional Ecologist, Department of Biodiversity, Parks & Attractions
@exploreparkswa

34 ALBANY for the History Buff

HEARTBREAKING | THOUGHT-PROVOKING | FASCINATING

If you love stepping back in time, Albany/Kinjarling should be a port of call. Learn about the local Menang culture, peel back the layers of the first European settlement in WA at King George Sound and walk in the footsteps of Australian diggers – Albany was many Anzacs' last sight of home before they headed off to the Great War.

ADWO/SHUTTERSTOCK

How to

Allow time Any one of these information-packed spots could be visited in an hour, but to really take it in and piece it all together, you need to go much slower and immerse yourself in the stories.

Go deeper Albany's Museum of the Great Southern and the informative **Kodja Place** (*kodjaplace.com.au*), in Kojonup on the highway to Perth, also have stories of the Noongar people.

EMMA JONES/SHUTTERSTOCK

Step back in time Board the 19th-century **Brig Amity** replica at the **Museum of the Great Southern**, overlooking the Princess Royal Harbour, and experience the journey from Sydney to King George Sound as this tiny ship battled perilous winds while it carried its small crew, convicts and animals to their new home. They anchored not far from the replica, where they established the first European settlement on the west coast of Australia in 1826.

The first European farm Established in 1827, **Strawberry Hill Farm** at Barmup is the oldest farm in WA. You can visit the original buildings as well as the visitor centre, completed in 2020, which aims to acknowledge that, for thousands of years before, Barmup (meaning 'place of tall trees' in Noongar) was a significant area for Menang people.

Australia's whaling past A visit to **Albany's Historic Whaling Station** at Discovery Bay provides an illuminating – and confronting – interactive experience as you board the whale chaser Cheynes IV and see the whale processing factory. While here, you can also visit the **Australian Wildlife Park** to see a range of wildlife, including bandicoots and wombats, and the Regional Wildflower Garden.

Coastal hikes and views Near the top of **Mt Clarence/ Corndarup** is the Desert Mounted Corps Memorial. Take the 3.2km heritage walk for spectacular views out across the town of Albany and the surrounding bays. The 4km Ellen Cove Boardwalk to Albany Port is a longer option, with the ruins of the Point King Lighthouse and the Mustafa Kemal Atatürk monument potential stops along the way.

Left *Brig Amity*
Below National Anzac Centre

A Place of Pilgrimage

The **National Anzac Centre** *(nationalanzaccentre.com.au)*, on Mt Clarence/Corndarup, is a state-of-the-art interpretation experience where visitors assume the identity of one of 32 Anzacs who left Albany in 1914 for the Great War. Through audio and multimedia presentations you'll be drawn into the Gallipoli campaign and onto the mud of the Western Front. The centre is adjacent to the **Princess Royal Fortress**, another treasure trove of military history.

Many believe that the first dawn service on Anzac Day was held in Albany in 1930, with a procession up a bush track to the top of Mt Clarence.

Listings

BEST OF THE REST

Outdoor Adventures

HMAS Perth Wreck

The HMAS *Perth* wreck near Albany is a good spot for recreational divers, with a 133m-long artificial reef and interpretive trail. Snorkellers and swimmers can also see the wreck from the surface.

Woody Island

Take a day trip to Woody Island out of Esperance or stay awhile and glamp or stop in a safari hut. Either way, don't miss snorkelling the pristine waters of Shearwater Bay.

King George Sound

From late May to October, whales often rest within King George Sound, making whale watching from Albany an excellent opportunity to see these creatures up close.

Wilson Inlet

For a serene and calming experience, enjoy a beautiful paddle from the Wilson Inlet to the centre of Denmark. Hire a kayak or paddleboat at the Rivermouth Caravan Park.

Kalgan Queen

Entertaining and very knowledgeable, Captain Jack of the *Kalgan Queen* will take you on a leisurely cruise around Oyster Bay and up the Kalgan River. Morning tea includes damper and local tastings.

Esperance Island Cruises

Visit some of the 105 islands that make up the Recherche Archipelago on a half-day scenic wildlife cruise out of Esperance. Each island has unique species, and snorkelling equipment is provided.

Barna Mia Nocturnal Wildlife Experience

Take a guided tour through this wildlife sanctuary in Williams for a chance to see a numbat (WA's animal emblem) or even a bilby, woylie or quenda.

South Coast Surfing

If you want to try riding the waves, take a lesson with an experienced instructor at Ocean Beach in Denmark; with small surf and a sheltered bay, the conditions are ideal. For the most part, however, surfing in this region isn't for beginners or the inexperienced.

Denmark Thrills Adventure Park

Smile, laugh and scream with excitement at this adventure park, home to the world's longest globe-riding track.

Unmissable Hikes

Bluff Knoll

Hike the highest (1099m) and best-known peak in the Stirling Ranges, a paradise for hikers and photographers, with incredible biodiversity, jagged peaks and wildflowers galore.

Esperance Island Cruises

Nancy Peak

This 5.5km loop walk offers sweeping views out to the Stirling Ranges. Reward yourself after your hike with a pizza and a local craft beer at historic Karribank Tavern.

Art Galleries

South Coast Woodworks Gallery

On Albany's main strip you'll find fine, intricate woodworks by nationally and internationally renowned local artisans.

Butter Factory Studios & Gallery

Set inside the characteristic Old Butter Factory, this Denmark gallery is all about community, showcasing regional artists and hosting workshops and guest artist exhibitions.

Petrichor Gallery

Lovely natural light illuminates the art at this gallery in Walpole. Exhibitions showcase the beauty of the natural environment across a range of mediums.

Makers Collective & Magic Marron Shop

An innovative cooperative in Walpole with a fabulous range of artworks, textiles and jewellery by talented locals, plus pond-to-plate marron.

Unique Flavours

Boston Brewing Co — $$

For an all-round great family day out, you can't go past Boston Brewing at Willoughby Park near Denmark. The brewpub food is consistently tasty, the craft beer flows and the wines from Willoughby Park are respected.

Garrison — $$$

Sitting atop Mt Clarence/Corndarup, Garrison has lovely views of Albany's waterways, a menu with plenty of local influences and a carefully selected wine list.

Bilby

Maleeya's Thai Café — $$

This place is described as the best Thai in WA. Asian herbs from its organic veggie garden are used to absolute perfection. Located in the idyllic Porongurup ranges.

Lucky Bay Brewing — $$

Claiming to be the most genuinely local craft beer in Australia, Lucky Bay Brewing is on every Esperance visitor's list. Serves up huge pizza portions, too.

Telegraph on Bremer — $$

With expansive gardens and views to the inlet, the Telegraph at Bremer Bay is housed in the lovingly restored original telegraph station. Breakfast on the veranda gets stellar reviews.

Bread Local — $

Esperance's renowned bakery brings ultimate beach town vibes with baked goods of a quality on par with some of Australia's best city bakeries.

Limeburners

With a spot overlooking Frenchman Bay, award-winning Limeburners is famed for its single-malt whiskies. While you're here, tour the distillery or try the tasting flight.

MONKEY MIA & THE CENTRAL WEST

COAST | LANDSCAPES | ADVENTURE

RESEARCHED BY STEVE WATERS

STEVE WATERS/CONTRIBUTOR

- **Keepers of the Flame** (p164)
- **A Long & Complicated History** (p166)
- **The Cliffs of Kalbarri** (p168)
- **The Park at the End of the Road** (p170)
- **A World Heritage Drive** (p172)
- **Shark Bay's Dolphins & Wallabies** (p174)
- **The Untamed Coast** (p176)
- **Listings** (p178)

STEVE WATERS/CONTRIBUTOR

MONKEY MIA & THE CENTRAL WEST

Trip Builder

This is a land where outback deserts collide to miraculous effect with the cerulean waters of the Indian Ocean. Here you can listen to Aboriginal storytellers, experience incredible wildlife on land and in the sea, and, often, simply just wander around and admire the view.

Practicalities

ARRIVING

Flights connect Carnarvon, Geraldton and Shark Bay with Perth. Buses between Perth, Port Hedland and Broome stop at Dongara, Geraldton and Carnarvon, with connections to Kalbarri and Shark Bay.

FIND YOUR WAY

Mobile (cell) phone coverage is limited outside towns and roadhouses north of Kalbarri. There's wi-fi at cafes, visitor centres and most accommodation.

MONEY

Most towns have at least one ATM, and credit cards are widely accepted; some out-of-the-way places only accept cash.

WHERE TO STAY

Place	Pros/Cons
Geraldton	Lots of motels and caravan parks, but not much variety.
Kalbarri	Good choice of B&Bs, holiday homes, motels and caravan parks.
Shark Bay	Several camp sites along the coast before Denham and a range of accommodation in town.There's a resort at Monkey Mia favoured by groups.

GETTING AROUND

Car The further north you venture, the more you need your own wheels. Perth has the best rental options.

Bus With a dose of creativity, a bus pass and several sleepless nights, you *could* get to *most* Central West locations. Sucker.

Bike/e-scooter You can rent either in Geraldton.

TOP: STEVE WATERS/CONTRIBUTOR
BOTTOM: BRENT HOFACKER/SHUTTERSTOCK

EATING & DRINKING

Geraldton has the best food scene, while Kalbarri, Carnarvon and Dongara-Port Denison also have reasonable choices. Even smaller towns have at least one supermarket, cafe and pub. Beyond Kalbarri, roadhouses are also an option.

Don't miss
Red spot emperor, kimchi and triple-cooked chips at Salt Dish (pictured; p179)

Must-try drink
The Hemingway Special at Old Man & the Sea (p179)

JAN–MAR
Hot and windy; Kalbarri and Geraldton are busy, fewer people up north.

APR–JUN
Settled weather; a good time for most places.

JUL–SEP
North's peak season; cool nights, good bushwalking, wildflowers.

OCT–DEC
Temps rising; fewer people until the December holidays.

35 Keepers of THE FLAME

SHIPWRECKS | TRAILS | ART

On Southern Yamatji Country, the laid-back port city of Geraldton has a maritime connection spanning five centuries and a continuous Indigenous one of over 400 centuries. Explore these fascinating relationships through the city's museums, memorials, galleries and self-guided trails. After you've soaked up some background info, relax by the beach or in one of Gero's plentiful food and beverage establishments.

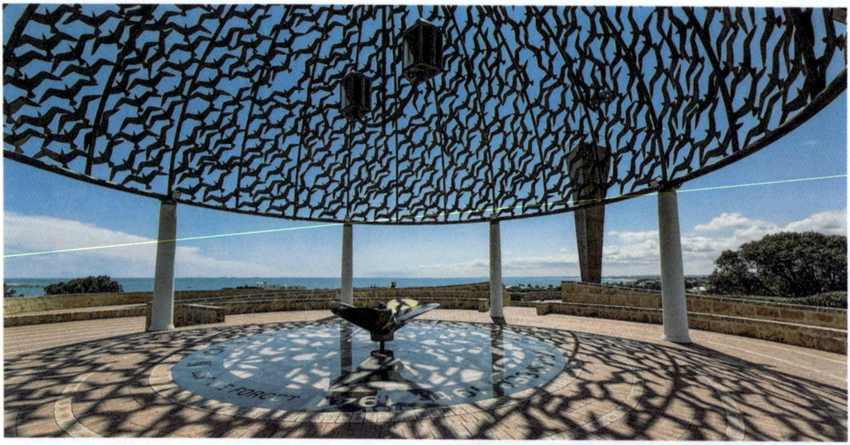

STEVE WATERS/CONTRIBUTOR

How to

Getting here and around Rent a car in Perth and take an Indian Ocean road trip via the Pinnacles (p88).

When to go November to February is high season, with great beach weather; April, May and September to November are milder and less crowded. Wildflowers bloom August to October.

More information Geraldton's visitor centre sells books on the region's history, including Stan Gratte's fascinating *Aboriginal History of Geraldton (Jambinu) and Surrounding Areas.*

ADWO/SHUTTERSTOCK

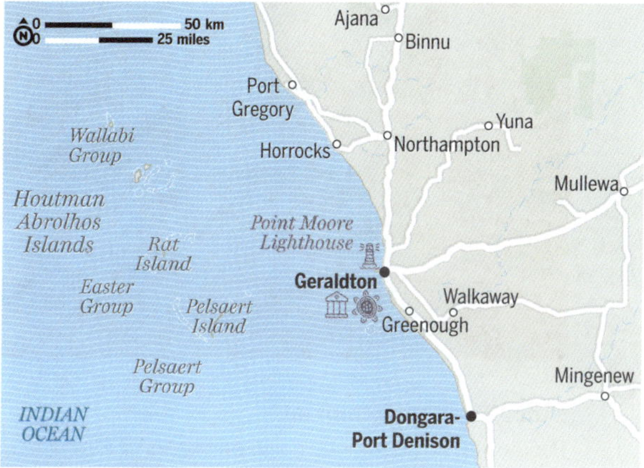

Left HMAS *Sydney II* Memorial
Below Point Moore Lighthouse

Shipping disasters More than 1000 ships have been lost off the WA coast. Many of the early wrecks, dating back to the 1600s, belonged to the VOC (Dutch East India Company) and strayed off course on their way to Java. The excellent **Shipwreck Gallery** at the waterfront **Museum of Geraldton** chronicles several, including the 1629 horror story of the *Batavia* (p167). The museum also showcases First Nations history, that of early settlers, and the area's unique endemic wildlife. Head out to the distinctive candy-striped **Point Moore Lighthouse**, erected in 1878, then climb the hill overlooking town, where the sombre **HMAS *Sydney II* Memorial** tells the WWII tale of the 1941 sinking of the cruiser in combat with the German raider *Kormoran*, killing all 645 crew. It was Australia's worst naval disaster. An eternal flame burns under the centrepiece Dome of Souls, and a poignant *Waiting Woman* sculpture looks out to sea.

Art and history trails Start at the wonderful **regional art gallery** with its interesting permanent Western Australian collection, then grab the public art trail map from the attached visitor centre. You can also wander the backstreets on a themed self-guided **Heritage Trail** (p179). For a different perspective, dedicate a day to the thought-provoking 195km **Yamatji Drive** across 14 culturally significant Indigenous sites in the town and surrounding hinterland. Finish at the excellent **Yamaji Art**, an Aboriginal-owned gallery showcasing and selling local Indigenous art and crafts.

Escape to the Houtman Abrolhos Islands

Sixty kilometres from land, the Houtman Abrolhos archipelago of 210 islands, rocks and coral reefs is an important refuge for wildlife including sea lions, green turtles, carpet pythons, migrating sea birds and Tammar wallabies. The surrounding waters, warmed by the Leeuwin Current, contain many tropical species of sea creature and the southernmost coral reefs in the Indian Ocean. The easiest way to experience this raw nature is on a 'fly and flipper' day trip from **Geraldton** *(shineaviation.com.au)* or **Kalbarri** *(kalbarriscenicflights.com.au)* with a landing on **East Wallabi** island and snorkelling at **Turtle Bay**. Multiday liveaboard dive tours are also available (p178).

A Long & Complicated History

INDIGENOUS AND COLONIAL HISTORIES COLLIDE

The human history of Monkey Mia and the Central West is a saga worthy of this most drama-filled of landscapes. It begins with one of the oldest stories of continuous human habitation on the planet and ends with an account that challenges the whole premise of European arrival in Australia.

Left Rock art, Mt Augustus/Burringurrah
Centre Captain Cook landing at Botany Bay
Right Replica of the *Duyfken*

STEVE WATERS/ALAMY

Since Time Immemorial

People first arrived on the northern shores of Australia at least 40,000 years ago but perhaps as long ago as 60,000 years. Finding out more is an archaeological detective story that's been pieced together using the traces of these long-ago people – layers of carbon (the residue of ancient fires) deep in the soil; piles of shells and fish bones marking the places where they hunted and ate; and paintings and engravings on remote rock walls.

These artworks tell stories of the Dreaming, that spiritual dimension where the earth and its human residents were created and the law was laid down. The descendants of these artists and fire-makers don't need carbon dating or university-trained archaeologists to know that their people have been here for a very long time – since the Dreaming, in fact – and the stories from this time go to the heart of the spiritual and cultural life of contemporary Aboriginal people.

Before the first European ships arrived along this stretch of coast in the 17th century, Aboriginal groups lived remarkably sophisticated lives for their time, surviving in one of the most hostile landscapes on earth. This was the land of the Yinggarda, Bayungu, Malgana, Thadgari, Thalanyji, Wajarri, Badimaya and Wilunyu. Each group lived in its own territory and maintained its own distinctive language and traditions. In places like Burringurrah (Mt Augustus), they left behind finely rendered artworks that tell their stories.

SUPERSTOCK/ALAMY

RUSSOTWINS/ALAMY

European Settlement

For decades in modern Australia, it was an article of faith that Captain Cook 'discovered' the continent and claimed it for Great Britain when he sailed into Botany Bay in 1770. The truth is rather different, and it all centres on the West.

Some historians say that Aboriginal peoples' first contact with the outside world occurred when a Chinese admiral visited Australia in the 15th century. Others say that Portuguese navigators mapped the continent in the 16th century. Whatever the truth of these stories, there's no doubt that Dutch ships began arriving along the WA coast in the 17th century, more than 150 years before Captain Cook first stepped ashore out east.

> These artworks tell stories of the Dreaming, that spiritual dimension where the earth and its human residents were created and the law was laid down.

In 1606 Dutchman Willem Janszoon sailed the speedy little *Duyfken* out of the Dutch settlement at Batavia (modern Jakarta) and found Cape York (the pointy bit at the top of Australia). Ten years later, another Dutch ship, the *Eendracht*, rode the trade winds, bound for the 'spice islands' of modern Indonesia. But the captain, Dirk Hartog, misjudged his position, and stumbled onto the island that now bears his name. Hartog inscribed the details of his visit onto a pewter plate and nailed it to a post.

But the Dutch had no interest in Australia. Their colonies were commercial interests, and nothing they saw convinced them to stick around. Nevertheless, their arrival was a precursor to later incursions that would devastate local Aboriginal communities.

The Batavia

The story of the Dutch ship *Batavia* is one of the more infamous in maritime history. After the ship sank off the Houtman Abrolhos Islands in 1629, the captain, Francisco Pelsaert, sailed off to find a rescue vessel in the Dutch East Indies. While he was away, mutinous crewmen raped and murdered the ship's passengers – men, women and children. When Pelsaert returned he executed the murderers. Only two youths survived; exiled to a local beach, they lived out their lives with local Aboriginal people. A **plaque** marks the spot where they came ashore, at Wittecarra Creek by Red Bluff Beach, south of Kalbarri.

36 The Cliffs of KALBARRI

CLIFFS | HIKING | WATER

West Coast Australia's promise to be the place where the outback meets the sea gets real at Kalbarri. This small, quiet seaside town is the launchpad for adventures on a grand scale, both out on the water and amid the epic cliffs, gorges and beaches of Kalbarri National Park. And wherever you go, the wildlife is as memorable as the scenery.

STEVE WATERS/CONTRIBUTOR

How to

Getting here and around Having your own vehicle is best. A shuttle meets Integrity Coaches at the Ajana turnoff on the highway.

When to go December to February is ideal for swimming but also busy; March to May has settled weather, while June to September is the best time for inland hiking. Wildflowers bloom August to October, and whales migrate June to November.

Top tip Down micro-brews and seafood in a courtyard with shark sculptures and live music at **Finlay's Kalbarri** (*finlayskalbarri.com.au*).

STEVE WATERS/CONTRIBUTOR

Sea cliffs South of Kalbarri, jaw-dropping viewpoints such as the **Natural Bridge** and **Eagle Gorge** mark the edge of the Australian continent as crumbling, 100m-high sandstone cliffs tumble haphazardly into the Indian Ocean. The whole area has a loose, primeval feel to it. The lookouts are connected by the wild (and shadeless) clifftop **Bigurda Trail** (8km one way), from which you might spot migrating humpback whales during the winter months.

Beaches Towards Kalbarri the cliffs eventually recede and some seriously beautiful beaches demand attention. **Red Bluff Beach** and **Chinaman's Beach** are good for swimming, **Wittecarra Creek** is revered by fishing folk, and **Blue Holes** is all about snorkelling. Surfers love the big left-hander at **Jakes Point**. Sunsets here are simply superb. While you can drive, the beaches are linked by the 8km dual-use **Melaleuca Trail**.

River cliffs and gorges The inland section of **Kalbarri National Park** has the impressive **Skywalk**, a pair of lookouts suspended over Murchison Gorge providing uninterrupted views of the Murchison River 100m directly below. The short, steep and stunning **Nature's Window hike** (800m return) leads to a photogenic natural hole in the orange sandstone cliffs. From here, the magnificent **Loop Trail** (9km, three hours) continues along the ridge, offering expansive gorge views before dropping down to the riverbank, where the route alternates between rock ledges and wildflower-strewn sandy tracks before climbing back up to Nature's Window. More short walks depart from **Z-Bend** car park.

Left Chinaman's Beach
Below Natural Bridge

Wild Kalbarri

Kalbarri Adventure Tours *(kalbarritours.com.au)* Paddle a canoe through the gorges of the national park.

Kalbarri Abseil *(kalbarriabseil.com)* Spend a rollicking day adventuring on the majestic gorge cliffs above the Murchison River, with plenty of swimming opportunities as well.

Reefwalker Adventure Tours *(reefwalker.com.au)* Whale watching and sunset cruises along the coast, plus fishing charters.

D'Guy Journeys *(dguyjourneys.com)* Seasonal wildflower tours around Kalbarri and the national park.

Blue Tongue Photography *(bluetonguephototours.com.au)* Three- to four-hour sunrise, sunset and after-dark photography tours to Kalbarri's epic coastal cliffs and gorges.

Feed the pelicans Find them along the foreshore at 8.45am every morning.

37 The Park at the End OF THE ROAD

WILDLIFE | COUNTRY | BEACHES

Venture beyond Francois Peron National Park and you'll fall off the map. This lovely low-profile park occupies the narrow tip of the Peron Peninsula in the Shark Bay World Heritage Area and is one dramatic natural formation after another. It's been the homeland of the Malgana, who call Shark Bay Gutharraguda (meaning 'two bays'), for at least 30,000 years.

NARAYAN MUKKAVILLI/SHUTTERSTOCK

How to

Getting here and around You'll need a high-clearance 4WD for most of Francois Peron due to sandy tracks; deflate your tyres to 20psi/1.5bar. Download 'Four Wheel Driving in Shark Bay' for more info.

When to go May to September are the best months. The rest of the year is hot, dry and windy.

Tours Indigenous-run **Wula Gura Nyinda Eco Adventures** *(wulagura.com.au)* offers excellent full-day and overnight camping tours to Francois Peron.

DOOLIN1989/SHUTTERSTOCK

Left Skipjack Point Lookout
Below Cape Peron

Pristine beaches Some of Western Australia's loveliest and most deserted stretches of sand wrap around the Peron Peninsula (known to the local Malgana people as Wulyibidi). If you're lucky you might be the only soul here. **Bottle Bay** and **Cattle Well** are simply gorgeous – great for swimming and kayaking. But the crowning experience awaits at **Cape Peron**, where bay and ocean currents collide below towering red cliffs and bottlenose dolphins drive their prey into the shallows, strand-feeding on the sparkling beach. At first glance it looks like a tumultuous rush of waters, but stick around and what's happening will soon become clear. Look out for mother dolphins teaching their calves to fish.

Scenic delights From Cape Peron the fabulous **Wanamalu Trail** (3.6km return) follows the clifftop south along the eastern peninsula to Skipjack Point. The magnificent views will have you lingering longer than the one-hour walk takes. Head off just after sunrise and you'll be rewarded with empty trails and pink seascapes; sunsets (from Cape Peron or the western bays) are busier but equally memorable. **Skipjack Point Lookout** provides expansive views of the coastline and, below, water so clear and blue it has to be seen to be believed. Here you might see dugongs, sharks, turtles, various rays and dolphins. Head back to the **Heritage Precinct** near the park entrance for a soak in an artesian hot tub.

Feeling Nature

The Shark Bay World Heritage Area is the traditional lands of the Nhanda and Malgana peoples. Local Aboriginal man Darren 'Capes' Capewell runs kayaking and SUP tours past the red cliffs of Cape Peron, looking for bush tucker on land and teaching you how to let Country talk to you. 'It's about feeling nature,' he says, 'more than it is just seeing it.' The experience with Capes is a mix of history, storytelling and pure fun, and his campfire-at-sunset 'Didgeridoo Dreaming' tours are magical. His favourite spot along this coast is **Big Lagoon**; he believes Shark Bay is the next big thing in kitesurfing; and he says the best sunsets are from aptly named **Sunset Beach** at Nicholson Point.

■ **Darren 'Capes' Capewell**
Wula Gura Nyinda Eco Adventures, Denham, Shark Bay
wulagura.com.au

38 A World Heritage DRIVE

DRIVING | DESERT | ADVENTURE

Discover ancient life forms, beaches made of shells, sparkling turquoise waters and the creatures that inhabit them on this drive into the unique Shark Bay World Heritage Area. This parched landscape of salt lakes and brilliant seas is like nothing you've seen so far...

WIRESTOCK CREATORS/SHUTTERSTOCK

Rise Above It All

One way to grasp the immensity (and downright weirdness) of the geography out here is getting airborne with **Shark Bay Scenic Flights**, which runs sightseeing tours across the peninsula, including over the Zuytdorp Cliffs, Steep Point and Dirk Hartog Island. Marvel at salt lakes, lagoons, manta rays and Shark Bay's skeletal 'fingers'.

How to

Getting around A 2WD vehicle is enough for Shark Bay Rd, but a 4WD will get you to the wilder national parks.

When to go May to September has the best weather and also the most visitors. Summers can be hot and windy.

Top tip Grab a copy of the *Animals of Shark Bay* pocket guide from the Denham Parks and Wildlife office to learn more about this UNESCO area's unique wildlife.

01 Dating back to 1884, Hamelin's **Telegraph Station** has a small museum and what may be the world's only living stromatolites (ancient coral-like life forms) in captivity.

02 You'll have to view the stromatolites at **Hamelin Pools** from a distance,as the access boardwalk was damaged by a cyclone. These cyanobacterial mounds are almost identical to organisms existing 3.5 billion years ago.

03 Stunning **Shell Beach** is where tiny, densely compacted cockle shells were once quarried as building material. The water here is often warm, very salty and a long way out.

04 Detour 4km to the brilliant **Eagle Bluff** lookout, where you might spy loggerhead turtles, manta rays, sharks and even dugongs in the transparent turquoise waters below the clifftop boardwalk.

05 Check out what inhabits the big blue beyond at Denham's **Ocean Park**, one of the West's best aquariums, where you can interact with sharks, turtles and stingrays.

39 Shark Bay's Dolphins & WALLABIES

WILDLIFE | COASTLINE | HISTORY

The Shark Bay World Heritage Area contains two of WA's most memorable wildlife experiences: observing wild dolphins at Monkey Mia and exploring the rewilding of Dirk Hartog Island/Wirruwana, its national park an ark for endangered species. Dirk Hartog offers a glimpse of a pre-European landscape, while the sight of a dolphin and calf in the Monkey Mia shallows is a guaranteed joy.

BENNY MARTY/SHUTTERSTOCK

How to

Getting here and around Rex flies daily from Perth to Shark Bay, where you can hire a 2WD (through carhire.net.au) for Denham and Monkey Mia. A shuttle (book ahead) connects with Integrity coaches at the Overlander Roadhouse.

When to go May to September has the best weather.

4WD to DHI You can drive to Dirk Hartog in a high-clearance 4WD via Steep Point (Australia's most westerly mainland extremity), crossing by barge from nearby Shelter Bay.

NATURE PICTURE LIBRARY/ALAMY

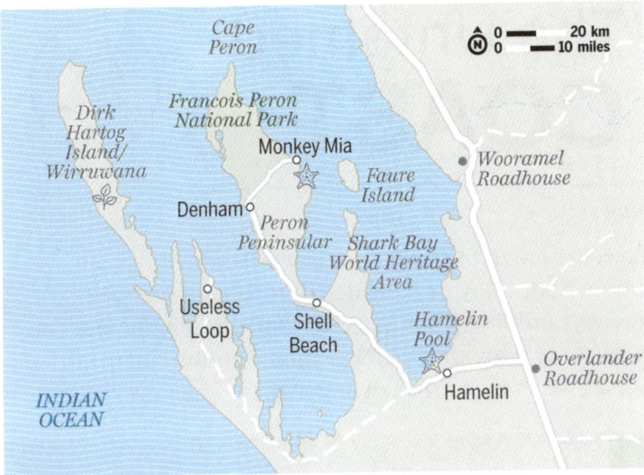

Monkey Mia dolphins Wild Indo-Pacific bottlenose dolphins have been arriving at Monkey Mia expecting a free feed for over 50 years, a phenomenon that's a huge hit with visitors. The first feed, around 7.45am, is the most popular. Don't expect to feed or touch the dolphins; this is handled by rangers and a small number of selected individuals. Most dolphin researchers would like to see the feeding phased out altogether, citing higher calf mortality rates caused by lack of hunting training from the hand-fed mothers. Supporters argue only 5 to 10% of the dolphins' daily food intake is from hand-feeding. The second and possibly third feedings, usually after the tour buses depart, are less crowded.

Dirk Hartog Island/Wirruwana This slim, wind-raked island, which runs parallel to the Peron Peninsula (p170), once attracted Dutch, British and French explorers. WA's largest island is now a national park with a wild, edge-of-the-world feeling. With feral goats, sheep and cats removed, the island's biodiversity is on the mend: native flora has been replanted and endemic animals such as the dibbler, banded hare-wallaby and rufous hare-wallaby have been reintroduced to restore the island to its 1616 (first European contact) splendour. Many of the species found here no longer survive on the mainland; you might also see dugongs and loggerhead turtles. Shark Bay Eco Tours and the island's eco lodge both run day tours from Denham.

Left Dolphins, Monkey Mia
Below Banded hare-wallaby

Dolphin Volunteering

Some visitors, after the all-too-brief feeding-time encounter with Monkey Mia's highly intelligent cetaceans, feel they want to participate further. If this applies to you, and you can set aside five to 14 days, consider **volunteering** *(sharkbay.org/place/monkey-mia/volunteering-monkey-mia)* your mornings to work with the dolphins. You'll get free entry to Monkey Mia, and it's amazing how much you'll learn in even this short amount of time. You'll assist with the feedings and interact with visitors while getting to know the dolphin family groups. It's the kind of deep-immersion wildlife encounter that will have you retraining to become a marine biologist.

40 The Untamed COAST

WAVES | SURFING | REMOTENESS

Beloved by locals, the coast north of Carnarvon is wild and windswept, receiving far fewer visitors than Shark Bay or Ningaloo, but this raw, elemental landscape has a stark remoteness missing from its better-known neighbours. You can dial up the isolation factor to 11 with an epic foray inland to Burringurrah (Mt Augustus), an ancient, massive lump of rock deliciously far from everywhere.

JACK KINNY/SHUTTERSTOCK

How to

Getting around You'll need your own vehicle; while a 2WD will work, a 4WD will work better! Rentals are available in Carnarvon, but you'll get a better deal in Perth.

When to go The big surfing swells arrive in winter, while summers are windy, ideal for kitesurfing.

Top tip Experienced 4WDers can follow sandy tracks along the coast beyond Gnaraloo to Coral Bay and eventually to Ningaloo.

PHOTO VOLCANO/SHUTTERSTOCK

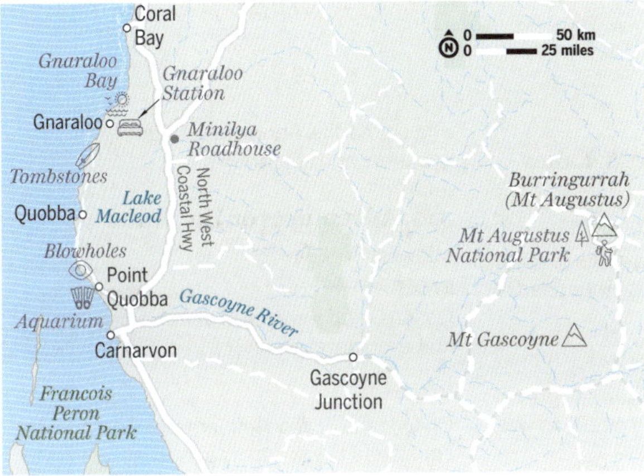

Left Blowholes, Point Quobba
Below Dunes, Gnaraloo Station

Quobba Coast North of Carnarvon, the North West Coastal Hwy turns inland, taking with it most of the traffic. Instead, follow Blowholes Rd to the Quobba Coast, a desolate shoreline that stretches from **Point Quobba** north to **Red Bluff**. This be the domain of surfers, fisherfolk and fire-in-the-sky sunsets. Stop at Point Quobba to snorkel the sheltered lagoon known as the **Aquarium** and see the impressive **Blowholes**, where swells force sprays of water through sea caves to howl out of narrow rock chimneys. At high tide water often covers the blowholes; an incoming tide is the best time to visit.

Tombstones North from Red Bluff at Gnaraloo, Tombstones has near-mythic status among surfers, who come here from mid-April to October. Promising one of the longest, roundest tubes in the world, Tombstones is a heavy, scary, left-hander reef break. Even if you don't surf it's fun to watch the experts. Other spots for experienced surfers include Gnaraloo Bay, Midgies, Turtles and Fenceline.

3 Mile and Gnaraloo Bay The perfect white crescent of legendary Gnaraloo Bay is as gorgeous as beaches come. Here you can snorkel, hike and kite-surf. Camp at laidback 3 Mile with its excellent snorkelling **lagoon** or grab a stone cabin and watch the sunset at the welcoming Homestead at **Gnaraloo Station**.

Bigger than Uluṟu

In Wajarri Country, 484km east of Carnarvon, **Burringurrah** (Mt Augustus; 1105m), a giant inselberg (literally, 'island mountain') rises 715m above the surrounding plain. Double the size of Uluṟu, it sees only a fraction of Uluṟu's visitors, not least because it's a long way from anywhere. A 49km loop road encircles Burringurrah's base, giving access to walking trails and rock art sites. Know your limitations: the challenging and shadeless but superb **Summit Trail** (12.5km return, five to six hours) has claimed several lives. May to August is the best season; the park is closed November to February because of incinerator-like temperatures. Approach from Carnarvon (six hours) or Meekatharra (five hours). A 2WD should make it.

Listings

BEST OF THE REST

Wildlife, Wildflowers & Lakes

Coalseam Conservation Park

In spring, visit this park on the Irwin River in Holmwood for carpets of everlastings (paper daisies) and ancient fossil shells embedded in its cliffs.

Greenough Wildlife & Bird Park

At this excellent sanctuary you can see grey and red kangaroos, dingoes and emus, as well as lots of birds and reptiles.

Hutt Lagoon

Visit this Insta-famous pink lake near Kalbarri in the middle of the day to see it at its most vivid.

Galleries & Museums

Geraldton Regional Art Gallery

The air-conditioned salons of this small gallery hold landmark works by Aussie greats including Norman Lindsay and Elizabeth Durack.

Gwoonwardu Mia

This Carnarvon icon has a gallery and shop featuring works by local Aboriginal artists, time-lapse stargazing and an ethnobotanical garden.

Central Greenough Historic Settlement

Greenough was quite a town in its 1860s heyday; some of its traditional stone buildings have been preserved.

Carnarvon Space & Technology Museum

In the shadow of a NASA Apollo-era tracking dish, this family-friendly museum explores the role Carnarvon played in early space exploration.

Shark Bay World Heritage Discovery Centre

This world-class museum has a gallery with stunning aerial photos and exhibits on marine and animal life, Aboriginal culture, early explorers and shipwrecks.

Adventures on the Water

Midwest Surf School

This Geraldton surf school has year-round lessons (and a choice of suitable beaches) to suit every level.

Red Bluff

On Quobba Station not far from Gnaraloo, the consistent break here is almost as famous as nearby Tombstones.

Batavia Coast Dive

Geraldton dive shop offering PADI courses and multiday trips to the Houtman Abrolhos Islands.

Eco Abrolhos

Liveaboard five-plus-day cruises diving and snorkelling the islands from February to November.

Shark Bay EcoTours

The Ocean Park aquarium mob near Denham runs brilliant boat tours and diving excursions to Steep Point and Dirk Hartog Island/Wirruwana and whale watching in August and October.

IAN GERAINT JONES/SHUTTERSTOCK

Coalseam Conservation Park

KiteWest

From October to April, KiteWest offers kite- and windfoil-surfing lessons and tours in Geraldton and Shark Bay.

Snacking & Brunching

Salt Dish $$

Fresh, innovative dishes and a killer wine list make Geraldton's coolest cafe perfect for a long lunch.

Banh Mi Up $

Hole-in-the-wall Vietnamese takeaway serving the best banh mi between Perth and Broome right on Geraldton's main street.

Little Leaf $$

Locally sourced produce mixed with love and turned into beautiful tapas and share plates and bowls in Kalbarri.

Jaffle Shack (Foreshore) $

Toasted sandwiches in all manner of gourmet flavours emerge from a shipping container on the Gero foreshore.

Shark Bay Cafe $

Refreshingly unpretentious early opener with lots of outdoor space; the croissants and bagels are great for brekkie.

Kestrel Cafe $$

Out at Carnarvon's One Mile Jetty, enjoy breakfast favourites with a view, plus Vietnamese-style lunches.

Best Sunset Drinks

Old Man & the Sea

Gero's only rooftop bar is perfect for sunset viewing, and not only because the cocktails come by the jug.

Shark Bay Hotel

Known in Denham as 'The Old Pub', Australia's most westerly boozer serves pub favourites and has the perfect sunset beer garden.

DAMIAN LUGOWSKI/SHUTTERSTOCK

Hutt Lagoon

Carnarvon Hotel

Grab a decent feed and watch the sunset over the Fascine bay.

Last Sunset

Overnight tours to Dirk Hartog include sun-downers on the island's western tip, where you'll be the last people in WA to see the sun set.

Self-Guided Trails

Heritage Trails

Walk or cycle around Gero's picturesque foreshore and backstreets following these downloadable trails. Themes include maritime history, the West End, public art and the waterfront. *trailswa.com.au*

Fruit Loop Trail

Download this 26km Carnarvon drive with nine stops including produce stalls, farms, ice creams and even a cactus garden. *australiascoralcoast.com/trip-ideas/itineraries/fruit-loop-drive-trail*

Thungara Trails

Six short walking trails weave through Dongara-Port Denison taking in historic and scenic spots. *trailswa.com.au*

■ **By Caoimhe Hanrahan-Lawrence**
Wiradjuri writer, currently living in Sydney on Wangal-Eora land

Australia's First Nations People

CUSTODIANS OF THE EARTH'S OLDEST CONTINUOUS CULTURES

Indigenous Australian cultures date back at least 65,000 years. Before European invasion in 1788, there were approximately 300 distinct language groups and 500 dialects. Now, Aboriginal and Torres Strait Islander peoples make up only 3.8% of Australia's population. Most live in urban areas, though some communities maintain traditional lifestyles in remote areas.

HOLLI/SHUTTERSTOCK

Left Invasion Day protesters
Centre Dried quandong fruit
Right Ice cream made with indigenous ingredients

Walking the Dreaming

Aboriginal culture and spirituality revolve around Dreaming and Dreamtime. The Dreamtime describes how things came to be. It details the creation of the natural world – rivers, mountains, plants, animals and everything in between.

The Dreaming explains why things are the way they are, such as the birth of the first platypus, how the echidna got her spines or the meanings of certain constellations. The Dreaming is always occurring, without a defined beginning or end. It tells people about how they should behave, about their culture and families, and about living from and respecting the land.

Dreamtime and Dreaming stories differ across nations, though some nations share the same or similar stories. These stories have been passed down through oral storytelling, dance and art, and now many stories have also been written down.

An important part of the Dreaming is that Aboriginal peoples are the custodians, not the owners, of the land they live on. Instead, the relationship between the land and the people is a reciprocal one, where the people care for the land because it cares for them.

Many of these Dreaming stories are connected to Songlines, which are paths walked by the spirits in the Dreamtime. Songlines serve many purposes, such as preserving history, detailing agricultural practices and mapping the land.

DALLASETTA/SHUTTERSTOCK

RUIJIE/SHUTTERSTOCK

Living off the Land

For many years it was assumed that Indigenous peoples were hunter-gatherer societies prior to invasion. However, Aboriginal testimonies and recent historical research indicate that Indigenous societies employed complex aquaculture and agriculture practices. Structures such as weirs and dams still exist.

> The Dreaming is always occurring, without a defined beginning or end.

Many Aboriginal and Torres Strait communities recognise different seasons from those in the European calendar. These seasons usually align with the area's weather patterns or relate to the local flora and fauna. The Wurundjeri people of Victoria recognise seven seasons, such as Biderap, which is sunny and dry, and Waring, when the wombat and the moth are by the creek. Understanding the Indigenous calendar in the area you are visiting may help you better prepare for the specific weather of the region. Knowing when to dress for the hot and windy, the wet and windy, or the cool and dry can make a big difference to your enjoyment of your travels.

Bush tucker (food) and bush medicine are still used today. Some bush tucker, such as pepperberry, quandong and Davidson's plum, is used in fusion cooking and can be found in restaurants.

The Difficult Date

The date 26 January, when the First Fleet of settlers arrived at Sydney Cove in 1788, officially became Australia Day in 1994. For Aboriginal and Torres Strait Islander peoples, 26 January is a more sombre occasion, marking the beginning of invasion, seizure of the land and erosion of culture. It is referred to as the Day of Mourning, Survival Day or Invasion Day. For many Indigenous people and their supporters, Invasion Day is a day of remembrance and resistance rather than celebration. The issue is contentious in Australia, and calls to keep or change the date occur every year.

Countries, Clans & Cousins

Individual clans exist within Aboriginal nations. Clans within the same language group usually speak dialects that are mutually intelligible. Within these clans are individual families, though Aboriginal families integrate the extended family more than most Western societies do. In some communities it is common to refer to your mother's sister as Mum rather than Aunty, and to call your first cousins your brother- or sister-cousins. Some people may use 'cousin' to refer to anyone within their clan, skin group or language group. 'Cuz' is also a term of affection among Aboriginal people even if they are from completely different nations.

> Family and community ties are vital to Aboriginal culture. Your family tells you who you are and where you come from.

Family and community ties are vital to Aboriginal culture. Your family tells you who you are and where you come from. Many peoples identify family ties by plant and animal totems. It is common to have your personal totem plus three further totems indicating your nation, your clan and your family ties. Sadly, much of this information has been lost, and it is a difficult journey for some people to find their family totems.

Aboriginal People Today

Across Australia, it is estimated that approximately 150 Aboriginal and Torres Strait Islander languages are still spoken, and there are continuing efforts to revive languages among Indigenous communities. It is now possible to listen to music, watch TV shows or take classes in a number of Indigenous languages. Aboriginal words are also present in the Australian vernacular. Animals such as koalas, dingoes, barramundi and galahs derive their names from Aboriginal languages, as do billabongs and boogie boards.

Similarly, Aboriginal words from different communities have spread through Australian Aboriginal English, the dialect of English spoken by many Aboriginal people across the country.

Around 62% of Indigenous Australians live on the East Coast. This may surprise some visitors to Australia who think that they do not see many Aboriginal people in the region. Others are confused when a light-skinned person identifies as Aboriginal. It is widely accepted among Aboriginal communities that your percentage of Aboriginality has

RICHARD T. NOWITZ/GETTY IMAGES

CHAMELEONSEYE/SHUTTERSTOCK

GREG WOOD/AFP/GETTY IMAGES

ANNIE 888/SHUTTERSTOCK

little bearing on your identity and involvement in the community. People with light skin and blond hair will proudly call themselves Blak or identify as Blackfullas. A common metaphor is that of a cup of tea: no matter how much milk you put in the cup, no matter how pale it becomes, it's still tea.

Since 1975 the first Sunday of July has marked the beginning of NAIDOC Week, which is dedicated to celebrating Aboriginal culture, history and perseverance. Communities, cities, schools and other institutions hold events that celebrate and build awareness about the rich and diverse Aboriginal cultures in Australia today.

Sorry Day (26 May) commemorates the formal apology from the Australian government in 2008 for its role in the Stolen Generations. From 1910 to the 1970s, Aboriginal children were forcibly removed from their families to integrate them into white society. Aboriginal people today still feel the effects of this policy through loss of culture, family ties and language.

Signs of Respect

An Acknowledgement of Country and a Welcome to Country are important statements that identify and thank the custodians of the land on which an event takes place. Anyone, Aboriginal or not, can give an Acknowledgement. Welcomes can only be given by Elders from that Country, or a member of the community who has been given permission by the Elders.

Elders and cultural teachers are usually referred to with 'Aunty' or 'Uncle' before their first name, in the same way that respect is conferred by the use of 'Sir' or 'Ma'am'. This recognises the knowledge and experience that Elders hold.

Far left Boomerang carving lesson
Left Aboriginal tools and weapons
Above left Traditional smoking ceremony performed at the opening ceremony for Naidoc Week
Above right Painted banners to celebrate Naidoc Week

NINGALOO COAST & THE PILBARA

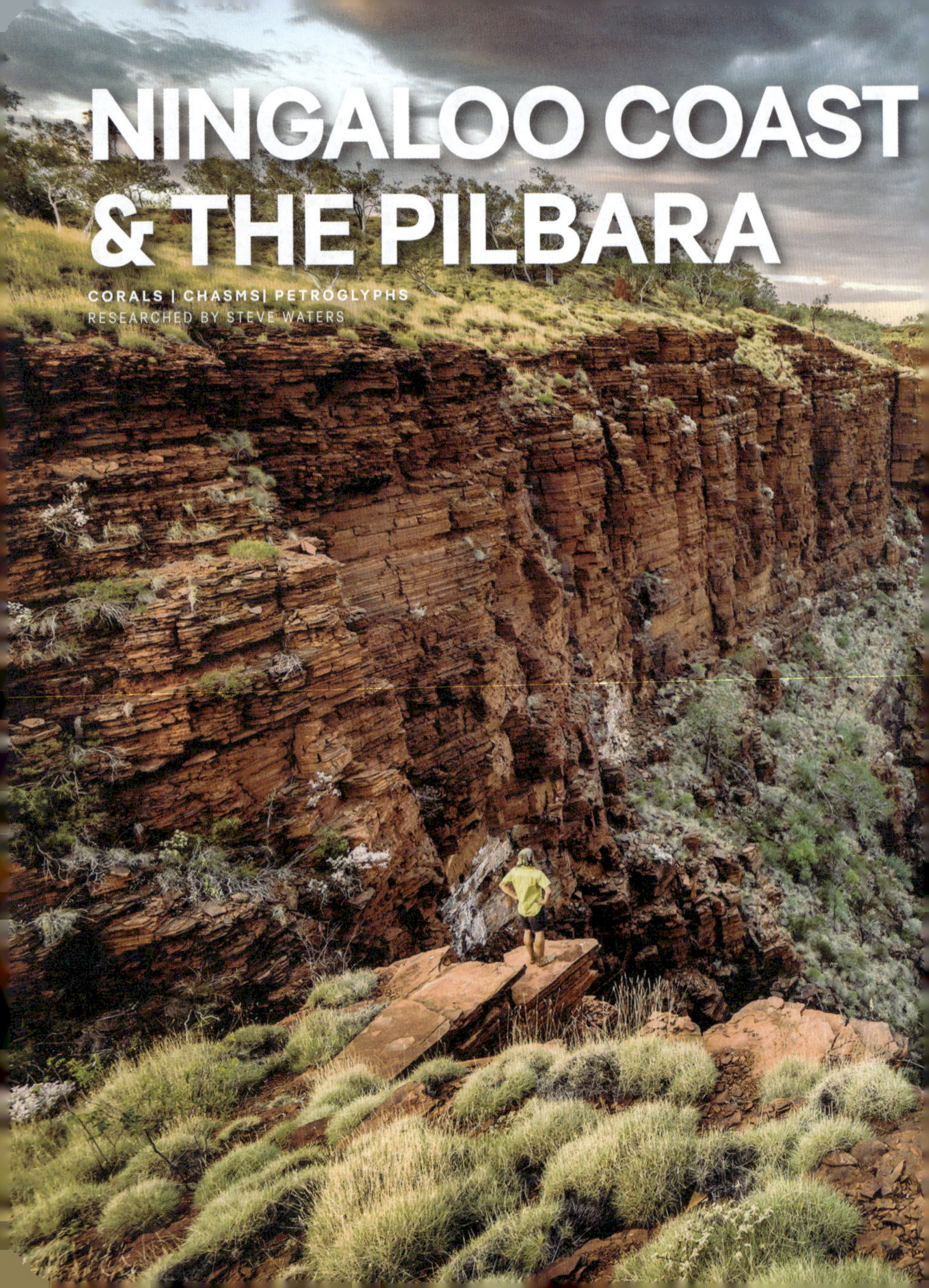

CORALS | CHASMS| PETROGLYPHS

RESEARCHED BY STEVE WATERS

- **More than Whale Sharks** (p188)
- **The Canyons of Cape Range** (p192)
- **Epic Adventures Inland** (p194)
- **The Pilbara's Great Mining Debate** (p196)
- **Indigenous Art in the Pilbara** (p198)
- **The Way of the Warlu** (p200)
- **Pits, Pearls & Pioneers** (p202)
- **Listings** (p204)

POSNOV/GETTY IMAGES

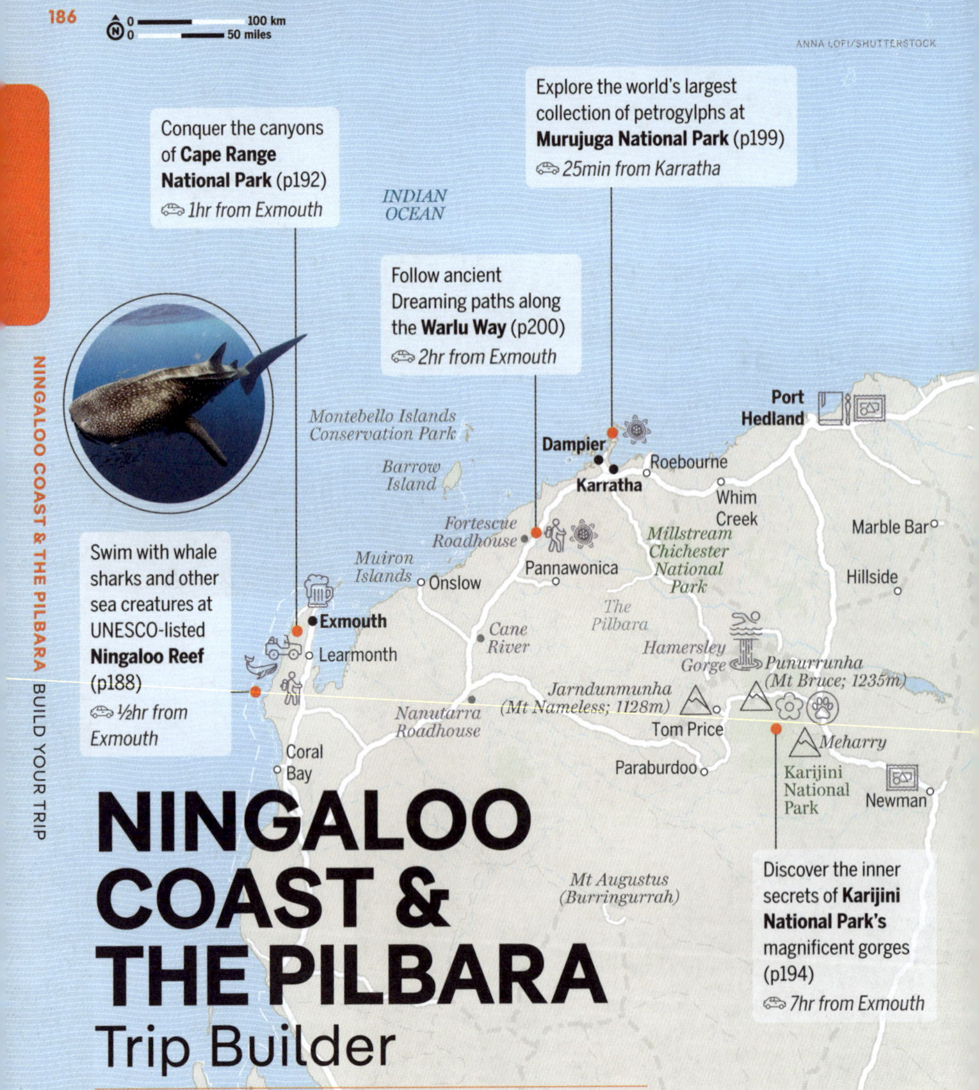

NINGALOO COAST & THE PILBARA

Trip Builder

Arguably, this region is home to the West's most epic landscapes: alongside the mines of the sun-blasted Pilbara you'll find the World Heritage Ningaloo Reef with its astonishing marine denizens, the exquisite chasms of Karijini and, at Murujuga, the largest collection of petroglyphs on the planet.

Practicalities

ARRIVING

Learmonth (Exmouth) Airport is the most useful for tourists, with daily Perth flights and accompanying shuttles into Exmouth (36km). Buses run between Perth and Port Hedland via coastal and inland routes.

FIND YOUR WAY

Get a GPS app AND a hard-copy road atlas such as Hema's Great Desert Tracks. Don't rely on mapping apps.

MONEY

The Pilbara coastal mining towns are expensive, especially for accommodation. Most travellers head inland and camp in the national parks.

WHERE TO STAY

Place	Pros/Cons
Exmouth	Has a good food scene and everything from motels and caravan parks to apartments and resorts.
Karijini National Park	Stay in the park near the attractions; lots of camping, some upmarket options and a restaurant.
Millstream Chichester National Park	Great bush camping under the Milky Way in sublime dark-sky country.

GETTING AROUND

Car As usual in WA, having your own vehicle is the best option. A 2WD will get you to most Pilbara attractions, but a 4WD will give you more flexibility.

Bus The Flying Sandgroper runs a hop-on, hop-off ('hoppa') weekly bus service between Exmouth and Karijini and will connect with flights and long-distance coaches. It'll also arrange accommodation and gorge tours.

TOP: : STEVE WATERS/CONTRIBUTOR, STEVE WATERS/CONTRIBUTOR

EATING & DRINKING

Exmouth has the hippest food scene between Perth and Broome. As with anywhere along the WA coast, seafood is the standout produce, with Exmouth prawns famous across the state.

Best boutique beer
Whalebone English Brown Ale (pictured top; p205)

Must-try seafood
Whalers' seafood platter, the best on the coast (pictured bottom; p205)

JAN–MAR
Filthy hot, loads of flies and possibly cyclones – avoid.

APR–JUN
Whalesharks are on. Get in early.

JUL–SEP
Fine weather; cold nights inland. Peak tourist season.

OCT–DEC
Warming up. Fewer travellers. Good deals.

41 More than Whale SHARKS

WILDLIFE | REEF | UNDERWATER

Most people come to Ningaloo Reef to swim with the whale sharks – and you should too. Stretching almost 300km, Ningaloo is the world's longest fringing reef, home to some of the richest marine life in the southern hemisphere. You can also plan your visit around humpback whales, manta rays and turtles.

WATERFRAME/ALAMY

How to

Getting there and around Exmouth is the main base for Ningaloo; it's connected by air to Perth and to just about anywhere by road. Coral Bay is also good.

When to go Whale sharks visit from mid-March to September and even later. For humpbacks it's June to October.

Tours Try Kings Ningaloo Reef Tours, Ningaloo Whale Shark-N-Dive or Three Islands Whale Shark Dive for whale shark and interactive whale tours.

FROZYGRAPHIE/SHUTTERSTOCK

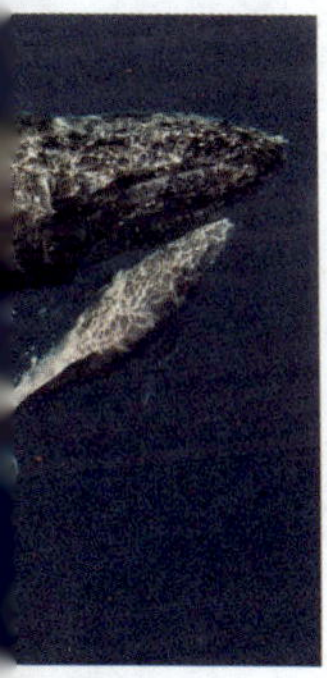

ELSALASS/SHUTTERSTOCK

Swimming with Whale Sharks

UNESCO World Heritage–listed Ningaloo is one of the few places in the world where solitary speckled whale sharks *(Rhincodon typus)* arrive like clockwork each year to feed on plankton and small fish. The largest fish in the world, whale sharks can reach up to 18m long and are believed to live 70 to 100 years. Those encountered at Ningaloo are mostly between 3m and 12m; a 12m whale shark may weigh as much as 11 tonnes and have a mouth more than 1m wide.

From March to August (and sometimes even as late as October), you can join a tour to snorkel alongside these extraordinary creatures.

Citizen Science

Once you're back on dry land, upload your amazing whale-shark pics to **Wildbook for Whale Sharks** *(sharkbook.ai)*, which will identify and track your whale shark. Similarly, **happywhale.com** will take your humpback images. Snorkellers and divers can add new meaning to saltwater adventures by collecting marine data for **reefcheckaustralia.org**.

Above left Snorkelling with a whale shark
Above Baby green sea turtle
Left Humpback whales

Humpback Whale Sightings

And you thought whale sharks were big! From May to October around 35,000 humpback whales *(Megaptera novaeangliae)* migrate along the WA coastline, heading north to their warm Kimberley calving grounds before returning south to feed on krill in the Antarctic summer.

Whale-watching tours from Exmouth go out to sea in hopes of sighting a classic breach. Your other option is to drive up to **Vlamingh Head Lighthouse** with a pair of binoculars.

Nesting Marine Turtles

Between December and March you can join a two-hour guided tour run by the **Jurabi Turtle Centre** *(exploreparks.dbca.wa.gov.au/site/jurabi-turtle-centre)* to see green and loggerhead turtles nesting on the beach; tours depart a few evenings each week, and advance bookings are essential. If you have five weeks to spare and a passion for conservation, consider volunteering with the **Ningaloo Turtle Program** *(ningalooturtles.org.au)*.

Drift Snorkelling at Turquoise Bay

If you're a strong swimmer (a necessary precondition), there's nothing quite like drift snorkelling at gorgeous Turquoise Bay, off Yardie Creek Rd on the western shore of Cape Range National Park, 63km from Exmouth. As the current carries you over coral bommies, watch for everything from bulbous brain corals to delicate branching staghorns. Avoid swimming when currents are strong, and don't miss the exit point or you'll be swept out to sea. From the Drift car park, head 300m south along the beach, then wade 40m into the water. Sadly, you'll see strong evidence here of the 2024–25 bleaching event.

Above & Below

More than 220 species of hard coral have been recorded in Ningaloo. While they're less colourful than soft corals (normally found in deeper water on the outer reef), hard corals are all about shape, with formations including bommies, plate corals, brains, fingers, bubbles and staghorns.

Spawning, where branches of hermaphroditic coral simultaneously eject eggs and sperm into the water, occurs en masse at neap tides after the March and April full moons. This underwater blizzard attracts krill and plankton, and in turn whale sharks, in addition to an already astonishing diversity of fish, rays, turtles and other marine life.

Snorkelling is the easiest way to see this wonderland. Because Ningaloo is a fringing reef, you can launch directly from shore at places like **Bundegi Beach**, **Lakeside** and **Turquoise Bay**; the latter offers both bay and drift snorkelling (p190). Hire snorkel gear from any of the dive shops in town.

From a kayak you might see turtles, dolphins and manta rays. Ningaloo has several dedicated moorings in the sanctuary zones of **Osprey**, **Tantabiddi**, **Bundegi** and **Maud** (Coral Bay) that allow you to tether your craft while you explore below, enjoying the best of both worlds.

In 2024–25 Ningaloo experienced its worst ever coral bleaching event. The underwater heatwave was particularly devastating to the shallower corals.

Left Ningaloo Reef
Above Turquoise Bay

42 The Canyons of CAPE RANGE

CANYONS | HIKING | EXPLORING

While most people head for the water, consider exploring inland for a different perspective on the remarkable Ningaloo Coast. Cape Range National Park starts at the water's edge then heads west across the dry coastal plain to the crumbing limestone hills, narrow gorges and truly amazing canyons of the range itself. Visiting involves a combination of scenic drives and impressive short hikes.

ROB BAYER/SHUTTERSTOCK

How to

Getting here and around Visit on a day trip from Exmouth or camp at one of the many coastal sites (book ahead). You'll need your own vehicle – 2WD is OK.

When to go Temperatures can exceed 50°C in summer. There's minimal shade on most hikes, so start early, and only attempt longer trails between April and October.

Wonderful wildlife Watch out for the rare black-flanked rock wallaby as well as dingoes, kangaroos and some of the park's 160 recorded bird species.

STEVE WATERS/CONTRIBUTOR

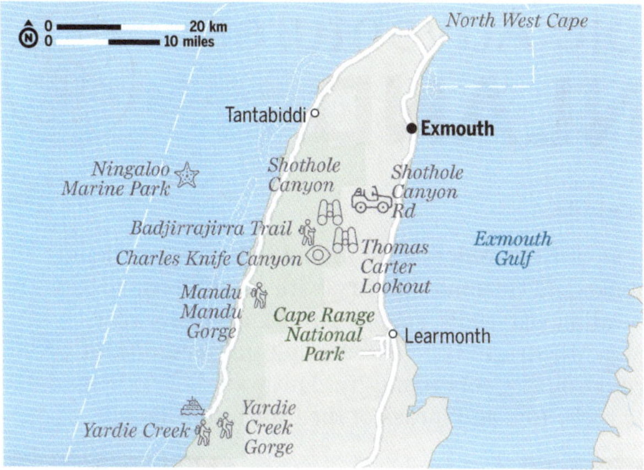

Scenic drives Around 15km south of Exmouth, the 12.5km-long, unsealed **Shothole Canyon Rd** runs deep into the heart of the canyon, meandering along a dry creek bed and passing some colourful, dramatic rock formations before reaching a picnic area and a short trail. Officially this road is 4WD only, but it's suitable for 2WDs with decent clearance during the dry months. Eight kilometres further south along the main road, the very scenic, 11km-long Charles Knife Rd – partly sealed and at times extremely narrow – ascends a knife-edge ridge via rickety corners; again, a 4WD is recommended. A rough track (passable by 2WD when dry) continues to **Thomas Carter Lookout** (311m), with great views over **Charles Knife Canyon**.

Hikes From near Thomas Carter Lookout, you can walk the 6.8km **Badjirrajirra Trail**. This scenic loop (two to three hours) wanders through spinifex and several steep, rocky gullies. If you don't want to do the whole loop, walk to the **Shothole Viewpoint** (about 4km return), which is the trail's scenic highlight. Other hikes include the pleasant, occasionally steep 3km return walk onto the picturesque rim of **Mandu Mandu Gorge** or the two walking trails at water-filled **Yardie Creek Gorge**: the gentle Nature Walk is 1.2km return and the more adventurous 2km return Gorge trail takes you high above – yep – the gorge. There's not much shade on any of these walks.

Left Yardie Creek Gorge
Below Shothole Canyon

Yardie Creek Boat Tour

A relaxing one-hour cruise up the short, sheer Yardie Creek Gorge is a fine alternative (or addition) to a more strenuous hike.

The steep rock walls are good places to see rare black-flanked rock wallabies. These cute little marsupials live in tiny, isolated populations across northwestern Australia, and this is one of the best places to see them anywhere in the country.

Departure times (and days) vary with the seasons; there are no cruises from early January to late March. See **yardiecreekboattours.com.au** for more information.

43 Epic Adventures INLAND

GORGES | WATERHOLES | CAMPING

After visiting Ningaloo, most travellers head inland to Karijini National Park on Banjima, Yinhawangka and Guruma Country, with magnificent gorges, lovely swimming holes, cascading waterfalls, snappy gums and elusive rock wallabies. Much less visited is Millstream Chichester, a culturally significant national park on Yindjibarndi Country comprising verdant waterholes along the Fortescue River and the rocky tors and mesas of the Chichester Range.

STEVE WATERS/CONTRIBUTOR

How to

Getting here and around It takes all day to drive to Karijini from Exmouth on sealed roads. Millstream is just over an hour from Dampier or 3½ hours (unsealed; 2WD OK if dry) from Karijini.

When to go Aim for April to October. Don't even think about heading out in the hot months (November to March).

Hoppa bus Those without vehicles can ride the Flying Sandgroper from Exmouth to Karijini (p187).

STEVE WATERS/CONTRIBUTOR

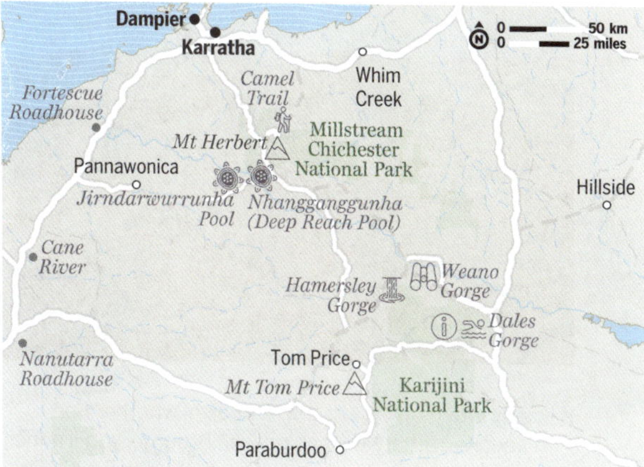

Karijini National Park The jewel of the Pilbara, Karijini draws visitors from across the globe to see its famous gorges. Among the most scenic are **Weano Gorge**, where you enter the sublime **Handrail Pool** through a tight rock passage, and nearby **Hancock Gorge**, where you descend via steel ladders to the slippery **Spider Walk** and the emerald-hued **Kermits Pool**, where it feels you're swimming deep within the earth. At the other end of the park, **Dales Gorge** is a visitor favourite. Take the **Rim Walk** to **Three Ways Lookout** for stellar clifftop views, then descend to the gorge bottom, following the stream back to **Fortescue Falls** and the tranquil **Fern Pool** just beyond. The folded rock strata at **Hamersley Gorge** are testament to the massive forces that created Karijini; cool off in the nearby **Spa Pool**. Spend a few days visiting all of Karijini's attractions.

Millstream Chichester National Park By the Fortescue River, peaceful Millstream is a lovely place to camp, with excellent dark-sky viewing. There's an unstaffed visitor centre and museum in the old pastoral **homestead**, and culturally significant **Jirndarwurrunha Pool** and **Nhangganggunha (Deep Reach Pool)** are close by. Towards Roebourne, **Mt Herbert** in the Chichester Range offers superb 360-degree views over tors, mesas and plains, while the nearby **Python Pool** provides a welcome cooling-off spot; the hot, rocky, 8km **Camel Trail** connects the two.

Left Karijini National Park
Below Fern Pool

Sacred Waters

The Yindjibarndi fought a long, brave battle for control of Millstream Chichester National Park, and the area is one of the most culturally important in WA. Two pools in particular carry deep significance. **Nhangganggunha (Deep Reach Pool)** is the resting place of the *warlu* (creation serpent). The water is deep and refreshing; access the pool via steps, and be sure to behave respectfully (no shouting, diving or splashing). No swimming is allowed at beautiful lily- and palm-fringed **Jirndarwurrunha Pool**, which is particularly sacred; reach it via a short, high-accessibility boardwalk from the old homestead. Other longer tracks lead to Nhangganggunha, though you can also drive.

The Pilbara's Great Mining Debate

MINING, THE ENVIRONMENT AND INDIGENOUS LANDS

The Pilbara's epic story has three major characters: First Nations people, the mining industry and an often pristine natural environment. It's truly a tale for our times. When these three characters meet, and very often collide, notable events ensue. Understanding this background will greatly enhance your visit.

Left The Pilbara
Centre Miners, the Pilbara
Right Geologists taking rock samples

ELECTRA/SHUTTERSTOCK

If you fly into many towns in WA's north, whether Port Hedland, Karratha, Newman or even Broome, you'll notice one thing straight away: signs of the fly-in, fly-out (FIFO) lifestyle remain ubiquitous. Large clutches of workers nonchalantly board their flights to remote mines and oil and gas plants, most in places few people have ever heard of. Some will be wearing their fluorescent orange or yellow 'high-vis' vests, required attire on-site and an understated badge of honour at city airports. It's a reminder that, regardless of the cyclical nature of the resources sector, mining remains the biggest game in town out West.

Environmental & Cultural Concerns

Perhaps because it's such a beautiful place, with so many sites of profound significance for First Nations people, the West Australian coast has seen many flashpoints. In the Pilbara, one controversial mining site is the Burrup Peninsula (p198) in the Dampier Archipelago, which is the location of millions of petroglyphs (rock art) believed to date from the last ice age. In 2007 Woodside Petroleum removed 170 petroglyphs to a seperate fenced-off area to better facilitate its Pluto A development. The Traditional Custodians saw this as a desecration and argued that the disruption of one petroglyph compromises the entire site.

More recently, another mining giant showed that very little has changed when it comes to mining companies and their dealings with Aboriginal groups. In 2020 Rio Tinto destroyed a cave housing two 47,000-year-old rock art shelters in Juukan Gorge in the Hamersley Range near Newman to facilitate expansion of its Brockman 4 iron ore mine. The cave was a sacred site for the Puutu Kunti

AUSSIE FAMILY LIVING/SHUTTERSTOCK

ADWO/SHUTTERSTOCK

Kurrama and Pinikura (PKKP) Traditional Custodians, providing direct evidence of continuous Indigenous occupation of the area for 47,000 years. Rio Tinto apologised and was fined. The PKKP people have since turned to France, where the famous Lascaux and Chauvet art caves have been painstakingly recreated, hoping that the same technology can be used to recreate Juukan in its entirety. Rio will be footing the bill.

The Yindjibarndi & Fortescue

Employment of First Nations people within the mining industry is very low. In 2008 mining magnate Andrew 'Twiggy' Forrest boldly promised support for 50,000 jobs for First Nations people. But even as Forrest's Fortescue Metals Group (FMG) was trying to increase Aboriginal employment in the mining industry, FMG's legal battles over mining leases on Yindjibarndi land (around Millstream Chichester National Park) told a different story. Recounted in fascinating detail by Paul Cleary in his book *Title Fight: How the Yindjibarndi Battled and Defeated a Mining Giant* (2021), the case pitted Indigenous Elders against the legal might of one of Australia's richest companies. Finally, in 2020, after more than a decade, the Yindjibarndi won their case in the High Court of Australia; its ruling recognised the Yindjibarndi's native title over many of the lands that FMG were seeking to mine. The outcome also effectively forces mining companies to more closely negotiate in good faith with native title holders.

The case pitted Indigenous Elders against the legal might of one of Australia's richest companies.

Saving Ningaloo

You'll still see 'Save Ningaloo' stickers around from one of Western Australia's most fiercely contested environmental campaigns. Bolstered by thousands of protesters, 'Save Ningaloo' successfully blocked development of a massive marina resort (slated for 2003) on a loggerhead turtle nesting ground.

In late 2012, BHP Billiton submitted a proposal to the state government to explore for liquefied natural gas 5km from Ningaloo's perimeter. This proposal was also rejected.

Apart from mining threats to Ningaloo, coral bleaching is an ever-increasing danger. In 2024–25 the worst and most widespread bleaching event on record devastated the reef's shallower corals.

44 Indigenous Art in THE PILBARA

ABORIGINAL CULTURE | PETROGLYPHS | ART

Aboriginal peoples have been living on this land for more than 40,000 years, and their remarkable stories are told across the region through art both ancient and modern. It begins with rock art on the Burrup Peninsula near Dampier and takes on an altogether more contemporary cast in the work of artists 67km away in Roebourne.

STEVE WATERS/CONTRIBUTOR

How to

How to go A 2WD will get you most places except the remote northern Burrup.

Guided tours Aboriginal-owned and -operated **Experience Murujuga** runs 90-minute tours at Nganjarli (Deep Gorge) Tuesday and Thursday.

When to go The best months are May to October.

Tasmanian tigers? Rock art tells an extraordinary story; see if you can find the thylacine, a species not seen on mainland Australia in 3200 years.

STEVE WATERS/CONTRIBUTOR

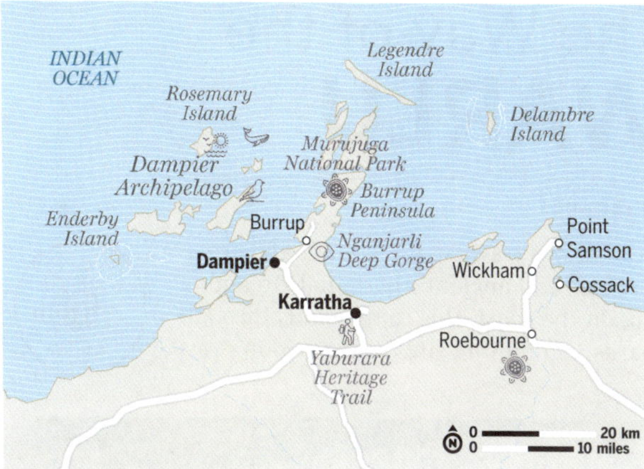

Left Rock art, Murujuga National Park
Below Nganjarli

Murujuga National Park Tucked away in the gorges of the Burrup Peninsula, UNESCO World Heritage–listed Murujuga National Park is home to what may be the world's largest concentration of rock art: there are an estimated 1 to 2 million rock engravings or petroglyphs in the park. Some date back 50,000 years, and at **Nganjarli** (Deep Gorge) alone, a veritable menagerie adorns the walls: fish, goannas, turtles, ospreys, kangaroos, the thylacine (once commonly known as the Tasmanian tiger) and more can all be seen from the boardwalk. The Traditional Custodians of the park come from five groups (Ngarluma, Yindjibarndi, Yaburara, Mardudhunera and Wong-Goo-Tt-Oo), collectively known as the Ngarda-Ngarli.

Yaburara Heritage Trail In the shadeless, rocky spinifex hills behind the Karratha visitor centre, these three trail loops (2.25km to 3.75km long) nicely complement the rock art of Murujuga with Yaburara rock art, stone quarries and shell middens, plus excellent lookout points. Bring plenty of water and start your walks early.

Yinjaa-Barni Art In Roebourne, just 39km up the road from Karratha, this Aboriginal-run gallery showcases the best in Pilbara art with a particular focus on works by Yindjibarndi artists. Pilbara painting styles are renowned for their bold, bright colours; styles vary from traditional to abstract. Don't rush a visit here: stay long enough to sit, watch the artists at work and have a chat.

Dampier Archipelago

The 42-island Dampier Archipelago has piercing blue sea and sky and islands littered with rocky outcrops, white-sand beaches and mangrove forests. The islands shelter rock wallabies, northern quolls and countless shorebirds, the same animals that appear in millennia-old rock art on the islands. Offshore, coral reefs, sponge gardens and underwater seagrass plains provide habitat for green, hawksbill, flatback and loggerhead turtles, as well as dugongs, dolphins, humpback whales and over 650 fish species. Most of the islands are uninhabited.

Dampier operators such as **Lethal Adventures** and **Pilbara Dive & Tours** offer boat tours that can include diving and snorkelling, fishing, sightseeing and sunset cruises.

45 The Way of the WARLU

DRIVING | DREAMING | LANDSCAPES

The Warlu Way tourist drives traverse the Pilbara and are a blend of modern traveller routes and ancient Aboriginal Dreaming stories. Starting and ending on the coast, this route winds through the landscapes, national parks and mining sites of the region's vast hinterland.

TRAVELLIGHT/SHUTTERSTOCK

Jarndunmunha (Mt Nameless; p205)

How to

Getting here and around You can join at many places along the route, from Coral Bay in the south to Cape Keraudren in the north.

When to go May to September has the best weather. It's fiercely hot and humid the rest of the year.

Choose your route Four route variations form part of the **Warlu Way** *(warluway.com.au)*; the inland ones are the most interesting.

The Dreaming Serpent

The *warlu* is a Dreaming serpent who travelled the Pilbara (roughly along the Fortescue River), creating waterways as he went. The *warlu* tourist routes, covering over 2500km, are dotted with interpretive signage. This drive combines elements of three of them, but you can pick and choose your own route.

FROM LEFT: JANELLE LUGGE/SHUTTERSTOCK, KARIJINI ECO RETREAT

01 The original Warlu Way started in family-friendly **Coral Bay** and so should you, for one final Ningaloo snorkel, saltwater swim and stunning Indian Ocean sunset, all by beautiful Bill's Bay.

02 The manicured oasis of **Tom Price**, WA's highest town, is surrounded by rust-red ironstone hills. It's the best place to refuel and stock up on groceries before camping in Karijini.

03 **Karijini Eco Retreat** is 100% Aboriginal owned and a model for sustainable tourism; sunsets from the on-site restaurant are sublime. The retreat makes a good base for exploring stunning Karijini National Park (p195).

04 Beguiling **Nhangganggunha (Deep Reach Pool)** in laid-back Millstream Chichester National Park (p195) is, according to lore, home to the *warlu*. This is dark-sky country; the Milky Way has never looked better.

05 The coastal reserve of **Cape Keraudren** marks the starting point of epic Eighty Mile Beach. This mesmerising, near-deserted 220km stretch of sand, sky and water is the longest on the continent.

46 Pits, Pearls & PIONEERS

MINING | HISTORY | GHOSTS

Mining in the mineral-rich Pilbara is on a such a huge scale that it assaults the senses. Superlatives are thrown around like confetti: the biggest port, the longest train, the deepest hole. But it can be a fickle game, and while some towns thrive, others see tumbleweeds rolling down their main streets. Compare the fortunes of two of the region's oldest towns.

STEVE WATERS/CONTRIBUTOR

How to

Getting here and around Port Hedland has daily flights to Perth and less frequent flights to other Pilbara towns; long-distance coaches ply both inland and coastal routes. You'll need your own vehicle for Cossack.

When to go Visit between May and October; it's hotter than hell otherwise.

Where to relax Point Samson just past Cossack makes a pleasant overnight break, with several lovely beaches, snorkelling and fishing and a great seafood platter at the pub.

STEVE WATERS/CONTRIBUTOR

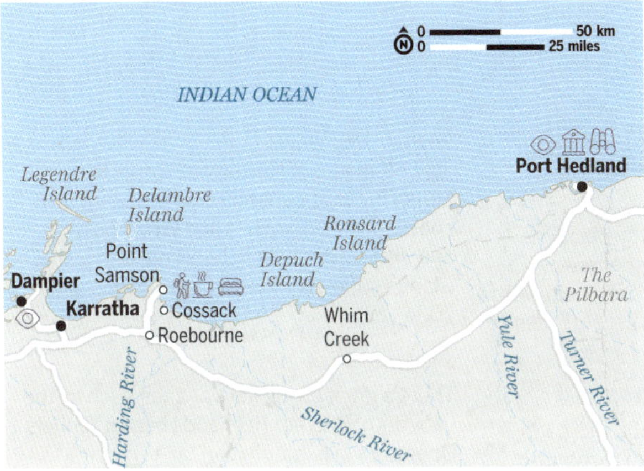

Cossack This former pearling port on Ngarluma land predated Broome, but after it was devastated by cyclones in the late 1880s it gradually declined; by the 1950s only ghosts remained. Many of the bluestone buildings date from the late 1800s, and some have been lovingly restored and repurposed as museum, cafe, gallery and accommodation. Download the **Cossack Heritage Trail** brochure and wander among the buildings, then drive out to the **Pioneer Cemetery**, its Japanese section a poignant memorial to Cossack's pearling past. Nearby, **Reader Head Lookout** has excellent views of the Harding river mouth and lovely **Settlers Beach** is worth a dip. At the time of research the local Aboriginal corporation, which now runs Cossack, was in a funding dispute with the state government and no businesses were open. Hopefully this will soon be resolved.

Port Hedland With its salt ponds and power lines, epic freight trains and giant mining machines, Port Hedland certainly won't win a beauty contest, but among the rust, the cloaking dust and the day-glo hi-vis it offers a fascinating glimpse of the boom-bust cycle of Australia's mining and resources obsession. Start with open-air **Don Rhodes Mining Museum**, with rusted trains, engines and mining machinery, then head for **Marapikurrinya Park** to watch phenomenally large iron-ore carriers and salt ships pass by; the helpful visitor centre lists shipping movements on its wall. At sunset visit **Redbank Bridge Salt & Train Lookout** to admire pink-tinted mountains of salt and those legendary ore trains trundling past.

Left Pioneer Cemetery
Below Reader Head Lookout

Mining Tours

Mt Whaleback Mine Tour Descend into Newman's BHP Mt Whaleback, the world's largest open-cut iron-ore mine, on a 1½-hour tour from Newman visitor centre.

Tom Price From the visitor centre, two-hour tours take you into the bowels of Rio Tinto's huge, open-cut Hamersley iron-ore mine.

Dampier Port Tour Run by the local Mission to Seafarers, these informative (and air-conditioned!) three-hour tours take you behind the scenes of Rio Tinto's Dampier Port operations.

Twilight Industry Tour Get up close with the world's largest bulk-loading port and learn about the mining companies that make Port Hedland tick.

Listings

BEST OF THE REST

Other Beautiful Beaches

Bill's Bay

Bill's Bay is Coral Bay's perfectly positioned town beach. Easy access and sheltered ultramarine waters make this a favourite with everyone from families to snorkellers (keep to the southern end).

Bundegi Beach

Within cycling range of Exmouth, this calm, chilled beach and nearby reef in Exmouth Gulf provide pleasant swimming, snorkelling, diving, kayaking and fishing.

Hearson Cove

A fine pebble beach with calm waters for swimming and a picnic area, Hearson Cove also has great mudflat exploring at low tide and, from March to November, Staircase to the Moon viewing.

Eighty Mile Beach

On the road to Broome is one of the most exquisite and most deserted beaches in the country (once you leave the camping area). And it's way longer than 80 miles.

More Watery Adventures

Glass-Bottom Boats

If you'd like to see the coral, but snorkelling isn't your thing, several companies run one- and two-hour and half-day glass-bottom boat tours out of Exmouth and Coral Bay.

Surfing

Dunes (aka 'Surfers Beach') off Mildura Wreck Rd is Exmouth's favourite break, though the more protected Wobiri south of Vlamingh Head is great for beginners. There's also a bommie out in Lighthouse Bay.

Muiron Islands

Just off the tip of North West Cape, the Muiron Islands contain some excellent dive spots such as Cod Hole and Whalebone and also some great snorkelling. Sadly, the islands suffered extensive coral bleaching in 2024–25.

Lighthouse Bay

There's great diving here at sites such as the Labyrinth, Blizzard Reef and Helga's Tunnels. Operators in Exmouth can take you out.

Art Centres & Galleries

East Pilbara Arts Centre

One of the state's most successful art collectives, Martumili Artists, has a beautiful gallery and workspace in Newman at which to admire the acclaimed, vibrant art of the Martu people.

Courthouse Gallery

More than a gallery, this leafy arts HQ is the centre of all goodness in Port Hedland. Inside are stunning local contemporary and Aboriginal art exhibitions.

CB_TRAVEL/SHUTTERSTOCK

Bill's Bay

NINGALOO COAST & THE PILBARA REVIEWS

Spinifex Hill Studios

This South Hedland studio and gallery has a range of styles, including those of Noongar, Banjima, Innawongka, Martu, Kariyarra, Nyiyaparli and Yamatji Pilbara cultural groups, plus works from the Torres Strait Islands.

Seafood & More

Bill's Bar $$

The courtyard at Bill's in Coral Bay is a fine spot to enjoy fish tacos, the catch of the day, the fabulous fish curry or a bucket of prawns – washed down with a boutique ale.

Social Society $

Everything is vegan or vegetarian and made from local organic ingredients at this Exmouth cafe – from poached eggs with green harissa and Halloumi to the 'bonzai bowl' for brekkie.

Soak $$

Enjoy great seafood and tasty tapas dishes on a deck overlooking Dampier's harbour. Yes, there are burgers too.

Karijini Eco Retreat Restaurant $$

Chefs serve up modern-Australian dishes often accented by bush tucker ingredients (bush tomatoes, wild herbs, wattle seed).

Silver Star Cafe $$

Across from Hedland's Courthouse Gallery is a 1939 Budd Zephyr stainless steel railcar; what better place for an impromptu brunch of diablo king prawns or grilled snapper?

Whalers Restaurant $$

This Exmouth institution has a mega seafood menu (but vegetarians and vegans get some loving too). Bookings recommended.

Craft Beers

Froth Craft Brewery

Party central, this rowdy Exmouth brewery does pale ale, IPA, amber ale and kölsch, as well as your usual burgers, fish tacos and parmies. Rock out to live music.

ZSTOCK/SHUTTERSTOCK

Prawns on ice

Whalebone Brewing Co

This lovely, family-friendly Exmouth courtyard is perfect for lazy Sunday sessions with a Squid Ink Stout, a prawn and pepperoni pizza, and perhaps some live performances.

North West Brewing Co

Order a paddle of six beers to taste this Karratha microbrewery's IPAs, lager and draughts. It also has a full menu of meals and bar snacks to make sure you don't drink on an empty stomach.

Mountains (Sort Of)

Punurrunha (Mt Bruce) **1235m**

In Karijini National Park, a well-marked trail (10km return, four to five hours) leads up to exceptional views from the summit cairn.

Jarndunmunha (Mt Nameless) **1128m**

Rising above Tom Price, this favourite sunset spot makes for a nice 4.5km workout (90 minutes return), or you can drive to the top in a low-range 4WD.

Meharry **1249m**

Getting to WA's highest peak is the adventure on a withering 4WD track out on Juno Downs near Newman. The 45-minute summit walk up a fire trail is an anticlimax.

BROOME & THE KIMBERLEY

SCENERY | ADVENTURE | DISTANCE

RESEARCHED BY STEVE WATERS

- **Beyond Broome** (p212)
- **The Inland Reef** (p214)
- **The Remote Duncan Road** (p216)
- **The Best of the Kimberley** (p218)
- **The Epic Gibb River Road** (p220)
- **Paradise Almost Lost** (p224)
- **Deep in the Kimberley** (p226)
- **Breathless in the Bungle Bungles** (p228)
- **The Best of Broome** (p230)
- **Listings** (p232)

ANJAHENNERN/SHUTTERSTOCK

BROOME & THE KIMBERLEY
Trip Builder

Mention the Kimberley to most Australians and their eyes light up: its remote red rock escarpments are a beloved setting for exploration. Wildly spectacular landscapes, timeless rock art and rich Aboriginal heritage: it's all front and centre here. Most adventures begin in Broome.

Explore natural beauty and Indigenous culture along the **Dampier Peninsula** (p212)
1hr from Broome

Walk the Songlines of the Goolarabooloo along the **Lurujarri Dreaming Trail** (p213)
30min from Broome

Catch that iconic image of camels, sand, sea and sunset at Broome's **Cable Beach** (p231)
10min from Broome

Change gears on the iconic **Gibb River Road** between Derby and Kununurra (p220)
2hr from Broome

SUE_PIX/SHUTTERSTOCK

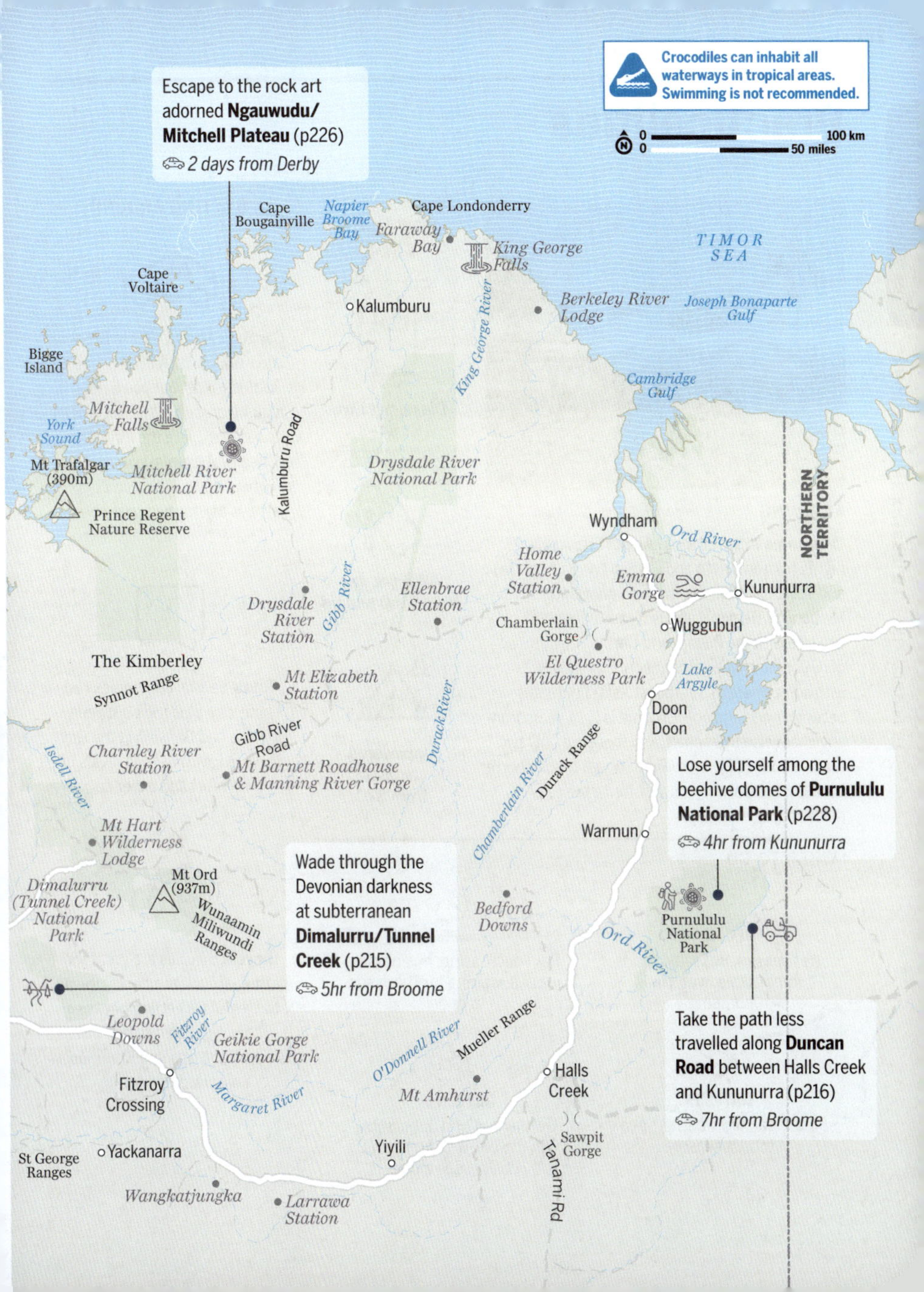
Crocodiles can inhabit all waterways in tropical areas. Swimming is not recommended.
0 100 km
0 50 miles
Escape to the rock art adorned Ngauwudu/ Mitchell Plateau (p226)
2 days from Derby
Lose yourself among the beehive domes of Purnululu National Park (p228)
4hr from Kununurra
Wade through the Devonian darkness at subterranean Dimalurru/Tunnel Creek (p215)
5hr from Broome
Take the path less travelled along Duncan Road between Halls Creek and Kununurra (p216)
7hr from Broome
TIMOR SEA
Joseph Bonaparte Gulf
Cambridge Gulf
Cape Londonderry
Cape Bougainville
Napier Broome Bay
Faraway Bay
King George Falls
Berkeley River Lodge
Cape Voltaire
Kalumburu
King George River
Bigge Island
Mitchell Falls
York Sound
Mt Trafalgar (390m)
Mitchell River National Park
Prince Regent Nature Reserve
Kalumburu Road
Drysdale River National Park
NORTHERN TERRITORY
Wyndham
Ord River
Home Valley Station
Emma Gorge
Kununurra
Wuggubun
Chamberlain Gorge
El Questro Wilderness Park
Lake Argyle
Doon Doon
Drysdale River Station
Gibb River
Ellenbrae Station
The Kimberley
Synnot Range
Mt Elizabeth Station
Durack River
Durack Range
Isdell River
Charnley River Station
Gibb River Road
Mt Barnett Roadhouse & Manning River Gorge
Chamberlain River
Warmun
Mt Hart Wilderness Lodge
Dimalurru (Tunnel Creek) National Park
Mt Ord (937m)
Wunaamin Miliwundi Ranges
Bedford Downs
Purnululu National Park
Ord River
Leopold Downs
Fitzroy River
Geikie Gorge National Park
O'Donnell River
Mueller Range
Fitzroy Crossing
Margaret River
Mt Amhurst
Halls Creek
Sawpit Gorge
St George Ranges
Yackanarra
Yiyili
Tanami Rd
Wangkatjungka
Larrawa Station

Practicalities

ALYBABA/SHUTTERSTOCK

ARRIVING

Broome International Airport has daily flights to/from Perth and Darwin (via Kununurra) and seasonal direct flights to Sydney and Melbourne. Regional airline Nexus connects Broome with the Pilbara and Derby. The number of direct international connections (usually with somewhere in Southeast Asia) fluctuates between none and one. Broome is light years from anywhere else by asphalt, and there are only two roads: south 2000km to Perth or not much shorter northeast to Darwin. Long-distance buses ply these routes.

HOW MUCH FOR A

Diesel per litre $1.84–3

4WD per day from $160 and up

Unpowered campsite from $20

WHEN TO GO

DEC–MAR
Wet season; unsealed roads impassable; waterfalls pumping.

APR
Rain decreasing; businesses reopen, waiting for the roads to open.

MAY–SEP
Fine, clear, dry weather; peak tourist season.

OCT & NOV
Getting hot and unbearable in the pre-Wet 'build-up'. Businesses close.

GETTING AROUND

Car You can rent cars in Broome and Kununurra. A 2WD is fine on sealed roads, but you'll need a high-clearance 4WD (not AWD!) to really explore the Kimberley. Check your rental contract for where you can and can't go; always ask for two spare tyres.

Tours Several companies run nine-day-plus trips between Broome and Darwin via the Gibb River Rd, with varying levels of comfort and expense.

Bicycle Bicycles are great for getting around Kimberley towns but awful for getting between them. You can hire bikes in Broome and at some Kununurra caravan parks.

EATING & DRINKING

Seafood features heavily on Broome menus, and authentic dishes are a fusion of Asian, Indigenous and European influences. Look for Broome-style seafood curries or make your own with spices from Yuen Wing (p234). Barramundi ('barra') is the hero fish in these parts – ensure it's wild caught; you'll taste the difference. The barra burger is the takeaway version, and these can range from sublime to depressingly mediocre. Elsewhere, remember that the Kimberley is cattle country: the steaks are large and plentiful.

Best wild barra burger
Blak Tapas (pictured; p235), Kununurra

Best beer
Chango (chilli/mango) at Matso's Broome Brewery (pictured; p234)

TOP: STEVE WATERS/CONTRIBUTOR, BOTTOM: STEVE WATERS/CONTRIBUTOR

CONNECT & FIND YOUR WAY

Find wi-fi at accommodation, visitor centres and many cafes in urban areas. Phone and wi-fi coverage between towns is minimal.

Don't rely on generic internet maps: they're notoriously inaccurate here. Have a good GPS app (Avenza, Garmin) and back it up with a quality paper map like Hema's *Great Desert Tracks*. Carry a satellite communications device.

WHERE TO STAY

Broome has far and away the biggest range of accommodation, with hostels, camping, caravan parks, motels, B&Bs and resorts. Kununurra has a reasonable selection, but elsewhere the choice is more limited. Some pastoral stations and Aboriginal communities offer rooms in converted shearers' quarters and homesteads along with bush camping.

Place	Pros/Cons
Broome	Lots of choice, but prices can be extortionate during the Dry.
Derby	Small selection of station stays, B&Bs, caravan parks; book ahead in high season.
Kununurra	Lots of choice, with big price swings between Wet and Dry.
Wyndham	A few options, including caravan park, B&B and station stay.

ROAD CONDITIONS

Check the Gibb and Great Northern Hwys at **mainroads.wa.gov.au**. Other minor roads can be checked on shire sites sdwk.wa.gov.au, swek.wa.gov.au, broome.wa.gov.au and hallscreek.wa.gov.au.

MONEY

Broome and the Kimberley are expensive. Try travelling in the shoulder season (April to mid-May, or October), camping and self-catering. Fuel, your biggest expense, is cheapest in Kununurra and eye-wateringly expensive on the Gibb.

47 Beyond BROOME

COAST | COMMUNITIES | CULTURE

Broome can be a destination in its own right, but it's also a great starting point for magical explorations of the Dampier Peninsula. Once you leave the highway, the world and its noise very quickly fade from view. This exceptional Country, wrapped in beaches, bays, headlands and red pindan cliffs, is Broome's best-kept secret.

NHOLAU18/SHUTTERSTOCK

How to

Getting around The Cape Leveque road is sealed for its entire length, but you'll still need a 4WD to visit many of the attractions, which are down sandy, deeply rutted side tracks.

When to go April to October; many places close outside this season.

Top tips A great resource is ardibeyondbroome.com.au. Book all community stays in advance and be aware communities can close suddenly. There is no longer public access to Cape Leveque itself.

PHILIP SCHUBERT/SHUTTERSTOCK

Broome's northern beaches Frequented mainly by anglers, locals and adventurous travellers, unsealed, sandy and usually corrugated Manari Rd runs roughly northwest of Broome through Goolarabooloo Country. Along the way you'll pass lonely beaches, tracking along a coast ripe with ancient dinosaur footprints. At **James Price Point/Walmadan** – whose Indigenous name honours the warrior who once lived here – you can walk the striking red pindan cliffs and feel as though you're standing at the edge of an entire continent. Set 35km from Cape Leveque Rd, Walmadan is right in the middle of the Lurujarri Songline.

Beagle Bay and Lombadina Beagle Bay's church, its mother-of-pearl altar dating from 1918, is definitely worth a look, but the beautiful tree-fringed Bardi community of Lombadina will entice you to linger, with fishing, whale-watching, 4WD, mud-crabbing, kayaking and walking tours. Don't miss the paperbark church and arts centre. Both communities are 2WD accessible.

Middle Lagoon and Gnylmarung Cool off at relaxed Middle Lagoon, a favourite with Broome families, or the even more relaxed Gnylmarung, nearby. Both offer beautiful beaches and protected crescent bays where days easily slip into weeks.

Pender Bay Exquisitely remote, this pristine encircled bay is an important calving ground for humpback whales; many can be seen offshore from May to November. The easiest access is from **Pender Bay Escape**, where Andrew is a font of whale knowledge; from **Smithy's** further down the track; or from **Goombaragin Eco Retreat**.

Left James Price Point/Walmadan
Below Camping, James Price Point/Walmadan

Lurujarri Dreaming Trail

The 82km Lurujarri Dreaming Trail follows a section of ancient Songline north along the coast from Gantheaume Point (Minyirr) to Coulomb Point (Minarriny). Each dry season the local Goolarabooloo people organise several nine-day guided walking trips, staying at traditional camp sites. There's a strong emphasis on sharing Aboriginal culture, with activities like spear-making, bush tucker hunting, fishing, mud-crabbing and native jewellery making.

The Songline (an oral memory map of stories, song and dance describing the landscape, handed down from generation to generation) stretches from Cape Leveque to the deserts south of Broome.

48 The Inland REEF

GORGES | HIKING | CAVES

As difficult as it is to imagine this far from the coast, today's limestone Napier Range was, some 380 million years ago in the Devonian Period, part of a western barrier reef. You can see the remnants of this Devonian reef close up at three small national parks and one intriguing cave system that are well worth the time to explore.

STEVE WATERS/CONTRIBUTOR

How to

Getting here and around Windjana Gorge and Dimalurru (Tunnel Creek) are accessed via 4WD-only Fairfield–Leopold Downs Rd (linking the Great Northern Hwy and Gibb River Rd). Danggu (Geikie Gorge) and Mimbi Caves are 2WD accessible from Fitzroy Crossing.

When to go May to September; parks may close outside this period.

Top tips You can only camp at Windjana and Mimbi. Bring a good torch and decent footwear (not thongs) for Dimalurru.

CATHERINE SUTHERLAND/LONELY PLANET

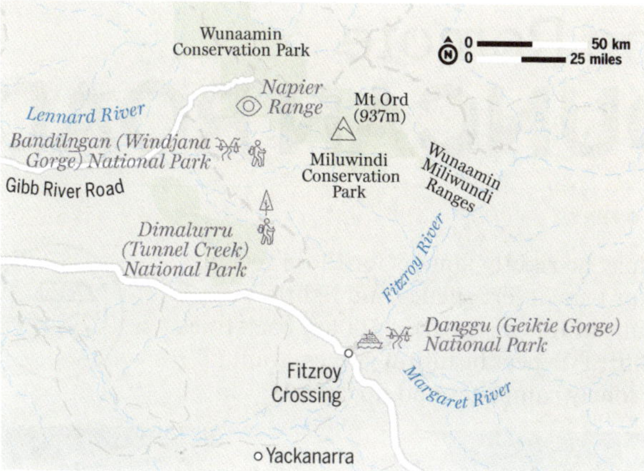

Left Bandilngan (Windjana Gorge)
Below Mimbi Caves

Danggu (Geikie Gorge) The easiest of the national parks to reach was also the most damaged in the Kimberley floods of 2022–23. It reopened in late 2025. There's now only minimal infrastructure, and no tours are presently operating, but you can still visit. The hope is that soon Bunuba-led cultural boat tours will once again traverse the 8km-long, wildlife-rich gorge below those iconic limestone cliffs.

Dimalurru (Tunnel Creek) This underground limestone cavern was carved over millions of years by water flowing under the Napier Range; it gained notoriety as the hideout of the Bunuba warrior Jandamarra. You can wade through the 750m-long cavern providing you have a good torch, as it's pitch black in the middle. There's rock art above the far entrance.

Bandilngan (Windjana Gorge) Stunning 100m cliffs line this gorge above the Lennard River, which contracts to a series of pools in the Dry. Sacred to the Bunuba, the pools are home to numerous freshwater crocodiles that can be spotted from the banks. Swimming is not allowed. There are several walking trails along the cliff base and into the gorge.

Mimbi Caves Lying 95km southeast of Fitzroy Crossing just off the Great Northern Hwy on Gooniyandi land located within Mt Pierre Station, this vast subterranean labyrinth is rich in rock art and fish fossils, and has a cultural heritage spanning 40,000 years. Book through Girloorloo Tours (p233).

Jandamarra's Story

Bunuba land stretches across the southern Kimberley, from Fitzroy Crossing to the Wunaamin Miliwundi (formerly King Leopold) Ranges. Jandamarra was a respected Aboriginal stockman on a local cattle station, and he became friends with an English stockman named Bill Richardson. When Richardson became a police officer, Jandamarra worked as his tracker. The late 19th century was a lawless time on the frontier, and captured Bunuba Elders asked Jandamarra to show his loyalty to his people. He shot Richardson, then waged a three-year guerilla campaign against the police and European settlers. Minko Mick, a police tracker from the Pilbara, shot and killed Jandamarra on 1 April 1897 outside Dimalurru (Tunnel Creek).

49 The Remote DUNCAN ROAD

4WD | EXPLORATION | DISCOVERY

The Gibb River Rd may be rightly famous for those seeking a Kimberley traverse, but for true desert silence and lightly trammelled tracks, take Duncan Rd (pictured), a 500km back track from Halls Creek to Kununurra. Expect beautiful gorges, tranquil billabongs, breathtakingly lonely campsites and no crowds.

JACK KINNY/SHUTTERSTOCK

Freshie or Saltie?

The Kimberley's two crocodile species are the extremely dangerous estuarine (saltwater) crocodile ('saltie'), growing up to 6m long, and the mostly benign freshwater crocodile ('freshie'), with a much narrower snout and a length of less than 3m. Freshies inhabit most inland water but won't attack unless provoked. Salties can be found in both fresh and salt water.

How to

Getting here and around You must have a 4WD; check if your rental company allows you to take the vehicle along this road.

When to go Duncan Rd is usually open, but May to September is easiest due to lower humidity.

What to bring There are no services on the entire unsealed Duncan – carry enough food, water, spare tyres and fuel for at least 600km. Check hallscreek.wa.gov.au for road conditions.

01 Surrounded by low, red sandstone buttresses and dense vegetation, **Palm Springs** is a beautiful, permanent pool on the Black Elvire River, 40km from Halls Creek.

02 The epitome of an outback oasis, **Sawpit Gorge**, 45km from Halls Creek, is encircled by craggy sandstone walls, eucalypts and even the odd sandy beach. It's a quiet, gorgeous spot.

03 At **Purnululu National Park**, spend hours taking in the eastern limits of the incredible Bungle Bungle range on the horizon – it's a view very few travellers see.

04 For much of the route north you'll be playing hide-and-seek with **Western Australia's border** with the Northern Territory. The last 50km before you return to the paved road are in NT.

05 The final stretch takes you past deep-blue **Lake Argyle**, Australia's second-largest reservoir. Watch for prolific birdlife, freshwater crocodiles and isolated marsupial colonies.

FROM LEFT: HEALTHYLAURACOM/SHUTTERSTOCK
TRAVELLING.ABOUT/SHUTTERSTOCK

The Best of the KIMBERLEY

03

01

04

02

05

01 Horizontal Falls
These extraordinary tides gush through narrow coastal gorges in the Buccaneer Archipelago. To the Dambimangari people, they're the Wongudd (creator snake).

02 4WDs
Don't leave home without one. The sealed Great Northern Hwy aside, most Kimberley tracks are rugged without rain and impassable with it.

03 Rock art
The Kimberley region is one of the oldest continuously inhabited lands on earth, and its incredible rock art tells the stories of the ages.

04 Gorges
Nothing screams 'Kimberley!' quite like a rich-red sandstone cliff-face set against the blue of a northern Australian sky.

05 Saltwater crocodiles
Lurking in many a Kimberley body of water, these ancient, fascinating creatures (p216) deserve your respect – never enter the water unless you're sure it's croc-free.

06 Brolgas
Graceful and ungainly in equal measure, the brolga is a classic Aussie bird and re-assuring presence in the

06

07

08

09

10

wetlands and rivers of the Kimberley's interior.

07 Dingoes
The Kimberley's apex predator lopes through undergrowth and across floodplains. It's best seen close to sunrise and sunset.

08 Cattle stations
Cattle stations the size of small European countries stretch across the Kimberley with farmstay accommodation and cattle musters central to outback lore.

09 Boab trees
Bulging at the base and with branches that make it look like it was planted upside down, the boab stands sentinel by many a Kimberley roadside.

10 Waterholes & waterfalls
A cooling oasis in a world of rock and sand: the waterholes and waterfalls here are classics of the Kimberley's escarpment country.

01 IMAGINE EARTH PHOTOGRAPHY/SHUTTERSTOCK, **02** PHILIP SCHUBERT/SHUTTERSTOCK, **03** PAULMICHAELNZ/SHUTTERSTOCK, **04** TOMACROSSE/SHUTTERSTOCK, **05** BINTURONG-TONOSCARPE/SHUTTERSTOCK, © **06** BIRDS COLLECTION/ALAMY STOCK PHOTO, **07** KATBRANCHART/SHUTTERSTOCK, **08** IMAGE PROFESSIONALS GMBH/ALAMY STOCK PHOTO, **09** BMPHOTOGRAPHER/SHUTTERSTOCK, **10** DAVID COWLES/SHUTTERSTOCK

50 The Epic Gibb RIVER ROAD

LANDSCAPES | WATERHOLES | ADVENTURE

On this 660km 4WD journey along Gibb River Rd, a former stock route between Derby and Kununurra, you'll cross rivers, pass beneath fabulous red-sandstone outcrops and see rock art stretching back millennia – all while traversing the glorious Kimberley.

STEVE WATERS/CONTRIBUTOR

How to

The route Start in Derby or Kununurra; both ends of the Gibb are now sealed for about 100km. Don't rush the trip: the detours are the best part.

Tips You'll need a high-clearance, preferably diesel, 4WD with two spare tyres, lots of water and food for a week. Rooms are expensive; camping is the better option. Check road conditions at travelmap.mainroads.wa.gov.au.

When to go May to September; most attractions start closing in October.

RINI KOOLS/SHUTTERSTOCK

Western Gibb

The Western Gibb is a relatively gentle precursor to what lies ahead. You will hardly hit full speed before, 4km out of Derby, you can pull over at **Mowanjum Art & Culture Centre**, where Mowanjum artists recreate Wandjina and Gwion Gwion images (p227). At the 119km mark the first of the Gibb's enticing detours, to **Bandilngan** (Windjana Gorge), branches away to the south. The popular gorge has a waterhole surrounded by a sandy beach, boulders and sandstone cliffs.

The revitalised **Mount Hart Wilderness Lodge** lies 50km north along a scenic road deep in the Wunaamin Conservation Park. Wash away the dust with an ice-cold beverage and peruse the pizza menu.

CATHERINE SUTHERLAND/LONELY PLANET

Dead Centre

Sadly, the Kimberley floods of 2022–23 severely damaged the tourist infrastructure at AWC's Mornington Wilderness Camp, one of the Gibb's brightest jewels, and it's been closed ever since. Hopefully the Fitzroy River gorges of Sir John and Dimond will be publicly accessible again one day. AWC closed Charnley River at the same time.

Above left Bell Gorge (Dalmanyi; p222)
Above Crossing the Pentecost River, Gibb River Rd
Left Windjana Gorge

One of the Gibb's most popular highlights is beautiful **Bell Gorge (Dalmanyi)**. A spectacular horseshoe-shaped plunge pool beckons below a small waterfall, usually only trickling in the Dry. The 29km detour from the Gibb can be rough, with several deep creek crossings.

Central Gibb

Along the central Gibb, you can grab fuel (diesel only), coffee and a toastie at tiny **Imintji**, which boasts a lovely campground and a tiny arts centre.

A flat stroll from a car park right on the Gibb, superb **Galvans Gorge** has a plunge pool perfect for washing away road dust. See if you can find the protective Wandjina.

If you've blown a tyre, go and see Nev at **Over The Range Repairs**, the only place on the Gibb where you can buy a new one.

Mount Barnett is a great (and actually the last) place to fuel up and grab a burger. You can pay for a welcome swim and/or camp at **Manning Gorge** ($10), 7km behind the roadhouse.

Kalumburu

Nearly 380km north of the Gibb River Rd on Balanggarra Country, isolated Kalumburu is WA's most northerly settlement. It's a picturesque Aboriginal community nestled beneath giant mango trees and coconut palms on the King Edward River. The original Catholic mission is still functioning and has a small museum. There's nearby rock art, a WWII bomber wreck and stunning hour-glass **Wongalala Falls** – with a large, perfectly circular plunge pool, the falls only opened to non-Aboriginal tourists in 2018. A community access fee of $50 is payable at the office. Camping is available at the mission or at several coastal outstations.

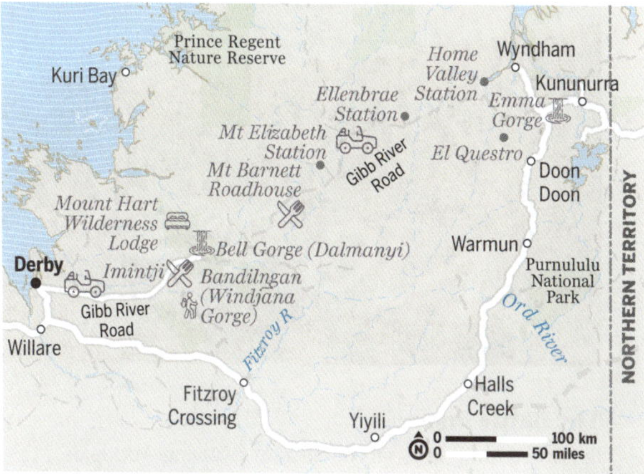

Historic **Mt Elizabeth**, a working cattle station in the heart of the Gibb, has a couple of interesting gorges: **Wunnumurra**, with a small waterfall and rock art, and wide **Warla** on the Hann River, great for swimming. Note that the legendary **Munja Track** is now closed.

Eastern Gibb

The eastern Gibb River Rd is gorgeous, although it's more difficult to escape the crowds here. One exception is the Kalumburu turn-off: take it for an adventure very few experience. (Check your insurance first.)

Along the main track, highlights include the scones at **Ellenbrae Station**, crossing the **Durack River**, and climbing though the **Pentecost Ranges** with panoramic views of the Cockburn Range, Cambridge Gulf and Pentecost River. Pass inviting **Home Valley Station** and cross the **Pentecost** – grabbing the obligatory snap of the rugged **Cockburn Range** in the background – before cliff-lined **El Questro Wilderness Park** looms on the right. While the Gibb is now busy and sealed, **Emma Gorge** is one last piece of magic before you come to the end of your trip: this sublime plunge pool and waterfall is one of the prettiest in the whole Kimberley.

Left Gwion gwion images, Kalumburu
Below El Questro Wilderness Park

FAR LEFT: ANDREW ATKINSON/SHUTTERSTOCK
LEFT: STEVE WATERS/CONTRIBUTOR

Paradise Almost Lost

THE BATTLE FOR JAMES PRICE POINT

Western Australia is a hotly contested frontier when it comes to the environment and mining. This is Australia's richest state for underground resources, but it also has few peers when it comes to natural beauty. When battle lines are drawn between the two, a fascinating story always results.

Left Protest signs, Jame Price Point
Centre Dinosaur footprints
Right Largetooth sawfish

PHILIP SCHUBERT/SHUTTERSTOCK

The Battle Begins

In 2005 a multinational consortium involving Woodside Petroleum, BP, Royal Dutch Shell and others partnered with the Western Australian government to announce plans for the world's biggest liquefied natural gas (LNG) station at James Price Point. It would have been lucrative for the state, providing jobs and tax revenues. But there was more than money at stake.

James Price Point (known to the local Goolarabooloo as Walmadan, for the warrior who once lived there) is a beautiful expanse of red pindan wilderness along the Kimberley coast 60km north of Broome. It has dinosaur fossils dating back 130 million years and is a playground for dolphins, dugongs and breeding bilbies. Humpback whales calve along the coastline, and the monsoon vine thicket backing the coast harbours a multitude of plant species. And, importantly, it was the traditional land of the Goolarabooloo.

Paradise Saved

James Price Point became one of Australia's defining environmental battlegrounds early in the 21st century. On one side was the powerful mining sector, backed by a government eager to show it was open for business. Arrayed against them were environmental groups and the Goolarabooloo people. It was a public relations disaster for the government, with images beamed around the country of local Indigenous peoples and others being forcibly removed by police as the bulldozers moved in.

LIVING ART BY MARGIE/SHUTTERSTOCK

AUSCAPE/GETTY IMAGES

In 2013 the Supreme Court of Western Australia overruled the WA environment minister and the WA Environmental Protection Authority to block the proposed Browse LNG plant at James Price Point. Eight years after proposing the development, Woodside Petroleum Ltd and its coalition partners announced that the refineries were not economically viable.

Their withdrawal was just as well. A 2016 University of Queensland study of the region's Cretaceous footprints concluded that they are the world's largest dinosaur footprint collection, with 21 species represented. The site may also contain the world's largest single dinosaur footprint. In 2017 further sauropod footprints were found here, measuring a massive 1.7m across, breaking the record for 'world's biggest' again. A 2019 Federal Court ruling also confirmed that 93.5% of the Kimberley is now under some form of native title protection.

> James Price Point became one of Australia's defining environmental battlegrounds.

Despite this, and despite the state government's policy to transition to net-zero carbon emissions by 2050, the mining lobby retains a powerful hold over government policy in the West. These interests can still trump the rights of Traditional Custodians and environmental concerns. In late 2021, close to Fitzroy Crossing, the Nyikina Warrwa Traditional Custodians stepped up their campaign to protect the sacred Martuwarra (Fitzroy) River, a habitat for the endangered freshwater sawfish.

In late 2021 it emerged that the WA government has not given up on the idea of an LNG plant, possibly even at James Price Point. The battle, it seems, may not be over yet.

Emu-Man

For many Australians, the very public struggle for the future of James Price Point introduced them for the first time to the remarkable natural heritage of the Dampier Peninsula. Of course, local Aboriginal Jabirr Jabirr and Goolarabooloo peoples have always known about these footprints on the beach: to them, the footprints represent the steps of Emu-man, their Dreaming ancestor, who lives today in the land, the people and their stories. For the moment at least, it's this kind of deep liquid time, rather than liquid natural gas, that won the day.

51 Deep in the KIMBERLEY

CAMPING | HIKING | ROCK ART

Even in the remote Kimberley there's a place considered remoter than most. In the far north, Ngauwudu (Mitchell Plateau) is a time-shrouded land of boab savannahs, lush hidden waterholes and rocky plateaus supporting groves of towering livistona palms. Wildlife and ancient rock art are plentiful, as are the corrugations along the one withering road in. Just getting here is the adventure.

AUSCAPE/UNIVERSAL IMAGES GROUP VIA GETTY IMAGES

How to

Getting here and around You'll need a well-equipped, high-clearance 4WD. Fill up at Drysdale River and check road conditions before setting off. Tours can fly in from Kununurra or Drysdale.

When to go Mitchell River National Park is usually open May or June until September, dependent on road conditions.

Wunambal Gaambera Country Purchase your **Unungu Visitor Pass** (*wunambalgaambera.org.au; 5-day pass adult/family $55/130*) for the **Ngauwudu Road Zone** (Munurru to Mitchell Falls), open April to October.

PHOTO VOLCANO/SHUTTERSTOCK

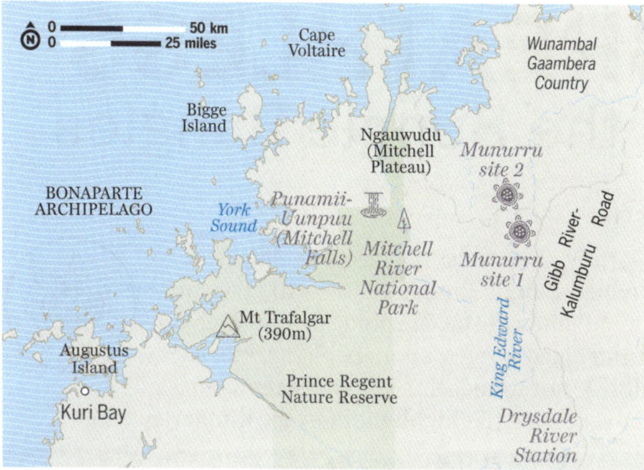

Ancient rock art There's incredible rock art right across the Kimberley, but the two Munurru sites are among the most vibrant and accessible. The first Munurru site has Wandjina and kangaroo depictions at the rear of a clump of sandstone boulders; Wandjina is an arresting and culturally significant rainmaker spirit found across the Kimberley. The second site features the unique Gwion Gwion images; elegant, stylised humanesque figures. Much debate surrounds the dating of the Gwion Gwion paintings, with estimates ranging from 12,000 to 45,000 years old. Both sites are accessed from the **Munurru campground** on the banks of the King Edward River.

The falls beyond time Mitchell River National Park contains the multitiered **Punamii-Uunpuu (Mitchell Falls)**. The easy 8.6km return trail from the dusty Mertens campground meanders through spinifex, woodlands and gorge country dotted with Wandjina and Gwion Gwion rock-art sites, secluded waterholes, goannas, wallabies and brolgas. The falls are stunning, whether trickling in the Dry or raging in the Wet (when they're only visible from the air). You can swim in the long pool above the falls, but swimming in the lower pools is strictly forbidden because of their cultural importance to the Wunambal people. Set out to explore it all early enough in the morning and it will feel like your own personal paradise, especially early or late in the season.

Left Gwion Gwion images
Below Punamii-Uunpuu (Mitchell Falls)

Bushwalking Wunambal Gaambera Country

The Wunambal Gaambera, whose tropical monsoonal lands extend to the west of Kalumburu, have established three riparian bushwalking 'corridors' that are open to hikers between July and October. A permit (wunambalgaambera.org.au; $110) is valid for 14 days along the Munurru (King Edward) River, Yirinni (Hunter) River or Lower Mitchell River. These river systems are rarely walked by whitefellas – you need to be totally self-sufficient and very experienced in hot, remote, off-track walking. Personal locator beacons, sat-phones and insurance covering helicopter evacuation are mandatory. The reward is the trip of a lifetime.

52 BREATHLESS in the Bungle Bungles

WALKING | SCENERY | WILDLIFE

Extreme and otherworldly, the sandstone 'beehive' domes of Purnululu National Park's fabled Bungle Bungle Range will take your breath away. On the traditional lands of the Gija and Jaru people, the orange cliffs, shady palm-fringed gorges, spinifex plains, searing sunsets and abundant wildlife – not to mention the sheer remoteness and inaccessibility – make a visit here the highlight of every Kimberley trip.

STEVE WATERS/CONTRIBUTOR

How to

Getting here It's always half the fun. Expect 53 unsealed, 4WD-only kilometres of pain, creek crossings and unbridled scenery from the asphalt north of Halls Creek.

When to go April to October, though the park could close anytime for heat, fire or floods.

Tips Book campsites online and check exploreparks.dbca.wa.gov.au/park/purnululu-national-park for the latest updates. Bring everything you need, including all fuel, food and water. There's wi-fi at the visitor centre. Don't expect phone reception.

STEVE WATERS/CONTRIBUTOR

STEVE WATERS/CONTRIBUTOR

Left Camping, 1st Finger
Far left: Bungle Bungle Range
Below left Piccaninny Creek

Northern gorges The most popular walk in this area is **Echidna Chasm**, a short scramble (2km return) up a dry creek into a knife-thin slot canyon, the narrow walls radiating various shades of orange against a sliver of sky. The northern highlight is the beautiful and underrated **Mini Palms Gorge**, a livistona palm sanctuary that's a 4.4km return trip from the Bloodwoods picnic area. The walk wanders through open woodland with lovely birdlife and good cliff views before heading into the inner sanctuary, where the vivid greens of the palms contrast against striking orange cliffs and the cloudless blue sky.

Lookouts There are several good vantage points around the park, though **Kungkalanayi** is a favourite at sundown. This central north–south ridge sprouts camp chairs around 4pm as people gather to toast the deepening red walls of the Bungles and the soft dusk glow of spinifex.

Southern gorges Assume action stations: the south is 'beehive central'. For a taster, the **Domes** easy 700m loop track gets you up close to the rock formations, but if you want to snag that classic Purnululu view, then head (with everybody else) to iconic **Cathedral Gorge** (2km return), where a massive orange overhang dwarfs a (usually stagnant) small pool. Escape the crowds by heading further up dry Piccaninny Creek to deserted **Whip Snake Gorge** (10km return). Start as early as possible to beat the heat.

Piccaninny Gorge Trail

This magnificent multiday trek follows the hot, meandering dry bed of **Piccaninny Creek** for several hours into a gorge system with towering orange cliffs, massive boulders and lovely shaded pools. The gorge is entered at the **Elbow**, and subsequent side gorges are labelled 'fingers'. Spring-fed **Black Rock Pool** usually provides drinking water, and there are pleasant campsites by **1st Finger** (13km from the car park). Expect lots of scrambling, and allow at least three days to explore the system. This is true wilderness without signage, amenities or tracks, so you must be familiar with navigating hot, rough terrain. Get permits ($20 per day) from the visitor centre.

53 The Best of BROOME

BEACHES | SUNSETS | FOOD

Broome (or Rubibi in local Yawuru) is like no other Australian town, where the iridescent colours of blue sky, red pindan and turquoise water burn into your brain as your body and soul shift into 'Broome time', where things happen when they feel like it or maybe not at all. Embrace the flow and find your own path.

METRIOGNOME/SHUTTERSTOCK

How to

Getting here and around Well connected by air, Broome is spread out and a long drive from anywhere else. It's too hot to walk far, but you can rent most things with wheels.

When to go Broome is hot and dry (May to September, peak tourist season) or hot and wet.

Off-season deals The town is much more relaxed during the Wet. If you thought sunsets were good from Cable Beach, try watching an electrical storm here.

STEVE WATERS/LONELY PLANET

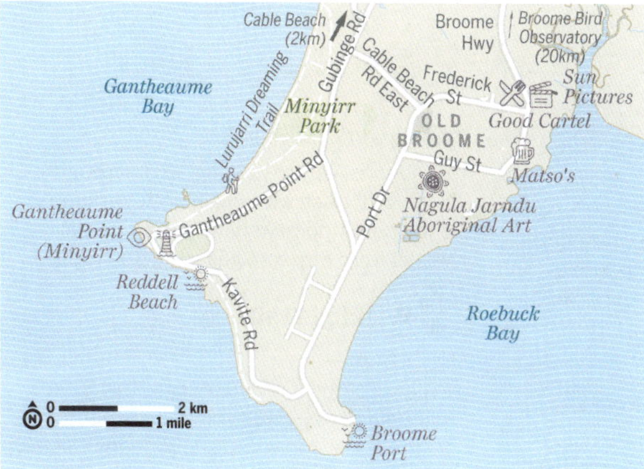

Left Gantheaume Pt/Minyirr
Below Roebuck Bay

The postcard shot Cable Beach's turquoise water, camels, sand and searing Indian Ocean sunset; yep, it's that good. Forget the tourist hordes, just do it once, then come back at sunrise for a swim when the beach is empty.

Sunsets beyond Cable Escape the crowds and watch pindan cliffs turn scarlet above **Reddell Beach**. Nearby, **Gantheaume Point/Minyirr** is beautiful at dawn or dusk. Not far away, and only visible at very low tides, is a 130-million-year-old secret: one of the world's most varied collections of **dinosaur footprints** *(visitbroome.com.au/see-and-do/dinosaurfootprints)*. Walking trails also lead through the red dunes of **Minyirr Park**, a spiritual place for the Yawuru people.

Nature's show The RAMSAR-recognised tidal mudflats of Roebuck Bay by the **Broome Bird Observatory** are where thousands of migratory birds, coming from as far away as Siberia, stop to rest and feed. It's a spectacular sight in a peaceful coastal setting.

Broome's story Yawuru local Johani Mamid of **Mabu Buru Broome Aboriginal Tours** *(broomeaboriginaltours.com.au)* runs excellent cultural tours in and around Broome, covering everything from the history of Broome and the lands here before the arrival of Europeans to indigenous bush foods.

The big screen Broome has a wonderfully retro feel at times, nowhere more so than at **Sun Pictures**, the world's oldest operating picture gardens, having opened in 1916. If only these walls could talk: the Sun building has witnessed war, floods, low-flying aircraft and racial segregation.

My Best of Broome

Broome has a unique vibe where remote outback Australia meets a laid-back beach town. Start your day with a killer coffee and breakfast bowl at **Good Cartel** (p235), then head to **Cable Beach** before the tourists.

The **Broome Bird Observatory** is a world-class destination if you're a birder or just love nature. Rent some binoculars there and roam the mangroves and pindan cliffs of Roebuck Bay.

There's plenty of great art galleries, but the standout for me is **Nagula Jarndu** (p232): the women there specialise in textiles, and I have a bunch of their screen-printed fabrics hanging up at home.

A Chango or two on the verandah at **Matso's** (p234) makes a great finish.

■ **Hamish McAlpine**
Kimberley Fire Manager, who's been lucky enough to work across most of its truly stunning places.

Listings

BEST OF THE REST

Written Words

Magabala Books

Broome's brilliant Indigenous publishers showcase Kimberley storytelling with a selection of novels, social history books, biographies and children's literature.

Kimberley Bookshop

Holds an eclectic collection of Kimberley stories – pearling, pioneers, cattlemen, WWII history – as well as natural history guides, recipes and bush tucker resources.

Art Cooperatives

Mangkaja Arts

Fitzroy Crossing collective uniting river and desert artists; known for a mix of bright acrylics, dot style and forays into printmaking, textiles and basket weaving.

Nagula Jarndu Women's Resource Centre

Broome studio gallery run by Yawuru women; showcases and sells beautiful screen- and block-printed textiles and other crafts.

Bidyadanga Artists

Brings together inspiration from the desert to the coast. Five language groups create acrylic artworks in WA's largest Aboriginal community, two hours down the coast from Broome.

Warmun Arts

Inspect traditional ochres and learn how each is used at this arts centre in the Great Northern Hwy community of Warmiun between Kununurra and Halls Creek.

Waringarri Aboriginal Arts

Kununurra centre hosting artists from the East Kimberley working in both traditional and contemporary styles. It also stocks works from Kira Kiro gallery in Kalumburu.

Walking Trails

Jetty to Jetty Trail

Created by local Yawuru people, this 3.4km self-guided trail takes you along Broome's Roebuck Bay foreshore and includes 13 stops at historical and cultural sites of significance. Download the Jetty to Jetty app to hear stories told by local Elders.

Joonjoo Botanical Trail

This 2.3km trail through Derby begins opposite the Gibb River Rd turn-off and has neat interpretive displays by the Nyikina people. It's a fascinating introduction to local ethno-botanical traditions.

Mirima National Park

Looking like a mini Bungle Bungles, the 'lost world' rock formations of Kununurra's Mirima NP are easily explored on several short trails with interpretive signage. The longest, a 5km circuit, takes 1½ hours.

PORTADOWN/SHUTTERSTOCK

Cable Beach

Amalia Gorge

On El Questro, a lovely riparian walk (3km return, two hours) heads upstream on rock slabs by dry waterfalls into a narrowing gorge that culminates in a beautiful plunge pool.

Paddling

Broome Adventure Company

Glide past turtles, hidden beaches and sea caves on these eco-certified coastal kayaking trips. It's a wonderful way to explore the superb coastline near Broome, free of crowds and all engine noise.

Go Wild

Undertake your own self-guided canoe trip (all gear provided) on the Ord River between Lake Argyle and Kununurra, with overnight stays at purpose-built camps along the riverbank. Allow three days to explore the river and nearby sights.

First Nations Tours

Mimbi Caves

Gooniyandi-owned Girloorloo Tours runs two-hour cultural trips through the subterranean labyrinth of Mimbi Caves, part of the ancient Devonian reef (p214). Tours include an introduction to local Dreaming stories, bush tucker and traditional medicines.

Luridgii Tours

Be guided through the gorges, thermal pools and Dreaming stories of Miriuwung Country by the Traditional Custodians on these 4WD cultural tag-alongs starting from Doon Doon Roadhouse. Also has cultural awareness tours.

Southern Cross Cultural Tours

Take an inspiring journey through Bardi Jawi culture and the mangroves, paperbark forests, salt plains, creeks and springs of the Dampier Peninsula.

JOHN CLUTTERBUCK/GETTY IMAGES

Gantheaume Pt/Minyirr, Broome

Uptuyu Adventures

Down in Nyikina Country on the Fitzroy River, 50km from the Great Northern Hwy, Neville runs cultural tours taking in wetlands, rock art, fishing and Aboriginal communities.

Kimberley Dreamtime Adventure Tours

Jarlmadangah Burru runs cultural tours based in Nyikina Mangala Country on Mt Anderson Station, 126km southeast of Derby. Camp under the stars, ride camels, fish, hunt, walk and learn about Aboriginal culture.

Waringarri Art & Culture Tours

Receive a Welcome to Country, explore bush foods and meet local artists on these informative 90-minute gallery tours in Kununurra. The 2½-hour culture tours around Mirima National Park are exceptional.

Just Over the Hills

These Balanggarra family-run 4WD tag-along tours showcase local culture and rock art in the remote northeastern Kimberley. Your 4WD needs to be in top condition.

Bundy's Cultural Tours

Bush tucker, bush medicine, spear-making and night fishing: they're all possible under the guidance of Bundy, a Bardi man who runs tours along the Dampier Peninsula.

Scenic Flights

Broome Aviation

Half-day flights over Cape Leveque and the Horizontal Falls from Broome. Full-day tours add Windjana Gorge, Bell Gorge and Mt Hart, Mitchell Falls or even the Bungle Bungles.

Fly Broome

Flies a loop from Broome out over the Dampier Peninsula and Buccaneer Falls to the Horizontal Falls, then lands at Cygnet Bay for a meal and pearl farm tour.

Horizontal Falls Seaplane Adventures

Operating out of Derby, these seaplanes land on Talbot Bay, where you'll transfer to high-powered speedboats for an adrenaline-packed ride through both sets of the Horizontal Falls.

HeliSpirit

The Kimberley's largest chopper outfit offers scenic flights over the Bungle Bungles, Mitchell Falls, Kununurra, King George Falls, Lake Argyle and anywhere else in the Kimberley.

Kimberley Dining

Papá Fuego $$

South American parilla in old Broome doing killer cocktails and the best meat dishes in town. Garlic prawns, rack of lamb and a glass of carménère – it doesn't get any better!

Johnny Sausage $$

You need to try Johnny's breakfast pasta at least once. You can also play it safe with baked eggs or ricotta hotcakes. It's inside Broome's Mangrove Hotel.

PumpHouse $$$

Enjoy a chilled beverage and tasty share plates as you watch the sun set over the Ord River from the deck of Kununurra's best restaurant.

Sampey Meats $

Carnivores can stock up for the Gibb with homemade jerkies, biltong and vacuum-sealed steaks at this excellent Derby butcher.

Wild Mango $

Hip and healthy offerings here in Kununurra include breakfast burritos, salads, pancakes, chai smoothies, strong coffee and homemade gelato.

Yuen Wing $

The best spice shop between Perth and Darwin is in Broome's Chinatown.

Wyndham Oasis $

Wyndham's only nosh house does a very respectable barra burger and just about everything else from tacos to parmas.

Wharf $$$

Whether it's tapas-style tasting plates or locally inspired mains, the seafood here behind Cable Beach is exceptional; try the barra wings and a Malay seafood curry or chilli crab.

Best Brews & Distills

Matso's Broome Brewery

There's only one order to kick things off here: a Chango (50/50 chilli/mango beer) and a smoked-croc souva (crocodile souvlaki). Live music on the veranda most afternoons.

STEVE WATERS/CONTRIBUTOR

Wyndham Oasis

Broome Closet

Love the name, love the cocktails – but watch out for that green-ant negroni!

Moontide Distillery

In Broome's Bilingurr, Moontide combines monsoonal Kimberley rainwater and native botanicals in its signature gins. Tastings and tours available.

Hoochery Distillery

Rum in the Kimberley sun – what could possibly go wrong? Out of Kununurra on Weabber Plains Rd, the tasting paddles will have you flying, with the generous steak sanga the perfect booze sponge.

Coffee & Cold Drinks

Good Cartel

Eat in or drive through early for excellent coffee and moreish breakfast rice bowls, then return for some serious dandan noodle lunch action at this Broome favourite.

Bay Club

The Mangrove Hotel's casual outdoor bar is perfect for a few early bevvies while contemplating Roebuck Bay. Filling bistro meals and live music complement excellent Staircase to the Moon viewing (p21).

Blak Tapas

Kimberley coffee, iced teas, mango smoothies, a killer barra burger and poke bowls are the hero offerings at this Indigenous-owned cafe and catering company complete with shady courtyard in downtown Kununurra.

Chi Mayi Kitchen

The fresh juices at this shady back-alley courtyard in Broome's Chinatown will take the sting out of Broome's midday sun. The barra tacos aren't bad either.

JASON KNOTT/ALAMY STOCK PHOTO

Matso's Broome Brewery

Station Stays

Home Valley Station

Leave the privations of the Gibb behind by pulling into Home Valley Station near the Pentecost Crossing, a hospitality training resort for young Balanggarra.

Ellenbrae Station

Some 70km east of the Kalumburu turn-off, the sign on the dusty Gibb proclaiming fresh scones is not a mirage: it heralds an Ellenbrae tradition. There are also quirky accommodation options.

Mt Elizabeth Station

This historic working cattle station bang in the heart of the Gibb has great bush camping, some motel-style rooms, several exploration-worthy gorges and a much-appreciated bar. Book ahead for the nightly communal dinner.

Drysdale River Station

Set 59km from the Gibb, Drysdale River is your last chance for fuel, meals, tyre repairs and a bed if you're heading to Ngauwudu (Mitchell Plateau). Check road conditions while munching an epic burger.

Practicalities

ARRIVING 238

GETTING AROUND 240

SAFE TRAVEL 242

MONEY 243

ACCOMMODATION 244

RESPONSIBLE TRAVEL 246

ESSENTIALS 248

Right Piccaninny Creek, Purnululu National Park (p229)

EASY STEPS FROM THE AIRPORT TO THE CITY CENTRE

Most domestic and international travellers arrive through Perth Airport, 16km east of the city. Check your ticket carefully as terminals T1 and T2 are on one side of the runway and T3 and T4 are on the other; you'll need to take the shuttle bus (free, every 20 minutes) to transfer between the two sides. Unless you're flying with Qantas, you'll probably be arriving at T1/T2.

AT THE AIRPORT

SIM CARDS You'll have more choice if you wait to buy a SIM in the city centre, and **Telstra** *(telstra.com.au)* has much wider mobile-phone coverage across WA than **Optus** *(optus.com.au)* and **Vodafone** *(vodafone.com.au)*, both of which have shops in Perth's international arrivals hall.

WI-FI There's fast, free wi-fi at Perth Airport; coverage reaches the T1/T2 train station, bus stops and Uber/taxi pickup points.

TENGKU MOHD YUSOF/ALAMY

CHARGING STATIONS Most dining areas and departure lounges have charging stations; bring an international adaptor.

ATMS All terminals have ATMs that accept foreign cards. Locate them via Perth Airport terminal maps *(perthairport.com.au)*.

CURRENCY EXCHANGE
There are several Travelex exchange counters at Perth Airport. Rates are generally comparable to those of the banks and forex bureaux in the city centre, and you may even be able to negotiate for a slightly better rate for large amounts and major currencies.

WHICH TERMINAL?

T1 International	All international flights (except Qantas)
T1 Domestic	Virgin Australia
T2	Jetstar, Rex, Nexus, regional WA
T3 & T4	Qantas (including international), Airnorth

GETTING TO THE CITY CENTRE

Train From T1/T2's Airport Central station trains to Perth take 18 minutes and cost around $5.

Bus and train From T3/T4 take loop bus 292 to Redcliffe Station; then it's a 15-minute trip to Perth.

Taxi/rideshare Trips take 20 to 30 minutes; fares start at around $50.

JAVIER CATANO GONZALEZ/SHUTTERSTOCK

HOW MUCH FOR A

Bus
$4.90
40min

Shuttle bus
$18–24
20–30min

Taxi
from $45
15–20min

SmartRider Card Available at T1's Smart Carte, most newsagents and Transperth InfoCentres; you'll save 10% on local public transport and ride free on Sunday.

Contactless fares You can use your credit card or digital wallet to tap on/off, but you will pay the full fare.

Border quarantine It's illegal to bring certain food, including fresh fruit, vegetables, raw prawns or honey, into WA regardless of whether you're on an international or domestic flight or driving from interstate. The Eyre and Victoria Hwys have border checkpoints, and your vehicle will be searched. There's usually a nearby picnic table for one last cook-up.

OTHER POINTS OF ENTRY

Cruise ships The Victoria Quay passenger terminal is in Fremantle, 18km southwest of Perth. Free shuttles to nearby Fremantle station meet each ship or you can walk there in 15 minutes. A train to Perth takes 30 minutes.

Interstate by air Other than the direct Melbourne–Margaret River (Busselton) Jetstar service three times a week and a daily Airnorth service from Broome and Kununurra to Darwin, the only other interstate direct flights not via Perth are Qantas' dry season (May to September) flights between Broome and Sydney/Melbourne.

Interstate by road Although several rugged desert tracks cross into WA from the Northern Territory and South Australia, there are only two paved roads. In the south the epic Eyre Hwy runs across the Nullarbor Plain from SA's Port Augusta to Norseman (around 1660km). Up north, the Victoria Hwy between NT's Katherine and Kununurra is a much lovelier 515km stretch of tarmac.

Interstate by train The gilded Indian Pacific runs weekly from East Perth across the entire continent to Sydney's Central, providing a 'tourism experience' rather than just a mode of transport. This luxurious cruise on rails takes five days.

TRANSPORT TIPS TO HELP YOU GET AROUND

Welcome to the land of the road trip. This is one place you really need your own wheels. North and inland the distances are vast; if you have limited time, consider doing a loop from Perth (north or south), where a 2WD will suffice, then fly to Broome and rent a 4WD for the Kimberley.

NORTH WEST COASTAL HWY
The main coast road north is sealed, well maintained and good for driving, with roadhouses at regular intervals, though don't expect a dual-lane carriageway or actually catching sight of the coast. The asphalt traverses very sparse country at the edges of deserts.

GREAT NORTHERN HWY
The main alternative to the coastal highway is the inland, mining-heavy Great Northern connecting Perth with Port Hedland, after which it continues to Broome and all the way to Wyndham in the East Kimberley. At almost 3200km, it's Australia's longest named road.

HOW MUCH FOR A

4WD (ute) rental per day: from A$155, more for one with a rooftop tent and camping gear

Diesel (Broome) per litre $2.07

Perth to Geraldton bus fare: about $75

4WD RENTAL When renting a 4WD, read the contract carefully. Ensure you get unlimited kilometres and two spare tyres. Check where you can and can't go: some companies restrict their 4WDs to the asphalt or to certain tracks. If renting in Broome or Kununurra, the Gibb River Rd (p220) should be fine, but Kalumburu probably won't be. Every rental car has a satellite tracker. If you void your contract conditions, you'll also void your insurance and possibly your deposit.

BUS A 3000km hop-on, hop-off bus pass from **Integrity Coaches** (*integritycoachlines.com.au/hop-on-off*) will get you to Broome via most coastal attractions (with connecting shuttles) or more quickly via the inland route. **TransWA** (*transwa.wa.gov.au*) is the main player south and east of Perth.

ELECTRIC VEHICLES Several companies rent electric vehicles in Perth, but whether you should take one on a road trip is another matter (even if you're allowed to). EV-charging companies spruik their 'EV highway' from Perth to Kununurra, but the infrastructure still lacks resilience, beset with breakdowns and vandalism.

DRIVING ESSENTIALS

Drive on the left; the steering wheel is on the right.

.05 Blood alcohol limit 0.05.

50 Speed limit from 50km/h in built-up areas to 110km/h in rural areas.

Slow down at floodways; the road will dip and might have water on it.

Take notice of 'Next fuel ... km' signs.

CHAMELEONSEYE/SHUTTERSTOCK

HAZARDS Road trains (articulated trucks stretching over 50m long), require careful overtaking.

If a police vehicle drives down the middle of the road with its lights flashing, pull over; a massive mining machine is heading your way.

Unfenced cattle, camels, donkeys, pigs and every flavour of jumping marsupial love being on the road at night. Do not drive at night, ever.

RELOCATE BY CAMPER A cheap way of getting between cities (eg Broome and Darwin) is with a rental-camper relocation. Typically you'll get a set number of days and kilometres for the trip, and you'll have to stay on sealed roads and avoid night driving. Look for deals online.

ROAD CONDITIONS Make a habit of checking road condition reports at **WA Main Roads** *(travelmap.mainroads.wa.gov.au)* and the local shires you'll be passing through, such as **East Kimberley** *(swek.wa.gov.au)* or **West Kimberley** *(sdwk.wa.gov.au)*. Roads can close anytime due to flash flooding, bushfires, accidents or maintenance work.

KNOW YOUR CARBON FOOTPRINT
A domestic flight from Perth to Broome would emit about 629kg of carbon dioxide per passenger. A bus would emit 60kg for the same distance, per passenger, while a normal car would emit 420kg (that's for the whole car, not per passenger).

ROAD DISTANCE CHART (KM)

	Perth	Margaret River	Albany	Geraldton	Denham	Exmouth	Port Hedland	Broome	Halls Creek
Margaret River	270								
Albany	418	343							
Geraldton	419	683	821						
Denham	823	1092	1229	408					
Exmouth	1249	1516	1654	833	683				
Port Hedland	1633	1906	1978	1339	1190	780			
Broome	2224	2498	2567	1930	1780	1370	612		
Halls Creek	2839	3113	3184	2546	2396	1987	1228	684	
Kununurra	3197	3472	3542	2904	2755	2345	1583	1044	358

SAFE TRAVEL

West Coast Australia is normally a safe destination; crime rates are comparatively low. Thefts are usually opportunistic; don't leave vehicles unlocked, even when filling them with fuel, and safeguard all possessions. International travellers are statistically more likely than locals to have a road accident.

SAFE SWIMMING International travellers and migrants are more likely than locals to drown in Australia. Most of the WA coast is not patrolled; ensure you know how to recognise a rip (undertow) and what to do if caught in one. Don't swim in muddy water, and never dive into unknown rivers or waterholes.

CROCS & STINGERS Assume all bodies of water in the Kimberley contain crocodiles (p216). Never swim anywhere unless you're reasonably sure salties aren't present. Stinging Irukandji and box jellyfish can be found anywhere north of Coral Bay between November and April and can cause severe reactions, even death. Wear a stinger suit. In the south, southern stingers and bluebottles cause milder irritation.

SNAKES WA has its fair share of the world's most venomous reptiles. Avoid walking around camp in open footwear at night (when many snakes are active), especially in the north. Snakes in the south are particularly feisty in spring after their winter dormancy. Always carry an inexpensive snake bandage when hiking, and know what to do with it.

Safer Driving Always carry spare fuel, food, water and tyres. Roads can close quickly for any number of reasons. Don't speed on unsealed roads, where it's much easier to lose control. Don't rely on internet maps (p211).

Bushfires Wildfires can happen anytime in WA but are at their most devastating in summer in the south and near the end of the Dry in the north. Don't light campfires during total fire bans.

FLOODING

From November to April, tropical low-pressure systems are possible along the coast between Exmouth and Kununurra. Some may develop into cyclones, but most will bring rainfall triggering flooding and road closures. Rains can wash away unsealed roads, and many such roads and tracks will be closed for up to six months every year. Never drive through floodwaters.

QUICK TIPS TO HELP YOU MANAGE YOUR MONEY

CREDIT CARDS Widely accepted, credit cards are essential for hiring a car and booking tours or accommodation. You can request cash advances over the counter at banks and from scarce ATMs, though you'll incur immediate interest. Charge cards (Diners Club, Amex) are not very useful outside five-star hotels. If travelling into the outback, carry cash for emergencies in case cards aren't accepted.

TIPPING

All Australian hospitality workers should receive a mandated minimum wage, so tipping is not expected, though it's common to round up a bill and leave the change.

ATMS

ATMs are on the decline across WA thanks to the rise in digital payments. If you can't find an ATM in a small town, try the local supermarket and ask for an eftPOS withdrawal.

CURRENCY

Australian dollar

HOW MUCH FOR A

Cup of coffee (Perth) $5.50

Pint of beer (Perth) from $11

Fish and chips for two (Perth) $30–50

SPLITTING THE BILL

A popular Australian dining phenomenon is when a group asks to split the bill (so each person only pays for what they individually consumed). Restaurants hate this practice as it's time-consuming, hence the 'no split bills' tag on some menus. If needed, ask for an 'itemised bill' and distribute costs at the table instead.

CHANGING MONEY Changing foreign currency is rarely a problem at banks and licensed moneychangers such as Travelex in Perth or Broome.

CARD SURCHARGES

You get the bill, pay with your card, then notice you've been charged slightly more than agreed. Welcome to the murky world of card surcharges, where vendors try to stick you for their bank costs, a soon-to-be-outlawed practice.

CASH

Covid hastened the demise of cash, and most businesses across the state now accept contactless payments. You'll even find vendors in far-flung markets proffering digital readers. Just keep cash handy for when comms are down.

DEBIT & TRAVEL CARDS

A debit card allows you to draw money from your home bank account. Any card connected to the international banking network (Cirrus, Maestro, Plus and Eurocard) should work with your PIN, but expect substantial fees.

Companies such as Wise, Revolut and Travelex offer travel cards in a number of currencies with minimal or zero transaction fees, but there are rules regarding top-ups and usage.

Always carry extra cash for when your card doesn't work or when only cash is accepted.

UNIQUE & LOCAL WAYS TO STAY

Perth, the South West and Broome have by far the largest and most varied selection of places to stay. Elsewhere, options are likely to include motels, caravan parks, national park campgrounds and possibly a pub, town apartment, B&B or roadhouse donga. While there are true boutique resorts in some beautiful off-grid locations, the term 'resort' is often commandeered by massive generic holiday parks.

HOW MUCH FOR A

National park campsite from $15 per person

Glamping tent $150–450 for two

Motel $135–240 for a double room

ELLINNUR BAKARUDIN/SHUTTERSTOCK

CARAVAN PARKS

The caravan park is a quintessentially Australian travel experience. If you're towing your own caravan or driving a camper van, you'll have a choice of powered or unpowered sites. Most caravan parks also have campsites for those with their own tent and some degree of on-site cabins for rent. The better ones have lots of shade, a swimming pool and a children's playground. They're great places to meet other travellers, including Australia's transitory army of grey nomads, who stay for weeks before moving on. Bookings are essential in high season.

AUSSIE MOTELS

The roadside motel is an Aussie classic imported from the US. Most are serviceable and without a whole lot of character but fine for the night. Others rise above their humble origins and a few are downright quirky. All have en suite bathrooms and some have a swimming pool and/or attached restaurant.

NICK RAINS/GETTY IMAGES

GLAMPING

Luxury safari-style tents offer proper beds, open-air en suites, verandas and lighting. They can be perfectly lovely or hideously overpriced and stuffy, as most don't have air conditioning. You'll find them on properties across the South West, on national park tourism concessions, at station stays, on the Dampier Peninsula and along the Gibb River Rd.

BILL BACHMAN/ALAMY STOCK PHOTO

STATION STAYS

A whole world of legend swirls around the Australian cattle station, and WA certainly has its fair share of vast, working pastoral leases where cattle roam across areas larger than some small European countries. As cattle markets fluctuate, a growing number of stations are turning to tourism to supplement their incomes, and it's possible to stay overnight and catch a glimpse of a much-loved Australian way of life.

Accommodation varies from shared digs in converted former shearers' quarters to more luxurious rooms in the homesteads that once were (or still are) the headquarters of outback station life. Some offer secluded bush camping areas, while others have invested in modern glamping setups. You're usually able to get a meal (and possibly a drink) and sit around the campfire swapping stories with strangers. If you're lucky your station might also offer activities showcasing daily routines, including the seasonal mustering (corralling) of cattle in preparation for transport to cities and export markets. You'll also probably meet the young jack- and jillaroos, trainee station hands from across the world.

You'll find station stays scattered across the northern hinterland, but they're especially common in the Kimberley along the Gibb River Rd and in the Pilbara, Murchison and Ningaloo areas.

BOOKING

Advance booking is always recommended. In Perth you'll always find something year-round, but book as early as you can for anywhere north of Geraldton from June to September. Many places in the Kimberley close entirely from October to April.

parkstay.dbca.wa.gov.au Most national park campgrounds must be prebooked; do so here.

WikiCamps app Loved by free campers; always ensure you're not camping on private land.

Booking.com Free cancellations and competitive pricing; good for finding rooms when none appear available.

australiasnorthwest.com/places-to-stay Great list of places across the Kimberley and Pilbara regions from top-end resorts to campgrounds and stations.

australiassouthwest.com The resource for WA's South West.

australiascoralcoast.com/plan/accommodation Good for Exmouth and Ningaloo.

destinationperth.com.au/places-to-stay The go-to for the capital.

Camps Australia (campsaustraliawide.com) A handy app with maps and information about campgrounds across Australia.

Farmstay Camping Australia (farmstayaustralia.com.au) and **WA Station Stays** (wastationstays.com.au) list some, but not by no means all, station stays.

FAMILY STAYS

Across West Coast Australia, every town has at least one caravan park and one motel, many with a swimming pool. Rooms or cabins often have interconnecting rooms that are ideal for families.

RESPONSIBLE TRAVEL

Tips to leave a lighter footprint, support local and have a positive impact on local communities.

ON THE ROAD

Aboriginal-owned businesses Wherever possible, seek out Aboriginal-owned and -run tours and businesses. Refer to waitoc.com for an expansive list.

Electric vehicles Car-rental companies are increasingly offering electric vehicles for hire. Charging stations are still a little thin on the ground north of Perth (see p240), but it's certainly an option in and around Perth and the South West.

Buy from the artist When purchasing Aboriginal art, always make sure that proceeds from the sale will go direct to the artist. Aboriginal-owned and -run art centres and cooperatives are the best places to make your purchase.

Car pooling If you plan on driving, consider getting together with other travellers to share a vehicle. It's a fun way to meet other people and is likely to help you go further; it also reduces each person's individual carbon footprint from the excursion.

BENOIT CAPPRONNIER/ALAMY

GIVE BACK

Broome opportunities Volunteer conservation postings are offered by Roebuck Bay Working Group, Broome Bird Observatory and Environs Kimberley.

Parks and Wildlife Service *(dbca.wa.gov.au)* Opportunities at national parks all over WA, from turtle tagging at Ningaloo to campground hosting at Windjana Gorge or track maintenance in the South West.

Gabyon Station *(gabyon.com.au)* This working sheep station accepts volunteers as part of the World Wide Opportunities on Organic Farms (WWOOF) program. Participants do a few hours of work each day in return for bed and board.

Australian Wildlife Conservancy *(australianwildlife.org/support-us/volunteer)* Be a campground host or help with wildlife censuses, weeding and supporter events at sanctuaries across WA and remote Australia.

Monkey Mia Conservation Park Work with the famous dolphins (p174).

DOS & DON'TS

Don't try playing the didgeridoo if you're female; in WA it's culturally men's business.

Do keep a respectful distance from wildlife, including while diving or snorkelling.

Don't take photos in Indigenous communities without permission, and dress modestly, covering your shoulders.

Don't look Aboriginal people in the eye while they're talking; listen and only shake hands if offered.

LEAVE A SMALL FOOTPRINT

Engine-free activities Wherever possible, hike, kayak or cycle to explore your natural surroundings. Take tours that aim for low or zero carbon emissions through their activities.

Carry out the trash Always carry out everything, including rubbish, that you bring into natural areas.

Clean your shoes If hiking anywhere in southwestern WA (especially Stirling Range National Park), clean your shoes and all other equipment to prevent the spread of an introduced fungus known as Phytophthora dieback; the fungus can be devastating for vegetation elsewhere.

ENTHUSIASTICPHOTOGRAPHERS/SHUTTERSTOCK

SUPPORT LOCAL

Buy local Buy locally made products and souvenirs, and buy direct from local producers where possible.

Eat local Avoid the chains and try the smaller locally run cafes and restaurants. Ask where the food you're about to order is coming from.

Drink local WA produces so much excellent wine and beer that you don't need to drink anything imported.

CLIMATE CHANGE & TRAVEL

Lonely Planet urges all travellers to engage with their travel carbon footprint, which will mainly come from air travel. While there often isn't an alternative, travellers can look to minimise the number of flights they take, opt for newer aircrafts and use cleaner ground transport, such as trains.

One proposed solution—purchasing carbon offsets—unfortunately does not cancel out the impact of individual flights. While most destinations will depend on air travel for the foreseeable future, for now, pursuing ground-based travel where possible is the best course of action.

The UN Carbon Offset Calculator shows how flying impacts a household's emissions:

The ICAO's carbon emissions calculator allows visitors to analyse the CO2 generated by point-to-point journeys:

RESOURCES

aachwa.com.au/art-and-art-centres

indigenousartcode.org

noongarculture.org.au

dbca.wa.gov.au

ecotourism.org.au

ESSENTIAL NUTS & BOLTS

PUBLIC TOILETS
The **National Public Toilet Map** *(toiletmap.gov.au)* has public toilet locations, including accessible toilets.

PHONE COVERAGE
Telstra has the widest mobile (cell) phone coverage, including most of the coast and some inland highways. Expect no coverage once you leave the tarmac.

GST TAX REFUND
You may be eligible for a refund of the GST component of large purchases. Find out more about the Tourist Refund Scheme (TRS) at abf.gov.au.

FAST FACTS

Time Zone
GMT+8 hrs

Country Code
61

Electricity
230V/50Hz

GOOD TO KNOW

The legal drinking age is 18.

Australia has a three-prong socket (it is different to the British one). Bring an adaptor.

Australia uses the metric system.

All visitors to Australia need a visa, except New Zealanders. For more information and to apply online, visit homeaffairs.gov.au.

ACCESSIBLE TRAVEL

Air travel Qantas offers discounted economy fares to people with disabilities and who have high-support needs, as well as to the carer travelling with them. Guide dogs travel free on Qantas, Jetstar, Virgin Australia and their affiliated carriers. Western Australia's major airports have dedicated parking spaces, wheelchair access to terminals, and skychairs to convey passengers onto planes via air bridges. Most smaller airports also have accessible toilets.

Public transport WA's suburban rail networks and the vast majority of urban buses are wheelchair accessible. Guide dogs and hearing dogs are permitted on all public transport.

Accommodation Legislation requires that new accommodation meet accessibility standards for mobility-impaired travellers. Many older establishments still lag behind.

Sights and attractions Many attractions, including many national parks, provide access for visitors with limited mobility. A number of sites also address the needs of visitors with visual or aural impairments.

Tour operators Discrimination by tourism operators is illegal. Ask each operator what's possible.

Lonely Planet Lonely Planet covers a whole range of accessible travel issues. Visit lonelyplanet.com/sitemaps/articles/accessible-travel to find out more.

NO GROG
Check alcohol restrictions when visiting remote communities. You may be breaking the law if you have booze in your vehicle.

SMOKING
Smoking is banned in all indoor public spaces and in some outdoor spaces where crowds congregate.

TAKEAWAY ALCOHOL
Many outback towns (including the whole Kimberley) have restrictions on alcohol type and strength, and purchase quantity, hours and days.

FAMILY TRAVEL

Sights and attractions Swimming with whale sharks, learning more about dolphins in Bunbury or Monkey Mia, and spotting migrating whales at Albany or Ningaloo.

Supplies Formula, disposable nappies and kid-friendly food can be found in most major towns.

Child car seats Car safety seats are available from car rental companies.

Concession Child concessions (and family rates) often apply to accommodation, tours, admission fees and transport.

Child-friendly meals Most cafes, pubs and restaurants offer children's menus.

GREETINGS

Usually a simple 'g'day', smile or nod suffices when passing people. Shake hands with non-Indigenous men or women when meeting for the first time. With Aboriginal people, be respectful, wait to be acknowledged and respond in a like manner. Some Aboriginal groups reserve handshakes for funerals.

PHOTOGRAPHY

For Aboriginal people, photography can be highly intrusive, especially when camera-toting travellers arrive in remote communities. Photographing cultural places, practices and images, sites of significance and ceremonies may not be welcomed. Respect is essential.

ALEXANDER_H_SCHULZ/GETTY IMAGES

LGBTIQ+ TRAVELLERS

Pridefest *(pridewa.com.au)* This 10-day festival runs in Perth in November, culminating in the Pride Parade.

Gay Perth *(gaysthattravel.com/perth)* Get the lowdown on Perth's small but dynamic gay bar, restaurant and entertainment scene.

LGBTIQ+-friendly? Like all Australian cities, Perth is LGBTIQ+-friendly, although attitudes tend to be more conservative in rural areas, especially in remote communities.

Gay marriage Same-sex marriages have been legally recognised in Australia since 2017.

Index

3 Mile 177
4WD tours 226-7
4WD travel 240, *see also* car travel, driving tours
  Broome 210
  Kimberley, the 216-17, 218, 220-3, 228
  Ningaloo Coast 193
  Pilbara, the 193
  South West 123

A

Aboriginal art 10-11, 166-7, *see also* Aboriginal art centres & galleries, rock art
  Kimberley, the 218
  Donnybrook Artisan Hub 136
  Kimberley, the 227
  Pilbara, the 198-9, 200-1
Aboriginal art centres & galleries
  Bidyadanga Community Art Centre 232
  Boola Bidi 136
  Brave New Works 147
  Courthouse Gallery 204
  East Pilbara Arts Centre 205
  Gwoonwardu Mia 178
  Japingka Aboriginal Art 49
  Mangkaja Arts 232
  Manjimup Arts Hub 136
  Mowanjum Art & Culture Centre 221
  Nagula Jarndu Women's Resource Centre 231, 232
  Spinifex Hill Studios 205
  Waringarri Aboriginal Arts 232
  Warmun Arts 232
  Yallingup Aboriginal Art 131
  Yamaji Art 165
  Yinjaa-Barni Art 199
Aboriginal culture 14, 124-5, 144, 166-7, 180-3
  Bilya Koort Boodja Centre 94
  Dreaming, the 166-7, 180-1, 200
  etiquette 183, 247
  history 166-7, 181, 215
  Kodja Place 156
  languages 114
  Pilbara, the 195
  tours 136
Aboriginal peoples 166-7
  Dambimangari people 218
  Gija people 70-1, 228
  Goolarabooloo people 213, 224-5
  Malgana people 170-1
  Menang people 156, 157
  Noongar people 17, 18, 58, 71, 78, 93, 98-9, 136, 144, 148-9, 156
  Wunambal people 226-7
  Yamatji people 164-5
  Yawuru people 230-1, 232
  Yindjibarndi people 194-5, 197, 199
accessible travel 101, 248
accommodation 244-5, *see also individual locations*
Acknowledgement of Country 5, 183
airports 238-9
Albany/Kinjarling 151, 156-7
amusement parks 127, 158
animals 148-9, *see also* sealife, *individual species*
Anzacs 157
aquariums 173, 177
architecture, 50-1, 95
art galleries, see also Aboriginal art centres & galleries, craft galleries, public art, rock art
  Bunbury Regional Art Galler 131
  Butter Factory Studios & Gallery 159
  Courthouse Gallery 205
  Denmark Arts Markets 147
  Geraldton Regional Art Gallery 178
  Peter Kovacsy Studio 131
  Petrichor Gallery 159
  REDSEA Gallery 131
  Sea Spray Art 89
  Sisters of Eve Gallery/ Studio 145
  South Coast Woodworks Gallery 159
  Walyalup Fremantle Arts Centre 49
ATMs 238, 243
Australia Day 181
Avon Valley 94-5

B

Bald Head 152
Bandilngan 215
Batavia 167
beaches 13, 66-9
  Bathers Beach 49
  Bennion Beach 67
  Bill's Bay 204
  Broome 213
  Bundegi Beach 191, 204
  City Beach 68
  Cottesloe Beach 54-5
  CY O'Connor Beach 68
  Eighty Mile Beach 13, 201, 204

000 Map pages

Emu Point 155
Fay's Bay 97
Floreat Beach 63
Francois Peron National Park 171
Gnarabup Beach 136
Gnaraloo Bay 177
Greens Pool 147
Hamelin Bay 122
Hearson's Cove 204
Kalbarri 169
Little Beach 155
Little Parakeet Bay 97
Little Salmon Bay 97
Madfish Bay 152
Mandalay Beach 155
Meelup Beach 121
Middleton Beach 155
Misery Beach 152
Peaceful Bay/Kwallup 154-5
Reddell Beach 231
Settlers Beach 203
Shell Beach 173
Shelley Beach 155
Smiths Beach 121
South Beach 67-8
Turquoise Beach 190
Twilight Beach 154
Two Peoples Bay 155
Yeagarup Dunes 123
Beagle Bay 213
beer 249, *see also* breweries
Bell Gorge 222
birdwatching 149, 169, 178
Broome 231
Kimberley, the 218-19
Pilbara, the 195
South West 129
Blowholes 177
boab trees 70-1, 219
boat travel 135, 158, 193, *see also* cruises
books 38, 164, 232
Bottle Bay 171
breweries 81, *see also* distilleries
Bartholomew's Meadery 147
Beerfarm 137
Boston Brewing Co 159
Cidery, The 137
Core Cider 103
Eagle Bay Brewing 115
Froth Craft Brewery 205
Gage Roads Brew Co 49
Little Creatures 81
Lucky Bay Brewing 159
Matso's Broome Brewery 234
Nannup Brewing Company 137
North West Brewing Co 205
Running with Thieves 81
Seasonal Brewing Co 74
Shelter Brewery Company 127
Whalebone Brewing Co 205
Wild Hop Brewing Company 115
bridges
Beedelup National Park 19
Matagarup 77
Northam 95
Broome 212-13, 230-1, **208-9**
accommodation 211
drinking 211, 234-5
food 211
money 211
navigation 211
planning 208-10
travel seasons 210
travelling to Broome 210
travelling within Broome 210
wi-fi 211
budget 240, 243, 244
Bundegi 191
Bungle Bungle Range 15, 217, 228-9
bus travel 240
bushfires 242
Busselton/Undalup 116, 126-7

C

camping 245
Canal Rocks 121
Cape Leeuwin 117, 132
Cape Leveque 212-13, 234
Cape Naturaliste 28, 121, 122, 132
Cape Peron 171
Cape Range National Park 192-3
car travel 240-1, 246, *see also* driving tours
road conditions 211, 216, 221, 241
safety 211, 241, 242
carbon footprint 241
Carnarvon 176
cattle stations 219, 223, 235, 245
Cattle Well 171
caves 132-3
Giants Cave 133
Jewel Cave 133
Lake Cave 133
Mammoth Cave 133
Mimbi 215
Mulka's Cave 93
Ngilgi Cave 133
cemeteries 91, 203
Central West 160-79, **30-1**, **162**
accommodation 163
activities 178-9
drinking 163, 168
food 163
itineraries 28-9, **28-9**
money 163
navigation 163
planning 162
travel seasons 163
travel to Central West 163
travel within Central West 163
wi-fi 163

Charles Knife Canyon 193
cheese 137, 147
churches 213
cinemas
  Kookaburra Cinema 102
  Luna Leederville 58
  Rooftop Movies 78
  Somerville Auditorium 78
Claisebrook Cove 77
climate 18-25, 36, 53, 242
climate change 247
conservation tourism 189
Coogee 69
cooking courses 113, 137
coral 9
Coral Bay 191, 201
Cossack 203
costs 240, 243, 244
craft galleries
  Cindy Poole Glass Gallery 145
  John Miller Design 131
  Jonathan Hook Ceramics 145
  Makers Collective & Magic Marron Shop 159
  Melting Pot Glass Studio 131
  Mermaid Leather 145
crocodiles 216, 218, 242
cruises 107, 158, 178, 193-4
currency 243
currency exchange 238
cycling 45, 96-7, 129, 136

D

Dalmanyi 222
Dambimangari people 218
Dampier Archipelago 199
Dampier Peninsula 212-13
Danggu 215
Darlington 101
Denmark/Kwoorabup 146-7
Department of Fire & Emergency Services (DFES) Education & Heritage Centre 77
Derby Boab Festival 23
Dimalurru 215
dingos 178, 182, 192, 219
dinosaurs 231
disabilities, travelling with 101, 248
distilleries 73, 81, 151, 159, 235 *see also* breweries
diving 8-9, 247, *see also* snorkelling
  Dampier Archipelago 199
  Monkey Mia 178
  Ningaloo Coast 191, 204
dolphin watching 79, 174-5
  Dampier Archipelago 199
  James Price Point/Walmadan 224
  Koombana Bay 127
  Matilda Bay 53
  Monkey Mia 171, 174-5
  Ningaloo Coast 191
  Perth 79
Donnybrook 117
Dreaming, the 166-7, 180-1, 200
drinking, *see* breweries, distilleries, *individual locations*
driving, *see* car travel, driving tours
driving tours
  Avon Valley 94-5, **95**
  Broome & the Kimberley 216-17, **217**
  Duncan Road 216-17, **217**
  Gibb River Road 220-3
  Great Northern Highway 240
  Karri Forest Explorer Drive 119
  North West Coastal Hwy 240
  Perth Hills 102-3, **103**
  Pilbara, the 193
  Shark Bay Road (Monkey Mia) 172-3, **173**
  South Coast 144-5, **145**
  South Perth 107
  South West 114-15, 123, **115**
Duncan Road 216-17
Dunsborough 114-15, **115**

E

Eagle Gorge 169
Eighty Mile Beach 13
Electric Lane 57
Emu-man 225
environmental issues
  Kimberley, the 224-5
  Pilbara, the 196-7
  South Coast 148-9
etiquette 247, 249
  Aboriginal culture 183, 247
  barbecue 62-3
  beaches 67
Exmouth 32-3
events, *see* festivals & events

F

family travel 76-7, 79, 245 249
  beaches 155
  Busselton 126-7
  Denmark/Kwoorabup 146
farmers markets 86, 105, 112, 150
farms (pick your own)
  Bickley Valley Asparagus Farm 106
  Carmel Cherry Farm 103
  Hoang Le's Strawberries 107
  Olio Bello 137
  S&R Orchard 106
  Orchard Perth 106
Fay's Bay 97

festivals & events
- Bloom Festival 24, 144
- Bridgetown Blues Festival 137
- Bunuru Festival 19
- Derby Boab Festival 23
- Djilba Wildflower Festival 144
- Entwined in the Valley 86
- Festival of Voice 147
- Fringe World 19
- Gourmet Escape 7, 113
- Laneway Festival 19
- Manjimup Cherry Harmony Festival 137
- Mardi Gras 19
- Margaret River Pro 20
- Margaret River Readers & Writers Festival 130
- Margaret River Region Open Studios 130
- Nannup Garden Festival 137
- Ord Valley Muster 21
- Perth Festival 19
- Red Earth Arts Festival 21
- Sculpture by the Sea 54-5
- Shinju Matsuri Festival 23
- Southern Art & Craft Trail 144
- Sunshine Festival 25
- Taste Great Southern 150
- Truffle Kerfuffle Festival 137
- Western Australia Gourmet Escape 113

films 39
firefighting 77
First Nations peoples, *see* Aboriginal peoples
fishing 129, 155, 169, 199, 204, 213, 233
Fitzgerald Biosphere 148-9
Flinders Bay 122
flooding 242
food 6-7, 37, *see also individual locations*
food tours 113, 135
forest bathing 118-19
Fremantle 48-9
'Fremantle Doctor' 37

G

gardens, *see* parks & gardens
Geikie Gorge 215
Geraldton 164-5
Gibb River Road 220-3
Gija Jumulu 70-1
glamping 244
glass-bottom boats 204
Gnaraloo Bay 177
Gnomesville 129
Gnylmarung 213
Gondwana Link 149
gorges
- Bell Gorge 222
- Broome & the Kimberley 218
- Danggu 215
- Emma Gorge 223
- Mandu Mandu 193
- Ngajarli (Deep Gorge) 199
- Purnululu National Park 229
- Sawpit Gorge 217
- Warla 223
- Windjana Gorge 221
- Wunnumurra 223
- Yardie Creek 193

Great Northern Highway 240
Greens Pool 155

H

health 53, 242
hiking 15, 23, 79, 155
- Bibbulmun Track 136
- Broome 232
- Bungle Bungle Range 229
- Burringurrah 177
- Cape to Cape Track 136
- Central West 179
- East Mt Barren 143
- Kalbarri 169
- Kimberley 227
- Lurujarri Dreaming Trail 213
- Monkey Mia 171
- Perth Hills 102
- Perth region 102
- Pilbara, the 192-3, 199, 200-1
- South Coast 142-3, 152, 157, 158-9
- South West 122
- Stirling Range National Park 143, 158
- Whistlepipe Gully 103

Hippo's Yawn 92
historic buildings
- National Hotel 49
- Perth 50-1
- Rottnest Island/Wadjemup 98-9
- Strawberry Hill Farm 157

history 98-9, *see also* Aboriginal culture
- Anzacs 157
- European settlement 167
- mining 203

HMAS *Sydney II* Memorial 165
honey 147
hot-air ballooning 95
Hutt Lagoon 178

I

ice cream 127
Imintji 222
Invasion Day 181
islands
- Dampier Archipelago 199
- Dirk Hartog Island/Wirruwana 174-5
- Heirrison Island 78
- Houtman Abrolhos Islands 165
- Rottnest Island 96-9
- Woody Island 158

itineraries 26-35
Avon Valley 94-5, **95**
Broome & the Kimberley 216-17, **217**
Kimberley, the 34-5, **34-5**
Margaret River 110, 132-3, **110**, **33**
Monkey Mia & the Central West 28-9, 172-3, **28-9**
Ningaloo Coast & the Pilbara 32-3, **32-3**
Perth 60-1, 74-5, **61**, **75**
Perth region 26-7, 102-3, **26-7**, **103**
South Coast 28-9, 144-5, **28-9**, **145**
South West 28-9, 110, 114-15, 130-1, **28-9**, **110**, **115**, **131**

J

James Price Point 213, 225-6
Jandamarra 215
jazz 46-7
jellyfish 242
Jurien Bay 89
Juukan Gorge 196

K

Kalamunda 101
Kalbarri 168-9
Kalumburu 222
kangaroos 78, 100-1, 153
Karijini National Park 187, 194-5
Katter Kich 90-3
kayaking 79
Beagle Bay 213
Broome 233
Margaret River/Wooditchup 134-5
Ningaloo 191, 204
Perth 79
Shark Bay 171
Swan Valley 86
Kimberley, the **208-9**
accommodation 211, 235
drinking 211, 234-5
food 211, 234-5
itineraries 34-5, 208-9, 216-17, **34-5**, **209**, **217**
money 211
navigation 211
planning 208-10
travel seasons 210
travelling to the Kimberley 210
travelling within the Kimberley 210
wi-fi 211
kitesurfing 179

L

lace 93
lakes
Honeymoon Pool 129
Hutt Lagoon 178
Lake Argyle 217
Lake Clifton 107
Lake Jasper 123
Lake Magic 92
Long Pool 129
Palm Springs 217
Lakeside 191
language 37, 182
Leederville 56-9
LGBTIQ+ travellers 249
lighthouses 117, 122, 132, 165, 190
literature 38, 164, 232
Little Parakeet Bay 97
Little Salmon Bay 97
Lombadina 213
Lurujarri Dreaming Trail 213, 231

M

Malgana people 170-1
Margaret River/Wooditchup 108-37, **110**
accommodation 111
activities 132-3
drinking 111, 136
festivals & events 113, 130
food 112-13, 136-7
itineraries 28-9, 132-3, **28-9**
money 111
navigation 111
planning 110
travel seasons 111
travel to Margaret River 111
travel within Margaret River 111
Margaret River Pro 20
markets 86-7, 105, *see also* farmers markets
marron 151
Maud 191
Maylands 74-5, **75**
mazes 127
Middle Lagoon 213
Mimbi Caves 215
mining 36, 196-7, 203, 224-5
Mitchell Plateau/Ngauwudu 226-7
mobile phones 248
money 36, 243
Monkey Mia 174-5
mountains
Jarndunmunha/ Mt Nameless 205
Mt Augustus/Burringurrah 177
Mt Clarence/Corndarup 157
Muiron Islands 204
museums
Albany's Historic Whaling Station 157
Carnarvon Space & Technology Museum 178

Central Greenough Historic Settlement 178
Don Rhodes Mining Museum 203
Miniature Soldier Museum 93
Museum of Geraldton 165
Museum of Natural History 87
Museum of the Great Southern 157
Power Up Electricity Museum 127
Shark Bay World Heritage Discovery Centre 178
Telegraph Station 173
music 38, 46-7

N

Nancy Peak 159
Napier Range 214-15
national parks & nature reserves
Beelu National Park 101
Cape Range National Park 192-3
D'Entrecasteaux National Park 155
Dirk Hartog Island/Wirruwana National Park 174-5
Fitzgerald River National Park 143, 148
Francois Peron National Park 170-1
Gloucester National Park 119
John Forrest National Park 101
Kalamunda National Park 101
Kalbarri National Park 168-9
Karijini National Park 195, 201
Millstream Chichester National Park 195
Murujuga National Park 199
Nambung National Park 88
Purnululu National Park 217
Serpentine National Park 105
Stirling Range 148
Torndirrup National Park 143
Two Peoples Bay Nature Reserve 155
Walpole-Nornalup National Park 143
Wellington National Park 129
William Bay National Park 147
Yalgorup National Park 107
Yanchep National Park 101
Nhangganggunha 201
Ningaloo Coast & the Pilbara 184-205, **186**
accommodation 187
drinking 187, 205
food 187, 205
itineraries 32-3, **32-3**
money 187
navigation 187
planning 186
traveling to Ningaloo Coast & the Pilbara 187
travelling within the Pilbara 187
travel seasons 187
Noongar calendar 73, 111, 141
North West Coastal Hwy 240

O

Omeo shipwreck 69
online resources 247
orcas 18, 152
Osprey 191

P

paddleboarding 135
parks & gardens
Araluen Botanic Park 63
Chevron Parkland 77
Claisebrook Cove 77
Coombe Reserve 53
Cottesloe Civic Centre 53
Esplanade Park 78
Hyde Park 78
Kings Park 63, 70-1
Langford Park 105
Marapikurrinya Park 203
Matilda Bay 53
May Drive Parkland 63
Origins Centre 136
Sir James Mitchell Park 63
Wellington Square 77
Pender Bay 213
Perth 16-17, 40-81, **42-3**
accommodation 45
activities 76-7, 78-9
drinking 45, 57-8, 79, 81
entertainment 46-7
food 45, 49, 52-3, 58-9, 62-3, 72-3, 74-5, 79-80
internet access 45
itineraries 26-7, 60-1, 74-5, **26-7**
money 45
navigation 45
planning 42-3
shopping 75
sights 54-5, 56-9, 66-9, 70-1, 76-7
travel seasons 44
travel to Perth 44
travel within Perth 44
wi-fi 45
Perth City Farm 77
Perth Hills 102-3, 104-5, 107
Perth region 82-107
accommodation 85
activities 106
drinking 85
food 85, 104-5
itineraries 26-7, 84, 94-5, 102-3, **26-7**
money 85
sights 86-7, 88-9, 90-3
travel seasons 85
travel to Perth region 85
travel within Perth region 85
wi-fi 85

Perth shopping 58
Piccaninny Creek 229
picnics 52-3
Pilbara, the, *see* Ningaloo Coast & the Pilbara
Pinnacles, the 88-9
podcasts 38
Point Quobba 177
Point Samson 202
population 16
Port Hedland 202-3
public art 55, 60-1, 95, **61**
  Bunbury murals 131
  Chainsaw Drive 145
  Collie Mural Trail 129
  Farm Gate Art Trail 145
  Northam Silo Art 95
  PUBLIC Silo 145, 153
  South West 131
  Tin Horse Highway 91
  Understory & Art Nature Trail 130
  Wellington Dam 129
Purnululu National Park 228-9

Q

Quobba Coast 177
quokkas 96-7

R

radio 38
rays 9
Red Bluff 177, 178
responsible travel 246-7
rock art 11, *see also* Aboriginal art centres & galleries
  Central West 177
  Kimberley, the 35, 218, 222, 223, 227
  Pilbara, the 33, 196-7, 198-9
Roebourne 199
Rottnest Island 96-9

S

safe travel 53, 121, 154, 211, 242
scenic flights 172, 234
Sculpture by the Sea 54-5
sealife 8-9
  Monkey Mia 165, 174-5
  Ningaloo Coast 188-91
  Pilbara, the 199
  South West 122-3
Shark Bay Road 172-3
Shark Bay World Heritage Area 170-1, 174-5
Shinju Matsuri Festival 23
shipwrecks 165
  Barque Mandalay 155
  Batavia 167
  HMAS *Perth* Wreck 158
SIM cards 238
slang 37
snakes 242
snorkelling 97, 154, 191, 204
  Coogee Maritime Trail 69
  Denmark/South Coast 147
  Ningaloo Coast 190
  South Coast 158
social media
Sorry Day 183
South Coast 138-59, **140**
  accommodation 141
  activities 154-5
  drinking 141, 151, 159
  food 141, 150-1, 159
  itineraries 28-9, 144-5, **28-9**
  money 141
  navigation 141
  planning 140
  sights 152
  travel seasons 141
  travel to South Coast 141
  travel within South Coast 141
  wi-fi 141
South West 108-37, **110**
  accommodation 111
  activities 118-19, 126-7, 134-5, 136
  drinking 111, 127, 136
  food 111
  festivals & events 130, 137
  food 114-15, 127, 136-7
  itineraries 28-9, 114-15, 130-1, **28-9**
  money 111
  navigation 111
  planning 110
  shopping 130-1
  sights 120-3, 128-9
  travel seasons 111
  travel to the South West 111
  travel within the South West 111
  weather 111
  wi-fi 111
street art, *see* public art
Strine 37
Sugarloaf Rock 121
surfing 20, 135, 177
  Ningaloo Coast 204
  Monkey Mia 178
  South Coast 158
  South West 135
sustainable travel 104-5, 148-9, 125
Swan Valley 86-7
swimming 121, 147, 242, *see also* beaches
  Aquarium 121
  Kimberley, the 217, 219, 223
  Lake Magic Swimming Pool 92
  Ningaloo Coast 189
  Perth 55
  Pilbara, the 195
  South Coast 147, 155
  South West 117, 121, 129

T

Tantabiddi 191
tipping 243
toilets 248
Tom Price 201
Tombstones 177
tours, *see also* food tours
  Aboriginal-led 175, 246
  Broome 231
  Kimberley, the 214-15, 233
  Margaret River/Wooditchup 113
  Monkey Mia 169, 175
  Ningaloo Coast 189
  Perth region 86
  Pilbara, the 198, 203
  Shark Bay 178
  South Coast 143, 144
  South West 118
travel seasons 18-25
travel to/from West Coast Australia 238-9
travel within West Coast Australia 240-1
Tunnel Creek 215
Turquoise Bay 191
turtles 190

V

vegan & vegetarian travellers 205
viewpoints
  Black Point 123
  Bungle Bungle Ranges 229
  Cape Peron 171
  Dave Evancs Bicentennial Tree 119
  Eagle Bluff 173
  East Mt Barren 143
  Gantheaume Point/Minyirr 231
  Gloucester Tree 119
  Granite Skywalk 143
  Lions Lookout 102
  Perth 81
  Reader Head Lookout 203
  Redbank Bridge Salt & Train Lookout 203
  Scarp Road 105
  Shothole Viewpoint 193
  Skipjack Point Lookout 171
  Thomas Carter Lookout 193
  Valley of the Giants Tree Top Walk 143
visas 248
volunteering 175, 190, 246

W

Wadjemup Project 99
WAITOC 14, 246
walking tours 60-1, 74-5, **61**, **75**
Warlu Way 200-1
water parks 79
waterbiking 79
waterfalls
  Beedelup Falls 119
  Broome & the Kimberley 219
  Horizontal Falls 218
  Lesmurdie Falls 103
  Punamii-Uunpuu (Mitchell Falls) 227
  Quinninup Falls 122
  Wongalala Falls 222
Wave Rock, *see* Katter Kich
weather 18-25, 36, 53, 242
Welcome to Country 183
Western Australian Indigenous Tourism Operators Council (WAITOC) 14, 246
Western Australia-Northern Territory border 217
whale sharks 20, 188-91
whale watching 18, 22, 78, 122, 152, 158, 169, 190, 199
wi-fi 238
wildflowers 22, 24, 64-5, 144, 148-9, 152-3, 178
wildlife 148-9, *see also* sealife, *individual species*
wildlife watching
  Houtman Abrolhos Islands 165
  Pilbara, the 192-3, 195
wildlife parks & centres 101, 127, 157, 158, 178, *see also* zoos
Wilson Inlet 158
Windjana Gorge 215
windsurfing 18
wineries
  Perth region 86-7, 92, 101, 103, 105, 106
  Margaret River/Wooditchup 113
  South Coast 147, 151
  South West 121, 127
Wittecarra Creek 169

Y

Yallingup 114-15, 121
Yeagarup Dunes 13
yoga 146-7

Z

ziplining 135
zoos 79, 127, *see also* wildlife parks & centres

'You will never get the red pindan dirt out of your clothes, your sandals, your car or your soul.'

STEVE WATERS

'I love meeting friends for a sunset picnic at Kings Park among the eucalypts, or catching a gig in the botanical gardens. A quintessential Perth experience.'

ROSAMUND BRENNAN

'Roos grazing around caravans, a simple camp brew, and a vibrant pink/purple sunrise over the Nornalup inlet. Pure bliss!'

EMMYLOU DZUBIEL

STEVE WATERS/CONTRIBUTOR, DAVID STEELE/SHUTTERSTOCK, RIC JACYNO/SHUTTERSTOCK

THIS BOOK

The 2nd edition of Lonely Planet's *Experience West Coast Australia* guidebook was written and researched by Steve Waters, Rosamund Brennan and Emmylou Dzubiel. Sarah Reid updated the First Nations Peoples essay. The previous edition was written by Fleur Bainger, Anthony Ham and Ariana Svenson. This guidebook was produced by the following:

Destination Editor
Jessica Lockhart

Coordinating Editor
Sarah Bailey

Production Editor
Kate Chapman

Cartographer
Hunor Csutoros

Image Researcher
Compton Sheldon

Cover Researcher
Giada de Agostinis

Thanks
Melanie Dankel, Lucy Jones, Kellie Langdon, Graham O'Neill, Gabrielle Stefanos, Saralinda Turner